Elastic Shape Analysis of Three-Dimensional Objects

Synthesis Lectures on Computer Vision

Editors
Gérard Medioni, *University of Southern California*
Sven Dickinson, *University of Toronto*

Synthesis Lectures on Computer Vision is edited by Gérard Medioni of the University of Southern California and Sven Dickinson of the University of Toronto. The series publishes 50–150 page publications on topics pertaining to computer vision and pattern recognition. The scope will largely follow the purview of premier computer science conferences, such as ICCV, CVPR, and ECCV. Potential topics include, but not are limited to:

- Applications and Case Studies for Computer Vision

- Color, Illumination, and Texture

- Computational Photography and Video

- Early and Biologically-inspired Vision

- Face and Gesture Analysis

- Illumination and Reflectance Modeling

- Image-Based Modeling

- Image and Video Retrieval

- Medical Image Analysis

- Motion and Tracking

- Object Detection, Recognition, and Categorization

- Segmentation and Grouping

- Sensors

- Shape-from-X

- Stereo and Structure from Motion

- Shape Representation and Matching

Boosting-Based Face Detection and Adaptation
Cha Zhang and Zhengyou Zhang
2010

Image-Based Modeling of Plants and Trees
Sing Bing Kang and Long Quan
2009

Elastic Shape Analysis of Three-Dimensional Objects

Ian H. Jermyn, Sebastian Kurtek, Hamid Laga, and Anuj Srivastava

ISBN: 978-3-031-00691-3   paperback
ISBN: 978-3-031-01819-0   ebook

DOI 10.1007/978-3-031-01819-0

A Publication in the Springer series
SYNTHESIS LECTURES ON COMPUTER VISION

Lecture #12
Series Editors: Gérard Medioni, *University of Southern California*
                Sven Dickinson, *University of Toronto*
Series ISSN
Print 2153-1056   Electronic 2153-1064

Elastic Shape Analysis of Three-Dimensional Objects

Ian H. Jermyn
Durham University

Sebastian Kurtek
Ohio State University

Hamid Laga
Murdoch University and University of South Australia

Anuj Srivastava
Florida State University

SYNTHESIS LECTURES ON COMPUTER VISION #12

ABSTRACT

Statistical analysis of shapes of 3D objects is an important problem with a wide range of applications. This analysis is difficult for many reasons, including the fact that objects differ in both geometry and topology. In this manuscript, we narrow the problem by focusing on objects with fixed topology, say objects that are diffeomorphic to unit spheres, and develop tools for analyzing their geometries. The main challenges in this problem are to register points across objects and to perform analysis while being invariant to certain shape-preserving transformations.

We develop a comprehensive framework for analyzing shapes of spherical objects, i.e., objects that are embeddings of a unit sphere in $\mathbb{R}^3$, including tools for: quantifying shape differences, optimally deforming shapes into each other, summarizing shape samples, extracting principal modes of shape variability, and modeling shape variability associated with populations. An important strength of this framework is that it is *elastic*: it performs alignment, registration, and comparison in a single unified framework, while being invariant to shape-preserving transformations.

The approach is essentially Riemannian in the following sense. We specify natural mathematical representations of surfaces of interest, and impose Riemannian metrics that are invariant to the actions of the shape-preserving transformations. In particular, they are invariant to reparameterizations of surfaces. While these metrics are too complicated to allow broad usage in practical applications, we introduce a novel representation, termed square-root normal fields (SRNFs), that transform a particular invariant elastic metric into the standard L^2 metric. As a result, one can use standard techniques from functional data analysis for registering, comparing, and summarizing shapes. Specifically, this results in: pairwise registration of surfaces; computation of geodesic paths encoding optimal deformations; computation of Karcher means and covariances under the shape metric; tangent Principal Component Analysis (PCA) and extraction of dominant modes of variability; and finally, modeling of shape variability using wrapped normal densities.

These ideas are demonstrated using two case studies: the analysis of surfaces denoting human bodies in terms of shape and pose variability; and the clustering and classification of the shapes of subcortical brain structures for use in medical diagnosis.

This book develops these ideas without assuming advanced knowledge in differential geometry and statistics. We summarize some basic tools from differential geometry in the appendices, and introduce additional concepts and terminology as needed in the individual chapters.

KEYWORDS

elastic Riemannian metric, shape model, shape metric, elastic registration, shape summary, modes of shape variability

Contents

Preface

Shape analysis of *three-dimensional objects* is a fast-growing discipline in its own right. Advances in technology for 3D scanners and 3D printers, and giant leaps in storage and transfer of large datasets, have focused attention on the need to develop tools for shape analysis of whole objects. Consequently, researchers have accelerated their efforts toward developing efficient mathematical representations and related computational tools for 3D shape analysis. This research has progressed in several directions, one of which relates to Riemannian frameworks and elastic shape analysis. This direction is the focus of this book.

One of the most difficult problems in comparing shapes, especially when seeking a comprehensive statistical solution, is the registration of points across objects. Such a registration is necessary, for instance, when measuring deformations, computing shape averages, or finding principal modes of variability in shape data. Many past and current methods presume this problem away, i.e., they assume that an optimal registration is already available, but that assumption is often not true in practice. Elastic shape analysis is a branch of shape analysis that performs both registration and shape comparison in a single, unified framework using a Riemannian approach. This book is an exposition on recent developments in mathematical representations, metrics, and computational solutions for elastic shape analysis of surfaces. To understand this approach, one needs a broad array of tools, ranging from geometry and calculus to finite-element analysis and computer programming.

This book is intended for a researcher or a graduate student in computer science, applied mathematics, statistics, biology, or a related discipline. It assumes a background in linear algebra and advance calculus, and will certainly be easier for those who have taken an introductory course in differential geometry. We have tried to keep the exposition self-contained by including some background material in appendices and throughout chapters as needed. However, this book is not intended to replace textbooks on the differential geometry of surfaces, as our focus is more on computational solutions in shape analysis.

Ian H. Jermyn, Sebastian Kurtek, Hamid Laga, and Anuj Srivastava
July 2017

Acknowledgments

Some of the research presented here was developed in collaboration with Prof. Eric Klassen of the Florida State University, Prof. Zhaohua Ding of Vanderbilt University, and Dr. Qian Xie of Amazon Inc. We are very grateful for their collaboration.

This research was supported in part by NSF grants: DMS 1621787, CCF 1617397, and DMS 1208959 to Anuj Srivastava, DMS 1613054 to Sebastian Kurtek, and Murdoch University's New Staff Startup Grant Scheme to Hamid Laga. Anuj Srivastava gratefully acknowledges support from a Durham University IAS Senior Research Fellowship (EU grant FP7-609412) and the Durham University Department of Mathematical Sciences.

The authors would like to thank: Nils Hasler for providing us with the 3D human shape models; Raif Rustamov and Maks Ovsjanikov for the discussion about functional maps and for sharing their data and results; the authors of the 2007 SHape REtrieval Contest (SHREC07), Watertight Models Track, and the authors of the TOSCA dataset for making their databases publicly available.

Ian H. Jermyn, Sebastian Kurtek, Hamid Laga, and Anuj Srivastava
July 2017

CHAPTER 1

Problem Introduction and Motivation

1.1 PROBLEM AREA: 3D SHAPE ANALYSIS

Shape is an important physical property that characterizes the external appearance of natural and man-made objects. It plays a central role in understanding and analyzing the roles of objects in their larger environments. For example, in the case of anatomical and biochemical objects, their shapes are important predictors of their functionality within the larger complex bio-systems in which they are situated. Understanding differences between shapes and modeling the variability within and across shape classes are, thus, fundamental problems and constitute building blocks to solutions in many application areas, ranging from computer vision and computer graphics to biology and anatomy. For instance, a study of the shapes of 3D anatomical structures and their growth patterns is of particular interest in understanding physiological abnormalities that may be linked to alterations in these shapes. Similarly, in the field of computer graphics, the growing availability of 3D models via online repositories has re-focused research efforts toward data-driven techniques for generating novel 3D shapes from existing ones. Data-driven techniques are also gaining momentum in the field of 3D reconstruction and modeling from images, range scans, and noisy point clouds. This process, however, requires powerful mathematical representations and efficient computer algorithms for capturing, modeling, and exploring the shape variability in vast collections of 3D data.

Shape analysis is a relatively old topic in computer vision, with papers and methods going back several decades. However, the early years of the new millennium saw a renewed focus on the area. This focus, which was application-oriented and data-driven, brought in new directions and tools. While the new interest was fueled by many factors, the most prominent was the increasing availability of large datasets of 3D shapes, especially in the fields of computer vision and medical imaging. It was also propelled by increases in computational power and storage, a growing interest in Riemannian methods, and a favorable atmosphere for the confluence of ideas from geometry and statistics. As a result, researchers developed novel approaches, based on mathematical tools that were new to this community, and made them practical using elegant computational solutions. The goal of this textbook is to cover some recent advances in analyzing the shape of 3D objects, with an emphasis on Riemannian frameworks and statistical analysis.

Even with the restriction to 3D objects, the degree of possible shape variability is enormous. This variability can arise in several ways. Topology can vary: shapes may have several pieces, or have different numbers of handles. Even if two objects share the same topology, they may have different geometries. For example, a deformed ball is topologically identical to a unit sphere but has a different geometry. Finally, objects may have different sizes, orientations, and positions. More specifically, the objects of interest may be observed under different scales or spatial configurations. For example, brain substructures observed in magnetic resonance images (MRIs) naturally vary in this way due to a subject's position in the scanner and the size of their individual substructure. In this book, we are interested in studying geometrical variability only, and thus we restrict our attention to objects with the same topology: we will consider only objects that consist of one piece with no handles. The boundaries of these objects are genus-0 surfaces, and can be viewed as embeddings of a sphere in $\mathbb{R}^3$. Despite the restriction, this is a rich class of shapes that includes the objects found in many of the important applications mentioned above. We note also that the techniques developed here can be adapted to objects with other topologies including quadrilateral, hemispherical, and cylindrical ones.

1.2   GENERAL GOALS AND CHALLENGES

What are the main tasks or tools required for shape analysis? Depending upon the application, there are many potential goals one could formulate. However, it seems reasonable to have a core set of tasks that any comprehensive method for statistical shape analysis must be able to accomplish. The following is a list of such tasks.

1. **Shape Metric and Deformations.** Perhaps the most fundamental task in shape analysis is quantifying the difference in the shapes of two objects. To accomplish this mathematically, we define a metric on an appropriate "shape space" that gives a "distance" between any two shapes. To give meaning to this distance, it is important to be able to associate to it an "optimal deformation." By definition, a "deformation" is a path of shapes leading from one shape to the other. We can use the metric to define the length of such a path; an optimal deformation is then the deformation of minimal length. If the length of the optimal deformation is equal to the distance between the two shapes, then we can think of the distance as measuring the "size" of the deformation needed to go from one shape to another. This requirement places a restriction on the original metric; modulo some extreme cases, it becomes possible to represent it using a "Riemannian metric," about which we will have a lot more to say in the sequel. In that context, the optimal deformation is known as a "geodesic path." Figure 1.1 shows an example of a geodesic path between two surfaces, computed under a particular metric to be described later.

2. **Shape Summary.** Given a set of objects, such as the ones shown in Figure 1.2, the method should be able to provide summary statistics, and in particular the mean and the covariance, of their shapes. The covariance can further be used to find the dominant modes of variability in the given set of shapes. One needs a formal mathematical representation of shapes, equipped with a proper shape metric, and associated computational tools, to

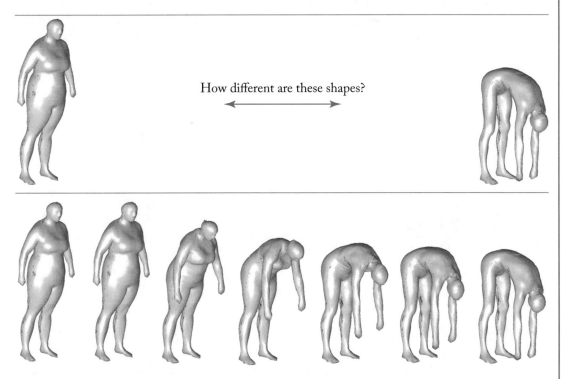

How different are these shapes?

Figure 1.1: Given two surfaces, our goal is quantify the difference in their shapes and find an optimal deformation (geodesic) from one to the other.

Figure 1.2: A population of human shapes in a neutral pose (left) and in various poses (right).

define, compute, and analyze these sample statistics. Figure 1.3a displays an example of summarizing a set of shapes using a metric-based approach. The summary here is in the form of a mean shape (center), and the three top principal modes of variation (shown in the three rows).

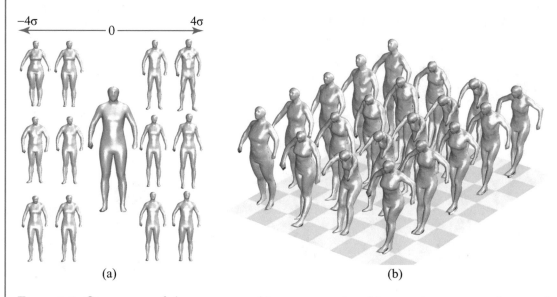

(a)   (b)

Figure 1.3: Given a set of shapes, one goal is to summarize this set using a mean shape and principal modes of variability (panel (a)). One can also learn a shape model, and then generate random samples from that model to study its effectiveness (panel (b)).

3. **Shape Modeling.** The approach should allow the definition of comprehensive, yet tractable, probability models for capturing essential variability in the shapes of a given set of objects. On the one hand, these shape models should be reasonable in complexity, leading to real-time statistical analysis of shapes; on the other, they should be powerful enough to capture the original variability and provide satisfactory class separation. One can use principal modes of variability in the data, first, to find lower-dimensional submanifolds where most of the data lies, and then to impose tractable statistical models on these submanifolds. Figure 1.3b shows examples of random shapes generated from a parametric shape model learned from training data.

4. **Shape Clustering, Classification, and Testing.** Given a shape metric, and probability models on a shape space, one can extend standard tools from pattern recognition and machine learning to the shape analysis context. For instance, one can develop techniques for shape estimation, shape-based clustering of objects, and hypothesis testing for shape classification.

5. **Real Applications.** Finally, an important goal has to be successful use of these tools on large datasets involving objects in real applications. Since a strong motivation for this work comes from the easy availability of shape databases, it is vital to demonstrate the success of any methods on these databases in order for them to be deemed useful.

Now that we have laid out a core set of tasks, the next questions are: *What makes shape analysis of 3D objects challenging? Why are the tasks of characterizing and analyzing shapes, and modeling shape variability, difficult ones?* Keep in mind that we are interested in shapes of boundaries of 3D objects, represented as 2D surfaces in $\mathbb{R}^3$. The main challenges are as follows.

1. **Registration of Surfaces.** Perhaps the most important aspect of shape comparison is registration. Registration is a matching of points across objects, i.e., it determines which point on one object matches with which point on the other (Figure 1.4). Registration is often a difficult problem to solve, especially across objects with large deformations and pose variability. A variety of techniques have been developed, depending on the context, for solving the registration problem. A major drawback of these past techniques is that registration is mostly performed independently of ensuing shape comparisons. In other words, the objective functions used for registration are different from the metrics used to compare and analyze shapes. It seems more natural to treat the two problems in a unified, comprehensive setup, using a single metric! In fact, that is one of the main accomplishments of the techniques presented in this book.

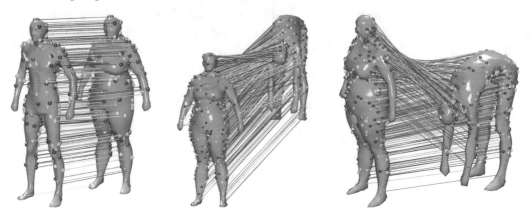

Figure 1.4: Registration of points across two surfaces that bend and stretch.

2. **Infinite-Dimensionality of Shape Spaces.** The objects of interest in this book, genus-0 surfaces, are elements of an infinite-dimensional space, and this requires the use of a Hilbert space structure to analyze that function space. Using this structure, one can represent any surface using a basis expansion and truncate the expansion to reach a finite-dimensional, albeit approximate, representation of a surface. These finite-dimensional representations can then be used for statistical analysis. The important questions are: What

should be the representation space of surfaces, and what Hilbert space structure should be used for shape analysis?

3. **Nonlinearity of Representations.** Shape representations frequently lead to nonlinear spaces, for a variety of reasons. For instance, shape is a property that is invariant to certain transformations such as rigid motion and global scaling. In the case of parametrized surfaces, it is also invariant to any reparametrization of a surface. This implies that shape spaces are quotient spaces of the original representation manifolds, in order to remove these nuisance transformations. The quotient spaces are not vector spaces and, thus, do not allow standard multivariate statistics to be applied directly. One has to utilize the geometry of these spaces, in conjunction with the chosen metric, to compute distances, take averages, or to perform Principal Component Analysis (PCA).

1.3 PAST APPROACHES AND THEIR LIMITATIONS

Perhaps the earliest known efforts in formalizing shape analysis came from D'Arcy Thompson who tried to relate the shapes of functionally similar objects. He explored the possibility of making shapes visually similar by applying transformations and making them closer than they originally appeared. His treatment of shapes appears in the form of a 1917 book titled *On Growth and Form*. Figure 1.5 shows examples, albeit using 2D objects, of using non-rigid transformations for matching two seemingly different but functionally similar objects. The left example considers Albrecht Dürer's face transforms, which were among Thompson's inspiration for studying shapes. Here, the transformation is applied to the coordinate system in which the object is represented and not to the object itself; the appearance of the object changes accordingly.

A large number of approaches in shape analysis abstract the important geometric properties of 3D objects into a set of numerical descriptors; examples are shape distributions [Osada et al., 2002], harmonic coefficients [Kazhdan et al., 2003], Zernike moments [Novotni and Klein, 2003], wavelet descriptors [Laga et al., 2006, 2007], and covariance descriptors [Tabia and Laga, 2015, Tabia et al., 2014]. Shapes are then compared using distance measures defined on the descriptor space [Laga and Nakajima, 2008]. The main shortcoming is that these representations are not invertible. That is, given an arbitrary point in the feature space, it is not possible to determine a shape or a set of shapes that correspond to that feature value. As a consequence, it is difficult to perform statistical analysis in the feature space and then map it back to the object space for inference.

In recent decades, perhaps the most prominent idea that laid foundations for statistical shape analysis in general is the work of Kendall [1977]. Instead of using descriptors, Kendall's approach represents objects with a finite set of *n* ordered points, called *landmarks*, sampled from the object's boundary and put in correspondence across objects. He then goes one step further and defines *shape as the property of an object that remains after variations due to translation, scale*

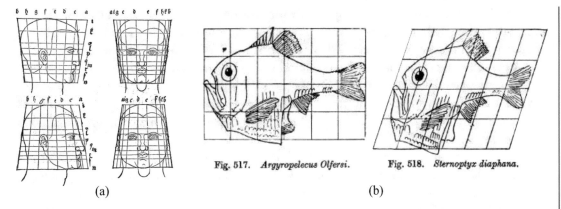

Figure 1.5: Examples from D'Arcy Thompson's work on measuring differences in shapes of related objects by means of simple mathematical transformations. The example in (a) is Albrecht Dürer's face transforms, which were among D'Arcy Thompson's inspiration for studying variation in shapes using non-rigid transformations. In panel (b) he compares the shape of an Argyropelecus olfersi with that of a Sternoptyx diaphana. The data are courtesy of Wikipedia Commons.

and rotation are factored out. This is known as Kendall's "shape space theory," introduced in 1977 [Kendall, 1977] and advanced by many others since [Dryden and Mardia, 1998, Kendall et al., 1999, Le and Kendall, 1993, Small, 1996], leading to multiple developments and applications, including the Active Shape Models of Cootes et al. [1995], in the case of 2D shapes, and to the 3D morphable models of Blanz and Vetter [1999] for 3D shapes.

There has also been remarkable success in the use of medial axis representations [Siddiqi et al., 2008], especially in medical image analysis [Bouix et al., 2005, Gorczowski et al., 2010]. These representations encode the pose-invariant topological properties of shapes. The main limitation here is that these techniques have been developed for pre-registered objects only. They do not solve for registration of points across objects using medial representations; instead, they use some off-the-shelf method for registering objects before analyzing their shapes.

There has been a tremendous amount of work on treating each object as a manifold and using its geometry to derive certain local features. These features are then matched across objects for registration and comparisons [Bronstein et al., 2009, 2010, Lipman et al., 2010]. These representations encode, simultaneously, the geometry and the topology of shapes. Their main advantage is that they are invariant under certain types of deformations (isometric or affine), and thus are suitable for finding correspondences between those kinds of shapes, e.g., shapes that only differ by bending. However, these methods do not provide a deformation (or geodesic) or any statistical modeling of variability across objects.

As we will see in subsequent chapters, treating the boundaries of objects as continuous surfaces, rather than discretizing them into point sets at the outset, provides more comprehensive solutions. Some approaches such as SPHARM or SPHARM-PDM [Brechbühler et al., 1995, Styner et al., 2006] tackle this problem by choosing special parameterizations, usually analogous to arc-length parameterization in the case of curves. Others restrict the type of reparameterizations that a surface can undergo to those that are area-preserving, such as Möbius transforms [Lipman and Funkhouser, 2009]. These represent major restrictions, and do not result in good registrations.

Once registrations have been computed, the next step is to find the set of transformations that align the surfaces. When dealing with rigid shapes, the transformations of interest are translation, scaling, and rotation. The problem is then referred to as rigid alignment. When using the L^2 metric for measuring closeness (and thus distances), and if the registration between f_1 and f_2 is known, such a rigid transformation can be found analytically using Singular Value Decomposition (SVD), leading to Procrustes analysis [Gower and Dijksterhuis, 2004], which forms the basis of the 2D Active Shape Models (ASM) of Cootes et al. [1995] and the 3D morphable models of Blanz and Vetter [1999].

In practice, however, such registrations are unknown, and better results are obtained if one simultaneously solves for the best registration and for the optimal rigid alignment. A popular solution to this problem is the Iterative Closest Point (ICP) algorithm [Besl and McKay, 1992, Chen and Medioni, 1992]. The algorithm iterates between two steps: (1) a matching step where registration is estimated by nearest-neighbor search using either point-to-point [Besl and McKay, 1992] or point-to-plane [Chen and Medioni, 1992] distances; and (2) an optimal alignment step using the estimated registration. Since its introduction, many variants of the ICP algorithm have been proposed. They aimed at improving various aspects of the original method, such as the speed and quality of convergence, by, for example, combining multiple distance measures with some local descriptors [Rusinkiewicz and Levoy, 2001]. Nevertheless, the ICP algorithm and its variants provide good results only when the poses of the shapes being aligned are initially close to each other.

When the poses are very different, the problem becomes very challenging since the search space for optimal alignment and registration is very large. In theory, however, three pairs of corresponding points are sufficient to define a rigid transformation that best aligns two shapes. This fact has been used in Chen et al. [1999], Papazov and Burschka [2011], and Rodolà et al. [2013] to derive RANSAC-based solutions. Their complexity, however, is high, of order $O(n^3)$ where n is the number of points being aligned. Aiger et al. [2008] introduced the four point congruent sets (4PCS) algorithm, which reduced the complexity of RANSAC algorithms to $O(n^2)$. It has been later optimized to achieve a complexity of order $O(n)$ [Mellado et al., 2014].

Many objects in nature, however, undergo non-rigid deformations composed of bending and stretching. In that case, the registration problem becomes even more challenging. Examples of methods that tried to solve the non-rigid registration problem include non-rigid variants of the ICP algorithm [Amberg et al., 2007] and deformation-driven techniques [Alhashim et al., 2015, Chang and Zwicker, 2008, Zhang et al., 2008].

1.4   OUR APPROACH: ELASTIC SHAPE ANALYSIS

As advocated earlier, a comprehensive approach to shape analysis involves performing registration and deformation in a single **unified** fashion. **Elastic shape analysis (ESA)** is a Riemannian approach that accomplishes exactly that for objects such as curves and surfaces. In ESA, one identifies an appropriate representation space for parameterized versions of the objects, and endows it with a Riemannian metric. The metric allows the definition of a geodesic, i.e., a shortest path, between two objects in the representation space. This path specifies the optimal deformation under the metric.

Registration is then handled by specifying an action of the reparameterization group on the representation space. The key idea is that the parameterizations of two surfaces define their registration; one changes the registration by reparameterizing the surfaces. This means that if we find the shortest path, not between the original two parametrized objects, but between all possible reparameterizations of those objects, then we simultaneously identify both the optimal registration of the objects, and the optimal deformation between them (as described by the shortest path). We also render the resulting registration and deformation independent of the original parameterizations. The result is therefore a registration and deformation of the corresponding *geometric* (i.e., unparameterized) objects.

The optimization over all possible reparameterizations can alternatively be viewed as finding a geodesic in the quotient of the original space by the group of reparameterizations (i.e., a geodesic between the orbits of the original objects under the reparameterization group), using a quotient Riemannian metric derived from that on the original space. As a matter of fact, one can also choose to introduce further invariances to, for example, translations and rotations, thereby incorporating alignment into the deformation as well. The space generated by taking these quotients is often known as a "shape space."

Central, then, to the implementation of the ESA program is the definition of a Riemannian metric on the space of parameterized objects that is preserved by the action of the relevant transformations, typically reparameterizations, translations, rotations, and perhaps scale. Key to the program's success in practical terms is the definition of a Riemannian metric that "measures" the types of shape changes that are important, and that renders computationally feasible the corresponding geodesic calculations.

These goals have been achieved in the elastic shape analysis of **curves** by using a particular member of the family of **elastic metrics**, in conjunction with a representation called the **square-root velocity function** (SRVF). The form of the elastic metric is extremely simple when expressed in terms of the SRVF: it becomes the L^2 metric [Srivastava et al., 2011]. This greatly facilitates computations, enabling sophisticated statistical analyses that require many geodesic calculations. Consequently, this method has been used in many practical problems [Laga et al.,

2012, 2014]. Critical to its utility is the fact that the mapping from the space of curves to the SRVF space is a bijection (up to a translation). Solutions found in the SRVF space using the L^2 metric can be uniquely mapped back to the original curve space, using an analytical expression. This is significantly more efficient than performing analysis in the curve space itself.

In the next chapter, we will review the elastic shape analysis of curves, and then use it as a starting point for the development of the elastic shape analysis of surfaces.

1.5 ORGANIZATION OF THIS BOOK

The rest of this book is organized as follows. We start Chapter 2 with a brief summary of the elastic shape analysis of curves in Euclidean spaces, and then introduce the elastic Riemannian metric for analyzing shapes of surfaces. This leads to the concept of square-root normal fields (SRNFs), an efficient framework for performing shape analysis using the L^2 norm. This chapter also describes the difficult problem of converting SRNF representations back to parameterized surfaces, and an approximate and computationally efficient solution to this problem.

Chapter 3 takes this fundamental framework and develops efficient algorithmic solutions for certain basic tasks, such as performing alignment and registration, and computing geodesics. Chapter 4 takes these basic tools and develops comprehensive solutions for statistical analysis, i.e., for capturing variability of shapes within and across shape classes, finding dominant modes of variability, and modeling this variability using parametric families on submanifolds of shape spaces.

Chapter 5 illustrates these ideas using various case studies, for example the statistical shape analysis of human bodies to model their variability, and the statistical shape analysis and modeling of anatomical parts for use in medical diagnoses. Examples are taken from well-known and well-used datasets: the TOSCA dataset, the SHREC07 watertight database [Giorgi et al., 2007], and the human shape database from Hasler et al. [2009a], and thus demonstrate the real applicability of elastic shape analysis.

Chapter 6 discusses and demonstrates some extensions of these ideas to shape analysis of surfaces with landmarks.

Finally, since the approach advocated here for shape analysis of surfaces is primarily a geometric one, the reader will need a certain amount of background in geometry to follow the details. In the appendices, we provide some background material on fundamental subtopics: differential and Riemannian geometry (Appendix A); in particular of surfaces in $\mathbb{R}^3$ (Appendix B); spherical parameterization of triangulated genus-0 surfaces (Appendix C); and landmark detection and matching on surfaces (Appendix D).

1.6   NOTATION

In order to help the reader, in this section we lay out the notation used in this manuscript. There is notation for general mathematical operations, and also specialized notation for representing objects, their spaces, and mappings between such spaces.

GENERAL MATHEMATICS

- Partial differentiation of a map f by a variable u will be denoted in various ways: $\frac{\partial f}{\partial u}$; $\partial_u f$; f_u.

- Composition of maps will be denoted by a circle $\circ$: if $f : X \rightarrow Y$ and $g : Y \rightarrow Z$, then $g \circ f : X \rightarrow Z$.

- We will often denote tangent vectors to a manifold at the point x by the notation δx, indicating an infinitesimal displacement of the point.

GEOMETRIC SPACES, OBJECTS, AND MAPS

Table 1.1: Spaces

Symbols	Explanation
D	Domain space of parameterized surfaces (usually S^2) or curves (usually S^1).
F	Set of parameterized surfaces (curves): smooth embeddings of D in $\mathbf{R}^3$ ($\mathbf{R}^2$).
C	Pre-shape space of surfaces (curves).
$C_f = C, S_f$	Pre-shape and shape spaces in f representation.
$\mathcal{Q}$	Space of SRNFs.
C_q, S_q	Pre-shape and shape space in SRNF representation.
Γ	Diffeomorphism (reparameterization) group of D.
$\mathcal{G}$	Space of Riemannian metrics on D.

Table 1.2: Objects

Symbols	Explanation
δX	Tangent vector to space $\mathcal{X}$ containing objects of type X, at X.
$M, T_p (M)$	A general manifold and its tangent space at $p \in M$.
$f \in F, S \in S$	Parameterized and unparameterized surfaces (curves).
$s = (u, v), ds$	Coordinate system on D; corresponding Lebesgue measure.
$n, \hat{n}$	Un-normalized and unit normal vector fields to a surface (curve).
$\gamma \in \Gamma$	Diffeomorphism (reparameterization) of D.
g	Riemannian metric induced on D by parameterized surface or curve (first fundamental form).
$\|g\| = \det(g),$ $\hat{g} = g/\|g\|$	Determinant of induced metric and "normalized" induced metric.
$r = \sqrt{\det(g)}$	Density with respect to ds of measure induced on D by parameterized surface or curve.
$J[\gamma]$	Jacobian of γ.
$\{b_i\}_{i \in I}$	Basis of $T_{id}(\Gamma)$.
$[f], [q]$	Orbits of f and q under rotation and reparameterization.
α_f, α_q	Geodesic paths in F and $\mathcal{Q}$, respectively.

Table 1.3: Maps and operators

Symbols	Explanation
$\|\cdot\|, \|\cdot\|$	Norm of a vector, L^2 norm of a function.
$\langle\cdot, \cdot\rangle, \langle\langle\cdot, \cdot\rangle\rangle_f$	Euclidean metric in $\mathbf{R}^3$, Elastic Riemannian metric on F.
$\langle\cdot, \cdot\rangle_2$	L^2 inner product between functions.
$(f, \gamma), (q, \gamma)$	Actions of Γ on F and $\mathcal{Q}$, respectively.
$Q : F \to \mathcal{Q}$	Forward mapping to SRNFs.
SRM	Square-root mapping.
$E_{inv}, E_{reg},$ E_{path}	SRNF inversion energy, registration energy, path-straightening energy.
$d_F, d_{\mathcal{Q}}, d_{S_f},$ etc.	Distance function on the space F of surfaces, on the space $\mathcal{Q}$ of SRNFs, on the shape space S_f, etc.

C H A P T E R 2

Elastic Shape Analysis: Metrics and Representations

In Chapter 1, we took a look at the long history of shape analysis, and the varied approaches that have been taken to it. We argued that elastic shape analysis (ESA), the approach taken in this book, has significant theoretical, and as a result, practical advantages over these older approaches. We explained how, by using parameterized objects, and an appropriate measure of distance between them, ESA produces a unified approach to the problems of shape registration and comparison, in contrast to other approaches. In this chapter, we will describe ESA, and the objects and structures involved, in mathematical detail.

The mathematics involved is differential and Riemannian geometry. For those not familiar with this material, Appendix A summarizes the key ideas and definitions; terms defined in the appendix appear in boldface the first time they appear in this or later chapters. However, we will not use these ideas in a very rigorous way; geometric intuition will be more important.[1] Let us begin!

2.1 SHAPES

It goes without saying, perhaps, that the objects of interest in shape analysis are "shapes." This word is used in many ways, and we too will be guilty of overloading its meaning. For our purposes, a shape will be an m-dimensional sub-**manifold**, possibly with boundary, of $\mathbb{R}^n$. This book is concerned with the case in which $m = 2$ and $n = 3$, and, in addition, in which the $m = 2$-dimensional submanifold, the "surface," is:

- closed, i.e., is the boundary of a $(m + 1) = 3$-dimensional submanifold; and

- simply connected, i.e., it has only one piece and no handles; in other words, it is connected and has genus 0.

We are thus concerned with 3D shapes that are "blobs." As an introduction, we will also discuss in some detail the case with $m = 1$ and $n = 2$ and subject to the same constraints, i.e., the case of closed planar curves. We will also briefly describe the general situation to emphasize that the approach is not limited to these cases.

---

[1]In particular, we will not concern ourselves with characterizing precisely the mathematical spaces that are needed to render everything rigorously well defined. It is worth remembering that it is only recently that the correct spaces were identified in the case of curves [Lahiri et al., 2015], but this did not impede progress in applications.

The shapes we have just described are unparameterized, i.e., they are purely geometric, whereas it was stated in the previous chapter that the starting point of elastic shape analysis is a space of *parameterized* objects of interest. Why introduce a parameterization, when there is none to start with? We will answer this question indirectly, by describing the framework of elastic shape analysis and seeing how parameterization helps.

2.2   ELASTIC SHAPE ANALYSIS

In elastic shape analysis, the genus-0 surfaces we have just mentioned will be represented by **embeddings**[2] of the 2-sphere $\mathbb{S}^2$ in $\mathbb{R}^3$, i.e., by parameterized surfaces. The unparameterized surface is then the image of $\mathbb{S}^2$ under such an embedding: if the embedding is $f : \mathbb{S}^2 \to \mathbb{R}^3$, then the surface is $f(\mathbb{S}^2) \subset \mathbb{R}^3$. (We will use the term "surface" to refer to both the embedding and its image, except where this would cause confusion.)

Clearly, there is an infinite set of embeddings, all of which share the same surface as an image. This multiplicity of representations may be dealt with by realizing that all these embeddings are related by the **group action** of the **Lie group** of **reparameterizations**, Γ, the **diffeomorphisms** of $\mathbb{S}^2$. The group Γ acts on $\mathcal{F}$ by composition: $\gamma : \mathbb{S}^2 \to \mathbb{S}^2$ acts on $f : \mathbb{S}^2 \to \mathbb{R}^n$ to give $(f, \gamma) \equiv f \circ \gamma : \mathbb{S}^2 \to \mathbb{R}^n$.[3] Notice that f and $f \circ \gamma$ represent the same unparameterized surface in $\mathbb{R}^3$ because $f \circ \gamma(\mathbb{S}^2) = f(\gamma(\mathbb{S}^2)) = f(\mathbb{S}^2)$. We can thus recover the space of genus-0 surfaces (unparameterized objects) from the space of embeddings (parameterized objects), as the **quotient space** of the latter by the action of Γ, the points of which are the **orbits** of the group action.

All of this remains true, *mutatis mutandis*, no matter what the domain D of the embeddings: it applies to surfaces ($D = \mathbb{S}^2$), but equally to closed planar curves ($D = \mathbb{S}^1$), or in general to $(m + 1)$-dimensional shapes in $\mathbb{R}^n$. We thus do not need to be specific at this point, and we will use the generic D for the domain of the embeddings from now on, unless its identity is important.

The quotient construction shows that we can use parameterized surfaces instead of unparameterized surfaces, but at the cost of an infinitely redundant representation. Why would we do this?

2.2.1   ENCODING OF REGISTRATION

One of the core tasks of shape analysis, as described in Chapter 1, is shape registration: creating a one-to-one correspondence between the points of two shapes. Parameterized objects are very natural in this context, because two parameterized surfaces f_1 and f_2 automatically provide a correspondence between the corresponding unparameterized surfaces: a point $x \in f_1(D)$ in one

---

[2]In practice, it will be hard to insist on embeddings as opposed to **immersions** (embeddings are bijective immersions); in fact, judging by the curve case, it is not even clear that we require the maps to be immersions; nevertheless we will persist in talking of embeddings rather than these more general possibilities.

[3]We denote the generic action of a group element g on an object f by (f, g) and function composition by $f \circ g$.

surface is registered to a point $y \in f_2(D)$ in another surface only if they are both images of the same point in the domain D, i.e., if and only if there exists $p \in D$ such that $x = f_1(p)$ and $y = f_2(p)$. We can thus encode different registrations of two shapes by picking different parameterized representatives for each of them. This turns out to be a very convenient way to encode registrations, and is one of the main reasons that parameterized objects are useful. The encoding of registrations in this way is illustrated in Figure 2.1.

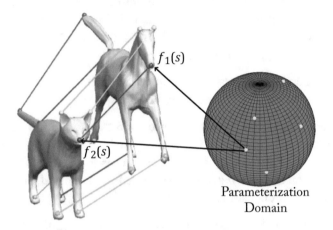

Figure 2.1: Registrations are encoded by parameterized objects via their domain. The fact that the points $f_1(s)$ and $f_2(s)$ are both images of the point $s \in \mathbb{S}^2$ means that they are registered.

At this point, though, let us note something important about this representation of registrations. Take a pair of registered points x and y as before, which by definition can be written $x = f_1(p)$ and $y = f_2(p)$ for some $p \in D$, and consider the two embeddings $f_1 \circ \gamma$ and $f_2 \circ \gamma$ produced by the action of a reparameterization. We note that $x = f_1(p) = f_1(\gamma \circ \gamma^{-1}(p)) = f_1 \circ \gamma(q)$ and $y = f_2(p) = f_2(\gamma \circ \gamma^{-1}(p)) = f_2 \circ \gamma(q)$, where $q = \gamma^{-1}(p)$. Thus, we see that if there is a $p \in D$ such that $x = f_1(p)$ and $y = f_2(p)$, then there is also a $q \in D$ such that $x = f_1 \circ \gamma(q)$ and $y = f_2 \circ \gamma(q)$. In other words, the pair f_1 and f_2 describe the same registration as the pair $f_1 \circ \gamma$ and $f_2 \circ \gamma$, in the sense that if two points are registered under one description, then they are registered under the other. Registration is thus invariant to the simultaneous action of Γ on the two embeddings involved. This point will be important as we move to the second key ingredient of ESA: the definition of a Riemannian metric on the space of parameterized objects.

2.2.2   RIEMANNIAN METRIC AND OPTIMAL REGISTRATION

As described in Chapter 1, ESA is based upon a **Riemannian metric** on the space of parameterized objects. A Riemannian metric measures the distance between infinitesimally close objects; alternatively, it measures the "size" of an infinitesimal change in (or "deformation of") an object.

A Riemannian metric can be used to define a distance between objects that are not infinitesimally close, by calculating the length of the shortest path between the two objects. (This is explained further in Section A.2.) The shortest path so found, known as a **geodesic**, then describes an "optimal deformation" from one object to the other.[4]

In ESA, however, we are not interested in distances and deformations between parameterized objects, but between unparameterized objects, i.e., shapes. In addition, we wish to find optimal registrations between these shapes. It turns out that in order to perform these functions (how this is done will be outlined presently, and detailed in the next chapter), a Riemannian metric on the space of parameterized objects should satisfy, insofar as possible, three general desiderata. We list these first, and then discuss them.

Interpretation: The metric should have an intuitive interpretation, and "measure" the types of changes in shape that are important in applications.

Invariance: The metric should be "preserved" by certain transformations: first, by the action of diffeomorphisms (reparameterizations) of the domain D of the objects; second, by translations and rotations.[5] The term "preserved" here means that if the same transformation acts on both objects, the distance between them remains unchanged. In mathematical terms, the transformations act by **isometries**.

Efficiency: Calculations involving the metric should be computationally feasible, with practically relevant time and space requirements.

The first and the last desiderata are natural enough, and need no great justification, even if many methods do not satisfy them. On the other hand, the second is rather technical, and demands some explanation.

The Riemannian metric in ESA is defined on the space of parameterized objects. Recall that any pair of parameterized objects implicitly defines two corresponding unparameterized objects, and a registration. The distance between two parameterized objects calculated using the metric will thus depend on both the unparameterized, geometric objects *and* the registration. This is a feature, not a bug, as it means that the Riemannian metric on parameterized objects will give us, simultaneously, a distance between unparameterized objects and their optimal registration. However, recall also that the simultaneous action of Γ, the group of reparameterizations of the domain D, on both objects, did not change the registration between unparameterized surfaces, as encoded by two parameterized versions of those surfaces. Therefore, in order for the

---

[4]The word "metric" is overloaded in mathematics. In our context, it can refer to a Riemannian metric, or to a function on pairs of points that satisfies the axioms of a metric space. The geodesic distance defined by a Riemannian metric satisfies these axioms, and so a Riemannian metric defines a metric. To avoid this clash of nomenclature, and to avoid having to use the adjective "Riemannian" continually, we will use the term "distance" to refer to a metric on a metric space, and "metric" to refer to a Riemannian metric.

[5]We have already described the action of diffeomorphisms, by composition on the right. Translations and rotations act on parameterized maps by composition too, but this time on the left: $f : D \to \mathbb{R}^n$ and a translation $\mathbb{R}^n \ni a : \mathbb{R}^n \to \mathbb{R}^n$ combine to give $f + a : D \to \mathbb{R}^n$, while a rotation $SO(n) \ni O : \mathbb{R}^n \to \mathbb{R}^n$ takes f to $Of : D \to \mathbb{R}^n$, where juxtaposition indicates multiplication by the rotation matrix.

distance between two unparameterized surfaces to depend *only* on the unparameterized surfaces and the registration between them, and not on the particular parameterized surfaces chosen to represent the unparameterized surfaces and the registration, the metric must be preserved by the simultaneous action of Γ on the two parameterized objects. This explains the first part of the second desideratum.

The second part of the second desideratum is a necessity if we wish our results to be independent of any special point or orientation in space: we should be able to translate, rotate, and scale two surfaces in the same way without altering the distance and the registration between them. In other words, the metric should be preserved by Euclidean transformations. Note that this does not mean that the distance between two objects remains the same if we translate or rotate *one* of them (or, in other words, that the distance between an object and its translated or rotated versions is zero); this is a different property, "geometric invariance," which we discuss in Section 2.2.3.

In addition, the second desideratum is essential in order to satisfy the third; we will see why as we discuss finding the optimal registration and deformation.

Optimal Registration and Deformation

Once we have a Riemannian metric on the space of parameterized objects that satisfies our desiderata, how do we use it to define a distance between *unparameterized* surfaces, while simultaneously finding their optimal registration and deformation? The essential idea is as follows; we will describe it in mathematical and algorithmic detail in Chapter 3.

Given two parameterized objects, we can represent all registrations between them by acting on one of them with all possible diffeomorphisms. (Note that we do not have to act on both objects with all possible pairs of diffeomorphisms in order to generate all possible registrations, because acting with the same diffeomorphism on both objects does not change the registration represented.) We can compute the distance between each of the resulting pairs of parameterized objects by finding the length of the shortest path from one to the other using the Riemannian metric. The pair of parameterized objects with the smallest distance between them then defines:

- a distance between the corresponding unparameterized objects (because it does not depend on the initial paramaterization of either object);

- an optimal registration of the corresponding unparameterized objects, defined by the parameterizations of the closest objects; and

- an optimal deformation between the corresponding unparameterized objects, defined by the geodesic between them.

It is here that we see why our second desideratum is essential for satisfying the third. If diffeomorphisms did not act by isometries, we could not minimize over reparameterizations of one object alone in order to find the minimizing distance, even though this would still be a search over all registrations. This is because the distance would depend not just on the registration, but on the individual parameterizations. It would then be tempting to think that we could simply minimize over all pairs of reparameterizations of both objects, which, although more complex computationally, would not be disastrous. However, this is not the case. The reason is that the "distance" between unparameterized objects so defined would not necessarily satisfy the triangle inequality: f_1 might be very close to f_2 in one parameterization, and f_2 in another parameterization might be very close to f_3, but this is no guarantee that f_1 and f_3 are close in any single parameterization. (In contrast, it is easy to prove that **isometric** actions do preserve the triangle inequality: we will see the proof in the next chapter, and further details are given in Appendix A.) It turns out that if reparameterizations do not act by isometries, then in order to define a distance between unparameterized objects that does satisfy the triangle inequality, we would have to minimize not only over continuous paths between them, but between all paths generated by arbitrary (i.e., not necessarily continuous) reparameterizations of every point in each continuous path. Such a task, needless to say, is computationally infeasible.

2.2.3   GEOMETRIC INVARIANCE

The invariances discussed so far ensure that the distance between two unparameterized objects, and their optimal registration, depend only on their geometry, and not on individual parameterizations or on arbitrary positions and orientations. These are necessities if we are to talk about *shape* analysis as such.

In many cases, however, we may also wish the distance to be invariant to various geometric transformations of the *individual* objects. In particular, we may require that the distance between two objects not change if either of the objects is translated, rotated, or scaled: that is, the distance, and hence the registration, should depend only on what we might call the "intrinsic shape" of the objects.[6] Look at Figure 2.2. It shows translated, rotated, and scaled versions of an object. Geometric invariance implies that the distance between any pair of these objects is zero. There are three standard methods for achieving such invariances.[7]

Intrinsic   The obvious method is to construct a metric that is invariant to such changes to begin with. The metrics we will use will all be constructed exclusively from derivatives of the parameterized objects, meaning that any additive constants disappear. Invariance is therefore automatic for translations.

Quotient   The second method is to define a new distance by calculating the minimum distance between all possible translations, rotations, or scalings of both objects: the result is then clearly independent of the initial positions, orientations, or scales of the objects. In this context, the fact that simultaneous rotation of both objects preserves the metric has an

---

[6]The word "shape" is often used to apply to what we are here calling "intrinsic shape."

[7]Under many circumstances, these three methods can all be used in such a way that they produce the same results, but not always. We will not go into the technical details of this.

additional advantage: it means one has only to minimize over the possible rotations of one of the objects.

Section The third method is to fix a "canonical" scale, position, or orientation for the objects, and to transform them all so that they satisfy this constraint. It turns out to be particularly easy to fix a canonical scale given the surface representations to be discussed later in this chapter.

Figure 2.2: Translations, rotations, and scalings of an object. If geometric invariance is respected, the distance between any pair of these objects is zero.

Due to the properties of the Riemannian metric and surface representations used in the ESA framework, as mentioned above under each method, we use intrinsic invariance to achieve translation invariance; the quotient construction to achieve rotational invariance; and a section to achieve scale invariance. We will refer to the process of rendering the distance geometrically invariant, and, in particular, the optimization over rotations, as "alignment." We will give further specifics about this process for curves and surfaces as appropriate, and will describe how it is implemented computationally in the next chapter.

2.3 BACKGROUND: ELASTIC FRAMEWORK FOR CURVES

Is it possible to find a metric for surfaces that satisfies our desiderata, and then implement the ESA framework just described? To guide us, we look first at the case of curves, where the elastic shape analysis program has already been successfully implemented.

The parameterized objects in this case are elements of the space $\mathcal{F}$ of absolutely continuous maps $f : D \to \mathbb{R}^n$, with domain $D = \mathbb{D}^1$, the interval, for open curves, or $D = \mathbb{S}^1$, the circle, for closed curves. Elastic shape analysis is then based on a one-parameter family of Riemannian metrics on $\mathcal{F}$ known as the "elastic metric," for reasons that will become clear. Although any member of this family could in principle be used for elastic shape analysis, there is one particular member that best satisfies the desiderata, as we shall see.

2.3.1   ELASTIC METRIC FOR CURVES

To express the elastic Riemannian metric, it is convenient to define a new curve "representation." A representation is a map from the space of objects, in this case, curves, to another space. By analogy with the idea of coordinates on a manifold, i.e., a map $x : M \rightarrow \mathbb{R}^n$, one may think of a representation as a different set of coordinates for the space concerned, except that a representation might not always be injective.

Let $\tau = \dot{f}$ be the derivative of the curve $f : D \rightarrow \mathbb{R}^n$, i.e., the unnormalized tangent vector to the curve (see Figure 2.3). We can then define the "speed" of the curve, $r = |\tau|$, and its "direction," $\hat{\tau} = \frac{\tau}{|\tau|}$. It turns out to be convenient to use, instead of r, its square-root, $\zeta = r^{1/2}$. The new representation is then

$$\zeta = |\tau|^{\frac{1}{2}} \tag{2.1}$$

$$\hat{\tau} = \frac{\tau}{|\tau|} . \tag{2.2}$$

The representation space therefore consists of pairs of maps $(\zeta, \hat{\tau}) : D \rightarrow \mathbb{R}_{>0} \times \mathbb{S}^1$.

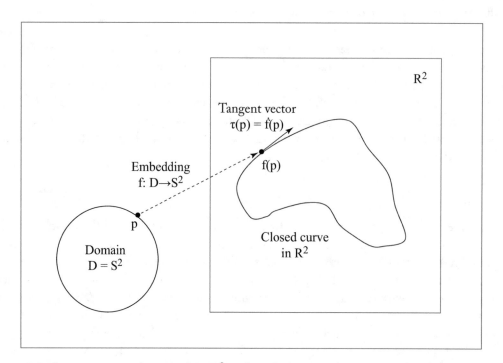

Figure 2.3: A parameterized curve f in $\mathbb{R}^2$ and its derivative, the unnormalized tangent vector $\tau = \dot{f}$, evaluated at a point $p \in D$.

In terms of this representation, the *elastic* Riemannian metric G on the space of such maps, is given by

$$G_{(\zeta,\hat{\tau})}((\delta\zeta, \delta\hat{\tau}), (\delta\zeta, \delta\hat{\tau})) = \int_D ds \left(\delta\zeta^2 + a\,\zeta^2 \langle \delta\hat{\tau}, \delta\hat{\tau} \rangle \right), \qquad (2.3)$$

where s is a coordinate on D (not necessarily arc length), ds is the corresponding Lebesgue measure, $(\delta\zeta, \delta\hat{\tau})$ is a tangent vector to the representation space at the point $(\zeta, \hat{\tau})$ (i.e., an infinitesimal change in $(\zeta, \hat{\tau})$), $\langle \cdot, \cdot \rangle$ is the Euclidean inner product on $\mathbb{R}^n$, and $a \in \mathbb{R}_{>0}$ is the family parameter. (There is also a possible overall scale factor, but this has no consequence for the current discussion.)

Having defined the elastic metric, we now explain it by showing that it satisfies our three desiderata.

Interpretation

A change in ζ means a change in r. This corresponds to a *stretching* of the curve: the infinitesimal distance between the points s and $s + ds$ is changed. A change in $\hat{\tau}$ corresponds to a *bending* of the curve: the direction of the infinitesimal interval $[s, s + ds]$ is changed. The metric thus has a very physical interpretation: it measures both stretching and bending, with the magnitude of the change being a combination of the measures of each. The presence of the stretching term explains the name "elastic metric," to contrast this metric with those used in previous work that did not allow stretching when matching curves to each other. We have thus satisfied the desideratum of interpretation.

Efficiency

If $a = 1$, the integrand in Equation (2.3) takes the same form as the Euclidean metric on $\mathbb{R}^n$ expressed in polar coordinates. This fact has a dramatic consequence. It means that the representation space endowed with the elastic metric with $a = 1$ is *flat*: its Riemannian curvature is zero. This means that we should be able to find "Euclidean coordinates" that can be used to express the elastic metric in particularly simple terms.

Using the analogy with polar coordinates, we can guess that such Euclidean coordinates should be given by

$$q = \zeta\hat{\tau} = \frac{\tau}{|\tau|^{\frac{1}{2}}}, \qquad (2.4)$$

and indeed this is the case. Calculating the map between tangent vectors, we find

$$\delta q = \delta\zeta\hat{\tau} + \zeta\delta\hat{\tau}, \qquad (2.5)$$

and thus, since $\langle \hat{\tau}, \delta\hat{\tau} \rangle = 0$, we find

$$\langle \delta q, \delta q \rangle = \delta\zeta^2 + \zeta^2 \langle \delta\hat{\tau}, \delta\hat{\tau} \rangle. \qquad (2.6)$$

The elastic metric in this new, *square-root velocity function* (SRVF) representation therefore takes the very simple form:

$$G_q(\delta q, \delta q) = \int_D ds \, \langle \delta q, \delta q \rangle = \|\delta q\|^2 \, . \tag{2.7}$$

This is the L^2 metric on the tangent space at the point q in the space $\mathcal{Q}$ of SRVFs. Note that it does not depend on q. We can immediately deduce that the distance between two points q_0 and q_1 is simply given by

$$d_{\mathcal{Q}}(q_0, q_1) = \|q_1 - q_0\| \, , \tag{2.8}$$

and that the geodesic between these two points is just the straight line between them:

$$\alpha_q(t) = (1 - t)q_0 + tq_1 \, . \tag{2.9}$$

The space $\mathcal{Q}$ of SRVFs, the image $\mathcal{Q}(\mathcal{F})$ of $\mathcal{F}$ under the map

$$Q : \mathcal{F} \to \mathcal{Q} \tag{2.10}$$

$$f \mapsto Q(f) = \frac{\tau}{|\tau|^{\frac{1}{2}}} \, , \tag{2.11}$$

is precisely the space $L^2(D, \mathbb{R}^n)$: $\mathcal{Q} \equiv L^2(D, \mathbb{R}^n)$.

These facts mean that the calculation of distances and geodesics in $\mathcal{Q}$ is trivial; indeed, $\mathcal{Q}$ is "Euclidean." Statistical analysis can thus proceed precisely as it would in $\mathbb{R}^n$, modulo technicalities due to the infinite dimensionality of $\mathcal{Q}$. Otherwise, more usually and more practically, a finite-dimensional subspace can be selected, and statistical analysis can take place there. We thus seem to have satisfied the desideratum of efficiency.

However, what we really want is not geodesics and statistical analysis in $\mathcal{Q}$, but geodesics and statistical analysis in $\mathcal{F}$. Fortunately, since the map Q is *bijective*, up to translation, there is a one-to-one correspondence between elements of $\mathcal{F}$ modulo translations, and $\mathcal{Q}$. Since $\dot{f} = \tau = |q|q$, the inverse of Q is given by

$$Q^{-1}(q)(s) = \int^s ds' \, |q|q + f_0 \, , \tag{2.12}$$

where f_0 accounts for the arbitrary translation. The consequence is that all geometric objects, and all the results of statistical analysis, can be calculated in $\mathcal{Q}$, and then can be mapped back to $\mathcal{F}$ using Q^{-1}. We thus really have satisfied the desideratum of efficiency.

There is one fly in the ointment, however. The above is true without conditions for open curves, but for closed curves, we face the problem that a geodesic in $\mathcal{Q}$ that runs between two closed curves may contain curves along its length that are not closed. Since the closure condition is nonlinear when expressed in terms of the SRVF, and since closed curves form a codimension-n subset of $\mathcal{Q}$, this seems inevitable. One approach to this would be to ignore it. A second would be to develop a method to find the shortest path between two SRVFs that does lie within the subset of $\mathcal{Q}$ corresponding to closed curves, and indeed such a method has been developed. We will not dwell further on this point, except to note that even in the case of curves, there are obstacles to the complete fulfilment of our dreams.

We have seen that the form of the elastic metric simplifies when $a = 1$. Is there any other argument for the use of this particular parameter value? After all, there is no *a priori* guarantee that it will produce reasonable results. The best answer at present is that this choice not only enables dramatic improvements in computational efficiency, and hence computation time, it also produces intuitively reasonable behavior in applications. In the end, this is what matters.

Invariance

The elastic metric is preserved by translations by design, because it only depends on $\dot{f}$. Since rotations only act on $\hat{\tau}$, and this always appears in a dot product, rotations act by isometries also.

The case of diffeomorphisms is more complex. Although the elastic metric is diffeomorphism-invariant for all values of a, we will only prove it here for the case of interest, when $a = 1$ and we can use the SRVF representation.

The group Γ of diffeomorphisms of D acts by composition on $\mathcal{F}$: $(f, \gamma) = f \circ \gamma$. The tangent vector $\tau = \dot{f}$ therefore transforms as $(\tau, \gamma) = \dot{\gamma}(\tau \circ \gamma)$. Equation (2.4) in turn means that Γ acts on $\mathcal{Q}$ via

$$(q, \gamma) = Q(f \circ \gamma) = \sqrt{\dot{\gamma}}\,(q \circ \gamma)\,, \tag{2.13}$$

where we note that we restrict attention to orientation-preserving diffeomorphisms, i.e., those with $\dot{\gamma} > 0$. Since this is a linear action, a tangent vector transforms as: $(\delta q, \gamma) = \sqrt{\dot{\gamma}}\,(\delta q \circ \gamma)$. As a result, we find that the metric transforms as follows:

$$G_{(q,\gamma)}((\delta q, \gamma), (\delta q, \gamma)) = \int_D ds\,\langle \sqrt{\dot{\gamma}}\,(\delta q \circ \gamma), \sqrt{\dot{\gamma}}\,(\delta q \circ \gamma)\rangle \tag{2.14a}$$

$$= \int_D ds\,\dot{\gamma}\,\langle \delta q \circ \gamma, \delta q \circ \gamma\rangle \tag{2.14b}$$

$$= \int_D ds\,\langle \delta q, \delta q\rangle \tag{2.14c}$$

$$= G_q(\delta q, \delta q)\,, \tag{2.14d}$$

where the penultimate line follows by a change of integration variable $s \mapsto \gamma(s)$. We thus see that Γ acts by isometries.

2.3.2 GEOMETRIC INVARIANCE

The fact that the metric only depends on $\dot{f}$ means that, in addition to being preserved by simultaneous translations of the two objects by the same amount, the metric is also preserved by separate translations of each object. Translation invariance is therefore immediate.

To render the distance invariant to the orientations of the objects, we will use the second method described in Section 2.2.3, and optimize over all possible rotations of one object. This is a well known problem with an analytical solution; we describe this in the next chapter.

We can render the distance invariant to the scale of the curves by first scaling both curves to have unit length, and then restricting attention to the subspace of unit length curves, $\mathcal{F}_1$, calculating distances and geodesics in this space. The SRVF representation allows us to do this without sacrificing efficiency as follows. Note that

$$\|q\|^2 = \int_D ds\, |q|^2 = \int_D ds\, |\dot{f}| = \mathcal{L}(f)\,, \tag{2.15}$$

the length of f. Thus, we see that $\mathcal{F}_1$ maps under Q to the unit sphere $\mathcal{Q}_1$ in $\mathcal{Q}$. This means that the scale-invariant distance between two curves can be calculated by computing the distance on the unit sphere; there is a simple analytical form for this, and for the corresponding geodesic (see Equation (A.7)), meaning that incorporating scale invariance is scarcely more difficult than not.

2.3.3   SUMMARY OF ELASTIC FRAMEWORK FOR CURVES

We have now seen that all three desiderata are satisfied by the elastic metric on curves. The definition of the metric itself leads to it having a clear and intuitive interpretation, and to it measuring "physical" changes in the shape of curves. Its form means that it is preserved by diffeomorphisms of D, as well as by rotations and translations. The satisfaction of the desideratum of efficiency depends on two facts:

- the space $\mathcal{Q}$ endowed with the elastic metric is *flat*, meaning that the metric can be transformed to a very simple, "Euclidean" form by a suitable choice of representation; and

- the map Q is *invertible* (up to trivial transformations) in a computationally feasible way, meaning that the results of analysis in $\mathcal{Q}$ can be transported back to $\mathcal{F}$.

Finally, geometric invariance is easily achieved due to a combination of the form of the metric, and the geometric interpretation of the norm of the SRVF.

Is the elastic metric the only metric that satisfies our desiderata? In general, this seems unlikely. However, if we restrict attention to metrics that are ultralocal in the first derivatives of the curve,[8] then it is possible that the elastic metric is the unique choice, in the same way that the Fisher-Rao metric is the unique choice for probability distributions [Bauer et al., 2016]. This would in turn mean that the elastic metric with $a = 1$ would be the unique *flat* metric satisfying these constraints. This, however, is a matter for further research.

The question now is whether we can achieve similar results in the case of surfaces.

---

[8]"Ultralocal" here means consisting of a single integral over the curve involving no derivatives of the ultralocalized quantity, in this case, involving no higher derivatives of the curve, e.g., no curvature.

2.4   ELASTIC FRAMEWORK FOR SURFACES

We have seen how the elastic metric on spaces of curves satisfied our three desiderata, and led naturally to the SRVF representation, a set of "Euclidean coordinates" for the space of curves in $\mathbb{R}^n$ that dramatically simplifies the computation of geodesics, and hence statistical analysis. Our goal now is to do the same for surfaces in $\mathbb{R}^3$ (i.e., the case $m = 2$ and $n = 3$), although we will see that the framework extends readily to other dimensions and codimensions.

The parameterized objects in this case are elements of a suitable space $\mathcal{F}$ of maps $f :$ $D \to \mathbb{R}^3$, where D can be the disc $\mathbb{D}^2$, the sphere $\mathbb{S}^2$, or other domains including cylindrical and quadrilateral. Let Γ be the set of all diffeomorphisms of D. As in the case of curves, it acts naturally on $\mathcal{F}$ by composition: $(f, \gamma) = f \circ \gamma$. Again, as in the case of curves, the map from embeddings to surfaces is not injective: two embeddings related by the action of Γ correspond to the same surface, so that the space of unparameterized surfaces can be thought of as the quotient $\mathcal{F}/\Gamma$.

How can we construct a metric on $\mathcal{F}$ that satisfies our desiderata? Let us first define some key quantities.[9] Let $s = (u, v)$ be coordinates on D. The partial derivatives f_u and f_v are then tangent vectors to the surface at the point $f(s)$. The unnormalized normal vector is then given by $n = f_u \times f_v$, where $\times$ indicates the cross product in $\mathbb{R}^3$.[10] The magnitude of n is $|n| = |g|^{\frac{1}{2}} = r$, the density with respect to $ds = du\, dv$ of the **induced measure** on D arising from the Riemannian metric g **induced** on D from the Euclidean metric on $\mathbb{R}^3$ by the map f, also known as the **pullback metric**. The tangent vectors and normal vector are illustrated in Figure 2.4.

2.4.1   SQUARE-ROOT MAP

Having defined these quantities, we can describe a first try at a metric. The approach taken by Kurtek et al. [2010] was to develop a new representation of surfaces such that the action of Γ preserves L^2 distances in the new representation space. The new representation was called the *square-root map* (SRM). The SRM q_{SRM} of a parameterized surface f is defined to be $q_{\text{SRM}} = r^{1/2} f$. The Riemannian metric is then taken to be the L^2 metric in SRM space. By construction, since $r = |g|^{\frac{1}{2}}$, the SRM is a half-density; the product of any two SRMs is thus a density, and transforms under diffeomorphisms of D in such a way that the L^2 metric is preserved. The SRM therefore satisfies the first part of the desideratum of invariance. Despite this success, the L^2 metric on SRMs fails to satisfy our other desiderata, as follows.

1. Translations do not act by isometries. In other words, the distance between two surfaces, and the distance between the same two surfaces translated by the same amount, will be

---

[9]Further explanation of this material is given in Appendix A.

[10] More generally, we can talk about the exterior derivative of f, df, and use the wedge product to define (abusing notation) $n = df \wedge df$, which is a 2-form on D taking values in $\mathbb{R}^3 \wedge \mathbb{R}^3$. If we then take the dual of this, both in $\mathbb{R}^3$ and D, we end up with an $\mathbb{R}^3$-valued 0-form on D, which is the unnormalized normal vector. It is this definition that generalizes to arbitrary m and n.

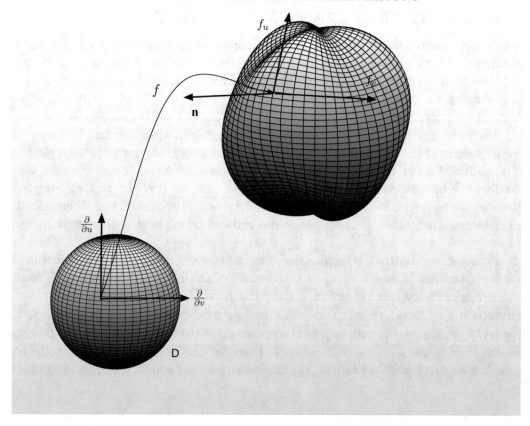

Figure 2.4: **A parameterized surface and its tangent and normal vectors.**

different. While invariance can be restored by centering all surfaces on a fixed point, the results depend upon the point chosen. This generates an unwelcome arbitrariness in the metric.

2. The metric does not have an intuitive interpretation in terms of the geometry of the surfaces concerned; it is certainly not the surface analogue of the elastic metric on curves.

3. Although the choice of the L^2 metric means that the computation of geometrical quantities, and hence statistical analysis, are very efficient in $\mathcal{Q}_{SRM}$, this efficiency cannot be exploited because the map from $\mathcal{F}$ to $\mathcal{Q}_{SRM}$ is difficult to invert; results obtained in $\mathcal{Q}_{SRM}$ cannot easily be transferred back to $\mathcal{F}$.

The next chapter shows how the SRM can be used to compute distances and geodesics between shapes. Nevertheless, although an interesting start, the SRM is clearly not the solution we are seeking. To go further, we will take a different approach. Rather than starting from a representation and imposing the L^2 metric upon it, we will instead generalize the proven elastic metric from the space of curves to that of surfaces, and then look for simplifying representations. It is to the development of such a metric that we now turn.

2.4.2   GENERALIZING THE ELASTIC METRIC FOR CURVES

The key intuitions behind the development of an elastic metric on $\mathcal{F}$ are that:

- the speed of a curve is equal to the square-root of the determinant of the Riemannian metric induced on its domain by its embedding in $\mathbb{R}^n$: $r = |\tau| = |\dot{f}| = \langle \dot{f}, \dot{f} \rangle^{1/2} = |g|^{\frac{1}{2}}$, where g is the induced Riemannian metric; and

- the dot product between the unit tangent vectors to a curve at any point is equal to the dot product between the corresponding unit normal vectors: $\langle \hat{\tau}, \hat{\tau} \rangle = \langle \hat{n}, \hat{n} \rangle$.

The representation of a curve in terms of its speed function and its unit tangent vector field can therefore also be thought of as a representation in terms of its induced Riemannian metric g and its unit normal vector field $\hat{n}$. As a result, the elastic metric on $\mathcal{F}$ can be viewed as a Riemannian metric on the product space of the space of Riemannian metrics on D and the space of unit normal vector fields. More specifically, the first term can be viewed as a Riemannian metric on the space of Riemannian metrics on D, while the second term can be viewed as a Riemannian metric on the space of unit normal vector fields, formed by integrating with respect to the induced measure generated by the induced metric.[11] This point of view is facilitated by the fact that there is a bijection between $\mathcal{F}$ and this product space, so that we can view the representation as a new set of "coordinates" on $\mathcal{F}$. Can we generalize this idea to the case of surfaces?

In the case of codimension-1 surfaces, such as those we are considering, there is still a unit normal vector field, $\hat{n} = n/|n|$, and a Metric on the space of such fields can still be defined by integrating against the induced measure $r = |g|^{\frac{1}{2}}$ on the surface domain D generated by the induced Riemannian metric g. This second term can therefore remain essentially unchanged when we move to surfaces. The question then naturally arises: is there a generalization of the first term in the elastic metric on curves that constitutes a Metric on the space of metrics on the surface domain, and on which the group of diffeomorphisms of the surface domain acts as isometries? Fortunately the answer is yes; it turns out that it has a long history.

Metric on Metrics

As part of his study of quantum gravity, DeWitt [1967] defined the following *unique, one-parameter family of diffeomorphism-invariant, ultralocal Metrics* on the space of Riemannian met-

---

[11]Henceforth, to avoid confusion, we will capitalize the word metric when referring to a Riemannian metric on an infinite-dimensional space, reserving the lower case for Riemannian metrics on finite-dimensional spaces.

rics on a manifold:[12]

$$G_g(\delta g, \delta g) = \int_D ds \, |g|^{\frac{1}{2}} \left[\text{tr}(g^{-1} \, \delta g \, g^{-1} \, \delta g) + \frac{\lambda}{2} \text{tr}(g^{-1} \, \delta g) \, \text{tr}(g^{-1} \, \delta g) \right], \qquad (2.16)$$

where, for positivity, $\lambda > \frac{-2}{m} = -1$ for 3D shapes.

In addition to the work of DeWitt, who studies this full Metric, the first term (i.e., the special case with $\lambda = 0$) has been much studied in the mathematical literature [Clarke, 2010, Ebin, 1968, Gil-Medrano and Michor, 1991]. The zero-dimensional version of this Metric, i.e., the above but with the integral removed, has been used more recently as a Riemannian metric on the space of positive-definite matrices, in Pennec and Lorenzi [2011].

Change of variables   It is convenient to change the variables in which the metric g is expressed. We can describe any metric by splitting it into its determinant, $|g|$, and a unit determinant metric, $\hat{g} = g/|g|$. We then define the variable

$$\zeta = \kappa^{-1} |g|^{\frac{1}{4}} = \kappa^{-1} r^{\frac{1}{2}}, \qquad (2.17)$$

where $\kappa = \sqrt{8m(\lambda m + 2)} = \sqrt{32(\lambda + 1)}$ for 3D shapes.

The Metric G can be re-expressed in terms of ζ and $\hat{g}$. The result is:

$$G_g(\delta g, \delta g) = \int_D ds \left[d\zeta^2 + \kappa^2 \zeta^2 \text{tr}(\hat{g}^{-1} \, \delta \hat{g} \, \hat{g}^{-1} \, \delta \hat{g}) \right]. \qquad (2.18)$$

The rewriting of the Metric G in these variables facilitates its intuitive interpretation, but we postpone discussion of this until we have defined the full elastic Metric for surfaces.

2.4.3   ELASTIC METRIC FOR SURFACES

When we combine the Metric on metrics given in Equation (2.18) with the metric on unit normal vector fields, we find the following full elastic Metric on the product space of Riemannian metrics and unit normal fields:

$$G_{(g,\hat{n})}((\delta g, \delta \hat{n}), (\delta g, \delta \hat{n}))$$
$$= \int_D ds \, |g|^{\frac{1}{2}} \left\{ \left[\text{tr}(g^{-1} \, \delta g \, g^{-1} \, \delta g + \frac{\lambda}{2} \text{tr}(g^{-1} \, \delta g) \, \text{tr}(g^{-1} \, \delta g) \right] + c \langle \delta \hat{n}, \delta \hat{n} \rangle \right\}$$
$$= \int_D ds \left[d\zeta^2 + \kappa^2 \zeta^2 \, \text{tr}(\hat{g}^{-1} \, \delta \hat{g} \, \hat{g}^{-1} \, \delta \hat{g}) + c \kappa^2 \zeta^2 \, \langle \delta \hat{n}, \delta \hat{n} \rangle \right], \qquad (2.19)$$

where $c \in \mathbb{R}_{>0}$.

We have thus reached the point in the elastic shape analysis of surfaces that we had reached for curves at Equation (2.3). We note the following points.

---

[12]"Ultralocal" means not including any derivatives of the metric.

- We have defined a new representation for surfaces $(g, \hat{n})$ in terms of the induced Riemannian metric g and the unit normal field $\hat{n}$.

- This representation is strictly analogous to the representation of curves as pairs $(\zeta, \hat{\tau})$. Indeed this latter is a special case of the former when the domain D is one-dimensional. This is revealed by re-writing the metric g as a pair $(\zeta, \hat{g})$, so that the surface representation becomes $(\zeta, \hat{g}, \hat{n})$. When the domain is one-dimensional, $\hat{g} \equiv 1$, and we see that the surface representation reduces to the curve representation.

- We have defined a Riemannian metric on the surface representation space that is a strict generalization of that on the curve representation space. This can be seen most clearly when the Metric is expressed in terms of the $(\zeta, \hat{g})$ variables.

As in the curve case, having defined the Metric, let us now see whether it satisfies our three desiderata.

Interpretation

The last term measures changes in the local "direction" of the surface, or, in other words, it measures "bending." This is essentially the same as in the curve case, and needs no further explanation.

The first two terms measure changes in the induced metric. The induced metric measures distances in the surface, and as such, changes in the induced metric correspond to "stretching." We therefore have a situation very similar to the elastic Metric for curves: the full elastic Metric for surfaces measures both bending and stretching of the surface.

Stretching in one dimension and stretching in more than one dimension are very different, however, with the result that there are two stretching terms in the elastic Metric for surfaces, but only one in the elastic Metric for curves. The difference arises because, in more than one dimension, a local piece of the surface has not only "size," like a local piece of a curve, but also "shape." This is made explicit in the second form of the full elastic Metric, Equation (2.19), via the split into two terms. The first term measures changes in the induced "area" of a local patch, via changes $\delta\zeta$ in the square-root of the induced measure. Changes in the "shape" of a local patch that do not affect local area do not affect this term. In contrast, the second term is not affected by changes in local area. Rather it measures changes in the "shape" of a local patch via changes in the relative magnitude and directions of the eigenvectors of a positive-definite, unit determinant form, $\hat{g}$, and then weights these changes by the local area. To summarize, the full elastic Metric for surfaces can be interpreted as a sum over the infinite set of infinitesimal surface patches making up the surface. For each patch, the first term measures changes in its area, the second term measures changes in its shape, weighted by its area, while the third term measures changes in its normal direction, again weighted by its area.

The full elastic Metric thus has an intuitive interpretation in terms of changes in the surface, that are a direct generalization of those in the case of curves. We can therefore say that this desideratum is satisfied.

Invariance

The induced metric and the unit normal field are both expressed in terms of derivatives of the surface. They are thus invariant to translation, and hence the Metric is too. The first two terms in the Metric do not transform under rotations, while the last term is expressed in terms of invariant inner products. The Metric is thus preserved by rotations.

We will not prove it, but the Metric on metrics, G, is preserved by the action of the group Γ of diffeomorphisms of D, as claimed by DeWitt. Similarly, since $\hat{n}$ is a scalar as far as diffeomorphisms are concerned, the last term is the integral of a density, and hence is preserved by Γ also.

Efficiency

The form of the full elastic Metric in Equation (2.19) is analogous to the form of the elastic metric on curves in Equation (2.3). The next step in the case of curves was to find a specific member of the parameterized family of elastic Metrics that had zero curvature, i.e., for which the representation space was flat. Such a Metric should admit a system of "coordinates" in terms of which it takes on L^2 form. For curves, we found such a representation, the SRVF, thereby greatly simplifying the calculation of all geometric, and hence statistical, quantities in the representation space.

The second crucial property of this representation was that it was invertible in a computationally tractable way. This enabled the statistical analysis carried out in the SRVF representation space, where the Metric is very simple, to be transformed back to the original, "physical" space of curves.

The bad news is that, to date, these steps have not been carried out for the full elastic Metric. As with the representation of a curve in terms of its speed and unit normal (or tangent) field, the $(g, \hat{n})$ representation *is* injective up to translations of $\mathbb{R}^n$ [Abe and Erbacher, 1975], i.e., different parameterized surfaces lead to different representations. However, *unlike* the case of curves, it is *not* surjective: not all pairs $(g, \hat{n})$ are consistent, in the sense that they can arise from a surface. Any other "coordinates" defined on this representation space would therefore suffer from the same drawback.

For this reason, we will not pursue here further development of the full elastic Metric. Rather, we will shortly see that useful progress can instead be made by using a *reduced* form of the elastic Metric. First, though, we pause to point out the full generality of the elastic Metric.

Higher Dimensions and Codimensions

The elastic Metric is not limited to two-dimensional domains, despite the use of terminology like "surface" and "area." The first term, the Metric on Riemannian metrics, takes the same form for m-dimensional domains D as it does for two-dimensional domains. For the second term, the Metric on unit normal fields, note that a normal vector field can be defined for any suitable codimension-1 map $f : D \to \mathbb{R}^{m+1}$ by generalizing footnote 10, and inner products taken in $\mathbb{R}^{m+1}$ can be used to define unit normal vector fields, and hence the second term of the elastic Metric. The discussion above thus applies to any codimension-1 surface.

To generalize further, rather than deal with the dual normal vector, it is better to define things in terms of the normal m-form of which the normal vector is the dual. Again, this can be done using the construction of footnote 10, with the usual vector inner product being replaced by a generalized inner product between m-forms. Unit normal m-forms can thus be defined, with the second term of the elastic Metric then being expressed in terms of unit normal m-forms rather than unit normal vectors.

The advantage of this formulation is that it remains valid when the codimension changes. For m-dimensional domains D immersed in $\mathbb{R}^{n+k}$, a normal m-form is defined in the same way as in codimension 1. Its dual, however, is no longer a vector, but a k-form, and the simplicity of dealing with vectors is lost. Nevertheless, an inner product between m-forms can be defined in $\mathbb{R}^{n+k}$ precisely analogous to that in $\mathbb{R}^{n+1}$, and hence unit normal m-forms can be defined, and hence an appropriate second term for the elastic Metric. At the other extreme, when $k = 0$, the normal m-form becomes trivial, and the third term of the elastic metric disappears.

The elastic Metric is thus completely general, applying to any dimension m of domain and codomain $n + k$ for $k \in \mathbb{N}$.[13]

2.4.4   REDUCED ELASTIC METRIC: SQUARE-ROOT NORMAL FIELD

We return, now, from the multi-dimensional heights, to the problem of 3D shapes. The elastic Metric defined at the beginning of Section 2.4.3 is the full generalization of the elastic Metric on curves to the case of surfaces. However, as explained at the end of Section 2.4.3, as it stands, its complexity means that it is hard to use in practice for the elastic shape analysis of surfaces.

Fortunately, there is a useful simplification of the Metric in Equation (2.19) for which it is possible, in principle and in practice, to find a representation analogous to the SRVF that reduces it to L^2 form. We will call this simplified Metric the "reduced elastic Metric." To find it, we take the limit $\kappa \to 0$ and $c\kappa^2 = a$ in Equation (2.19), i.e., we drop the second term. This gives:

$$G_{(g,\hat{n})}((\delta g, \delta \hat{n}), (\delta g, \delta \hat{n})) = \int_D ds \left[d\zeta^2 + a \, \zeta^2 \, \langle \delta \hat{n}, \delta \hat{n} \rangle \right], \tag{2.20}$$

---

[13]When $k < 0$, the induced metric is degenerate, and the first term of the elastic Metric disappears as well. A different approach is therefore needed, but these cases have a very different character anyway.

where $a \in \mathbb{R}_{>0}$. Notice that all reference to $\hat{g}$ has disappeared. We have therefore effectively reduced the representation space from triples $(\zeta, \hat{g}, \hat{n})$ to pairs $(\zeta, \hat{n})$.

The observant reader will now notice that both the representation and the Metric have the same form as in the case of curves. As in that case, when $a = 1$, the integrand has the form of the Euclidean metric on $\mathbb{R}^n$ expressed in spherical coordinates. We should therefore be able to re-express it in the corresponding Euclidean coordinates for each point in D, and thus transform the reduced elastic Metric to L^2 form. We therefore define the "square-root normal field" (SRNF).

Definition 2.1   The square-root normal field (SRNF) $q : D \to \mathbb{R}^3$ is defined as

$$q = \zeta \hat{n} = r^{\frac{1}{2}} \hat{n} = \frac{n}{r^{\frac{1}{2}}} = \frac{n}{|n|^{\frac{1}{2}}} \ . \tag{2.21}$$

Now, since

$$\delta q = \delta \zeta \hat{n} + \zeta \delta \hat{n} \tag{2.22}$$

and $\langle \delta \hat{n}, \hat{n} \rangle = 0$, we find, exactly as in the curve case, that the reduced elastic Metric can be written as

$$G_q(\delta q, \delta q) = \int_D ds \, \langle \delta q, \delta q \rangle = \| \delta q \|^2 \ . \tag{2.23}$$

As expected, this is simply the L^2 metric, and so we have succeeded in finding a simplifying representation for the reduced elastic Metric. The space $\mathcal{Q}$ of SRNFs, given by $\mathcal{Q} = Q(\mathcal{F})$, where Q takes a surface to its SRNF, is thus a subset of $L^2(D, \mathbb{R}^3)$.

As a special case of the full elastic Metric, the reduced elastic Metric also exists for higher-dimensional domains, and codimensions other than 1. For codimension 1, it is also straightforward to see that the SRNF representation maps the reduced elastic Metric to the L^2 metric, as before.

We now investigate whether the reduced elastic Metric and SRNF representation satisfy our desiderata.

Invariance

Invariance is easily dealt with. The reduced elastic Metric inherits its invariance from the full elastic Metric. It is therefore invariant to translations (because the representation is expressed in terms of derivatives), and is preserved by rotations and diffeomorphisms of D. The latter can be seen to be a consequence of the transformation of q under the action of a diffeomorphism. We know, by definition, that $(f, \gamma) = f \circ \gamma$, i.e., elements of Γ act by composition on surfaces. If we now compute $Q(f \circ \gamma)$, we find:

$$(q, \gamma) = Q(f \circ \gamma) = \sqrt{J[\gamma]} \, (q \circ \gamma) \ , \tag{2.24}$$

where $J[\gamma]$ is the Jacobian of γ, i.e., the absolute value of the determinant of its derivative. (Note the close analogy with Equation (2.13).) Thus, like the SRVF, the SRNF q transforms as a half-density, and so Equation (2.23) is preserved by the action of diffeomorphisms. The reduced elastic Metric therefore satisfies this desideratum.

Interpretation

The interpretation of the reduced elastic Metric similarly follows from that for the full elastic Metric. The reduced elastic Metric measures "bending" in the same way as the full elastic Metric. However, it does not measure stretching in the same way. It lacks the second term of the full elastic Metric, which measures changes in local patch shape. It therefore, apparently, only measures changes in the area of a local patch, an important, but nevertheless "reduced," measure of change in the surface. The reduced elastic Metric therefore satisfies the desideratum of having a clear, "physical" interpretation.

Why do we use the word "apparently" here? This is because the relationship between changes in the area, shape, and direction of a local patch is non-trivial, and it is not clear at the time of writing, at least for closed surfaces that are generic (i.e., that do not possess a high degree of symmetry), whether there are any globally consistent changes in the shapes of local patches that do not also change either the area or direction of some patches. We will discuss this issue in greater depth now, as we turn to the third desideratum, efficiency.

Efficiency

As in the case of curves, it is clear that the process of finding distances and geodesics in the space $L^2(D, \mathbb{R}^3)$ is efficient, not to say trivial. Equations (2.8) and (2.9) apply equally well to $L^2(D, \mathbb{R}^3)$. This is a Hilbert space, with distances given by the norm of differences, and geodesics given by affine lines. However, two difficulties arise.

The first arises for closed surfaces, and is similar to that arising for closed curves: the constraint of closure places nonlinear constraints on the SRNF of a closed surface. These must be imposed if geodesics and distances are to exist in the space of closed surfaces only, which is desirable to the same degree that it is for curves.

The second difficulty is more significant, and arises for surfaces only. For curves, the map from $\mathcal{F}$ to $L^2(D, \mathbb{R}^n)$ is invertible: every SRVF corresponds to an open curve and vice-versa; the two spaces are isomorphic. This enabled any computation performed in $\mathcal{Q}$ to be transformed back to $\mathcal{F}$. For surfaces, however, it is not clear that the map Q is either surjective, i.e., that every point in $L^2(D, \mathbb{R}^3)$ corresponds to a surface, closed or not; or whether it is injective, i.e., whether, even if an SRNF does correspond to a surface, that surface is unique.

This threatens our program for three reasons. First, a geodesic between two points in $L^2(D, \mathbb{R}^3)$ that do correspond to surfaces, may contain points that do not correspond to a surface at all. Second, even the points that do correspond to surfaces may correspond to more than one. Third, partly as a consequence, we do not know how to invert the map Q to obtain even one surface corresponding to a given SRNF. If we cannot mitigate these difficulties, then the goals we have set seem out of reach.

One approach is to abandon computation in $L^2(D, \mathbb{R}^n)$ altogether, and instead pull the L^2 Metric back to $\mathcal{F}$, and perform computations there [Tumpach et al., 2015, Xie et al., 2013]. This solves the first and third of the above difficulties, of course, but not necessarily the second: the reduced elastic Metric may be degenerate; to avoid this, one could also try to use the full elastic Metric. The downside of all these procedures is that they are computationally extremely intensive, meaning that the resulting techniques are not really practical. We will describe these methods more fully in the next chapter; in this chapter, we will focus on an alternative method that maintains computational efficiency by introducing an approximation. As with the SRVF representation for curves, this computational efficiency is actually the main *a priori* motivation and justification for the use of the reduced elastic Metric (as opposed to the full Metric), coupled of course, *a posteriori*, with the fact that this choice produces reasonable and intuitive behavior in applications.

Before we delve into the details of this alternative method, however, we will tie up the loose ends of the theory by looking at how geometrical invariance is achieved for surfaces.

2.4.5   GEOMETRIC INVARIANCE

The situation for surfaces is much the same as it is with curves. The (reduced) elastic Metric is invariant to translations of either surface, because it is expressed in terms of derivatives. Invariance to rotations will be achieved by optimizing the distance over all possible rotations of one object (made possible by the fact that the Metric is preserved by rotations); this problem again has an analytical solution, to be described in the next chapter.

We will once again achieve invariance to scale by scaling both objects. We scaled curves to have unit length; we will scale surfaces to have unit area, subsequently restricting attention to the subspace of unit area surfaces, $\mathcal{F}_1$. What is the nature of this subspace? Note from Equation (2.21), that $|q|^2 = r$, the induced measure. We therefore see that the L^2 norm of an SRNF, $\|q\|^2 = \int_D ds\, |q|^2 = \int_D ds\, r$, is simply the area of the corresponding surface, just as the squared norm of an SRVF was the length of the corresponding curve. Thus $\mathcal{F}_1$ is a subspace of the unit sphere in $L^2(D, \mathbb{R}^3)$, which means that, just as in the case of curves, we can compute scale-invariant distances between two SRNFs by computing distances on the unit sphere, for which there is an analytical form. Modulo the difficulties discussed in Section 2.4.4, then, achieving scale invariance for surfaces is no more difficult than it is for curves.

2.4.6   SRNF INVERSION PROBLEM

We now return to the practical question of efficiency. Ideally, in order to take full advantage of the simplicity of the reduced elastic Metric in the SRNF representation, we need to be able to find, given $q \in L^2(D, \mathbb{R}^3)$, a surface f such that $Q(f) = q$; this is the inversion problem. Unfortunately, not only is the solution to this problem unknown, it is not even known whether a solution always exists, and if it does exist, whether it is unique: for a given $q \in L^2(D, \mathbb{R}^3)$, the problem may have no solution (if Q is not surjective and $q \notin \mathcal{Q}$); or it may have several solutions (if Q is not injective). The problem can be formulated and analyzed in several different ways; here we describe two.

1. Given a map $\hat{n} : D \to D$ and a function $r : D \to \mathbb{R}_{>0}$, when are these the Gauss map $\hat{n} = n/|n|$ and area form $r = |n|^{1/2} = \det(g)^{1/2}$ of an immersion $f : D \to \mathbb{R}^3$? If such an f exists, is it unique (up to translation)?

2. Given $q : D \to \mathbb{R}^3$, does the differential equation $n = |q|q$ have a (global) solution, and is it unique (up to translation) [Michor and Bryant, 2013]?

In the first case, as we have already mentioned, it is known that if we are given $(\hat{n}, g)$, rather than just $(\hat{n}, r)$, then f, if it exists, can be reconstructed up to translation [Abe and Erbacher, 1975, Eschenburg et al., 2010]. This is also true, up to an additional global scaling, when we are given only the "conformal class" of g [Hoffman and Osserman, 1985], i.e., we know $(\hat{n}, \hat{g})$. Unfortunately, little seems to be known about the nature of the solution in the case at hand. The problem was stated by Arnold [1990], but in a 2004 book listing Arnold's problems and their subsequent elucidation or solution [Arnold, 2004], the same problem still appears, without commentary.

In the second case, a global solution clearly does not always exist, at least in degenerate cases (if g is constant, for example [Michor and Bryant, 2013]). The discussion in Michor and Bryant [2013] does lead to the conclusion that the equation is locally solvable, but this is not sufficient for us: we require a global solution. Even if a global solution does exist, it may not be unique. In degenerate cases, any flat area of the surface could be subjected to an area-preserving diffeomorphism, while for open surfaces, one may find distinct, non-degenerate cases that share the same Gauss map and area form [Klassen, 2011]. If the solution is to be unique, then, it can be so only for non-degenerate, closed surfaces.

Clearly these questions are highly non-trivial, and we will not attempt to answer them directly here. Instead, we will develop an approximate "inversion" method that circumvents the above difficulties. We address the problem in an indirect way, by developing a method that, given $q \in L^2(D, \mathbb{R}^n)$, finds an $f \in \mathcal{F}$ such that $Q(f) = q$, if one exists, or an f whose image $Q(f)$ is the closest, in the reduced elastic Metric, to q, if one does not. This approach has some attractive properties as described next.

- If Q is bijective, i.e., both surjective and injective, then the method will reproduce the correct inverse map Q^{-1}.

- If $q \in \mathcal{Q}$, then even if Q is not injective, the method will still find a point in the preimage, i.e., one of the surfaces corresponding to q. In actual use, for example when computing a geodesic, continuity will frequently ensure that this is the point of the preimage that we require.

- Finally, even if Q is not surjective and $q \notin Q$, the method will still find a surface whose SRNF is the best possible approximation to q. In actual use, for example when computing a geodesic, the hope is that this will produce a result close to that which would be obtained by explicitly constraining the path to lie in Q.

We will achieve these results by formulating SRNF inversion as an optimization problem: find an element $f \in \mathcal{F}$ whose image $Q(f)$ is as close as possible to the given $q \in L^2(D, \mathbb{R}^3)$ under the L^2 norm. An efficient numerical procedure will then be used to solve this problem.

Inversion as Optimization

We begin by defining an energy function $E_0 : \mathcal{F} \to \mathbb{R}_{\geq 0}$ (actually the square of the distance in $L^2(D, \mathbb{R}^3)$) by

$$E_0(f; q) = \|Q(f) - q\|^2 . \tag{2.25}$$

Finding an $f \in \mathcal{F}$ such that $Q(f) = q$ is then equivalent to seeking zeros of E_0. We denote by f^* an element of $\mathcal{F}$ satisfying $E_0(f^*; q) = \min_{f \in \mathcal{F}} E_0(f; q)$.

From a computational point of view, it will be easier to deal with deformations of a surface, rather than the surface itself. We therefore set $f = f_0 + w$, where f_0 denotes the current estimate of f^*, and w is a deformation of f_0. The task is then to minimize

$$E_0(w; f_0, q) = \|Q(f_0 + w) - q\|^2 , \tag{2.26}$$

with respect to w. One can view f_0 as an initial guess of the solution or a known surface with shape similar to the one being estimated. If no initial guess is possible, one can set f_0 to be the unit sphere, or even set $f_0 = 0$.

Note that for a given q, a minimizing surface f^* can exist even when there is no $f \in \mathcal{F}$ such that $Q(f) = q$. Thus, even though there is no guarantee that Q is surjective, we are still able to map points in $L^2(D, \mathbb{R}^3)$ back to $\mathcal{F}$. What is more, because we will perform minimization using an iterative descent method, we can, by starting the descent for similar q, $q' \in Q$ from similar initial points f_0, $f_0' \in \mathcal{F}$, help to ensure that the inverted surfaces we find are, if not uniquely determined, at least consistent with each other. This is particularly important when trying to invert a whole geodesic, for example. In that case, in addition, the path that we find in $\mathcal{F}$, if projected back to Q, would be in some sense the "closest" path to the original geodesic in $L^2(D, \mathbb{R}^3)$ that lies entirely in Q. These are precisely the desirable properties listed earlier. Let us now describe the minimization process in more detail.

Numerical Optimization

In practice, we will minimize E in Equation (2.26) over $\mathcal{F}$ by minimizing successively over two sets of "moves."

1. The first set of moves consists of transformations of f under rotations and diffeomorphisms, i.e., under the action of the group $SO(3) \times \Gamma$. We will find the rotation and diffeomorphism that results in the greatest reduction in E, i.e., we will minimize E over the

action of $SO(3) \times \Gamma$ on $\mathcal{F}$. However, because of the invariance properties of the L^2 metric under the action of $SO(3) \times \Gamma$ on $\mathcal{Q}$, we have

$$\|Q(O(f,\gamma)) - q\| = \|O(Q(f),\gamma) - q\| = \|Q(f) - O^{-1}(q,\gamma)\| ,$$

where, from Equation (2.24), $(q,\gamma) = \sqrt{J[\gamma]}\,(q \circ \gamma)$, with $J[\gamma]$ the Jacobian of γ. We can thus equally think of minimizing E over the action of $SO(3) \times \Gamma$ on q, and this is what we do in practice.

2. The second set of moves consists of very small (in the L^2 norm) changes in w. We will find the small change that results in the greatest reduction in E. The solution to this problem is of course well known: the small change should be in the direction of the negative gradient of E with respect to w, i.e., standard gradient descent.

To perform the minimization, we thus iterate the following two steps. At iteration $i \in \mathbb{N}$:

1. Given w_i and q_i, we find the rotation O_{i+1} and a diffeomorphism γ_{i+1} that minimize:

$$E(O_{i+1}, \gamma_{i+1}, w_i; f_0, q) = \|Q(f_0 + w_i) - O_{i+1}(q_i, \gamma_{i+1})\|^2 . \tag{2.27}$$

We then define $q_{i+1} = O_{i+1}(q_i, \gamma_{i+1})$.

2. Given q_{i+1}, we use gradient descent to find the deformation w_{i+1} that minimizes:

$$E(w_{i+1}; f_0, q) = \|Q(f_0 + w_{i+1}) - q_{i+1}\|^2 . \tag{2.28}$$

The algorithm is initialized with the choices $w_0 = 0$ and $q_0 = q$. Note that the first set of moves is not strictly necessary, since $\mathcal{F}$ is closed under the action of $SO(3) \times \Gamma$. Separating out these transformations, however, permits large "leaps" in $\mathcal{F}$, thereby helping the algorithm to search more rapidly.

Step 1: Optimizing over rotations and diffeomorphisms   The first minimization is performed using the approach described in Jermyn et al. [2012]. That is, we find the best rotation O using singular value decomposition, given a fixed γ. Then we find the best γ by a search over the space of all diffeomorphisms using a gradient descent approach. In practice, however, restricting the search over Γ to the space of rigid rotations, $\Gamma_0 \equiv SO(3)$, is sufficient to achieve good reconstruction accuracy, while being considerably computationally more efficient.

Step 2: Optimizing over small changes   To minimize E with respect to w using a gradient descent approach, we need the directional derivative of E with respect to w. Since $\mathcal{F}$ is an infinite-dimensional vector space, we will approximate the derivative using a finite basis for $\mathcal{F}$.

We therefore set $w = \sum_{b \in B} \alpha_b b$, with $\alpha_b \in \mathbb{R}$, and where B forms an orthonormal basis of $\mathcal{F}$. The directional derivative of E at $f_0 + w$ in the direction of b, $\nabla_b E(w; f_0, q)$, is then given by:

$$\nabla_b E(w; f_0, q) = \frac{d}{d\epsilon}|_{\epsilon=0} \|Q(f_0 + w + \epsilon b) - q\|^2$$
$$= 2\langle Q(f_0 + w) - q, dQ_{f_0+w}(b)\rangle . \tag{2.29}$$

Here dQ_f denotes the differential of Q at f. This can be evaluated using the following expression:

$$dQ_f(b) = \frac{n_b}{\sqrt{|n|}} - \frac{n \cdot n_b}{2|n|^{5/2}} n , \tag{2.30}$$

where $n_b = (f_u \times b_v) + (b_u \times f_v)$. To improve numerical accuracy, the second term can be replaced by the more stable $\frac{\hat{n} \cdot n_b}{2\sqrt{|n|}} \hat{n}$, resulting in

$$dQ_f(b) = \frac{1}{\sqrt{|n|}} \left(n_b - \frac{\hat{n} \cdot n_b}{2} \hat{n} \right) . \tag{2.31}$$

Finally, the update is determined by the gradient $\nabla E_0(f_0; q) = \sum_{b \in B} (\nabla_b E(b; f_0, q)) b$ obtained using Equations (2.29), (2.30), and (2.31).

A naive implementation of this procedure results in the algorithm becoming trapped in local minima, as is normal for descent-based algorithms. We will see, however, that this problem can be overcome by carefully engineering the orthonormal basis B of $\mathcal{F}$, and combining it with a multiscale and multiresolution representation of the elements of $\mathcal{F}$ and $L^2(D, \mathbb{R}^3)$. These developments will be described in subsequent sections.

Basis Formation

We have not so far specified the orthonormal basis B to be used to represent elements of $\mathcal{F}$. To do so, we first restrict our attention to closed genus-0 surfaces, i.e., we set $D = \mathbb{S}^2$. Since elements of $\mathcal{F}$ are then smooth maps of the form $f : \mathbb{S}^2 \to \mathbb{R}^3$, we can use spherical harmonics (SHs), in each coordinate, as the basis. Let $\{Y_i : \mathbb{S}^2 \to \mathbb{R}\}_{i \in I}$, with I some index set, be the real-valued spherical harmonic functions. Then, a basis for $\mathcal{F}$ is given by $\{Y_i e_a\}_{i \in I, a \in \{1,2,3\}}$, where $\{e_a\}_{a \in \{1,2,3\}}$ is the standard orthonormal basis for $\mathbb{R}^3$. We will refer to the resulting basis as $B = \{b_j\}_{j \in J}$, for J some index set.

By definition, an arbitrary genus-0 surface can be represented with the basis B. However, complex surfaces will require a large number of basis elements in order to capture all of the surface details. Nevertheless, by using a spherical wavelet-based multiresolution representation, the optimization problem of Equation (2.26) can still be solved in a computationally efficient manner.

Alternatively, depending on the context and the availability of training data, it may be more efficient to use a principal component basis instead of a generic basis: given a set of example shapes, we can compute its PCA in $\mathcal{F}$, and then use the leading components to construct a (partial) basis. In the case of human shapes, for instance, there are several publicly available datasets that can be used to build a PCA basis. In our experiments, the number of PCA basis elements required to represent a typical surface to a given accuracy is of the order of 100. This is significantly smaller than the number of spherical harmonics elements needed, which is typically more than 3,000.

One can also combine the PCA and SH bases in order to account for shape deformations that have not been observed in the training dataset. It is also possible to use different bases for the surfaces themselves and their small or large deformations. This can improve efficiency, but we will not explore this idea further here.

Multiscale Representation of SRNFs
Experiments reveal that the gradient descent method at a fixed resolution finds it difficult to reconstruct complex surfaces that contain elongated parts and highly non-convex regions, such as the ones shown in Figure 2.6. Note, however, that such parts often correspond to the high frequency components of the surface. This suggests the use of a multiscale approach where one reconstructs first the low frequency information, which corresponds to a rough approximation of the surface and can serve as an initialization to the reconstruction of the more accurate and detailed surface.

Let q be the SRNF of an unknown surface f, and let q_s be the SRNF of a unit sphere f_s. The geodesic between them under the L^2 metric is the linear path $\beta(\tau) = (1 - \tau)q_s + \tau q$ for $\tau \in [0, 1]$; let the corresponding path in $\mathcal{F}$ be $\alpha(\tau)$ such that $f_s = \alpha(0)$ and $f = \alpha(1)$. One can then treat β as a multiscale representation of the SRNF q. In practice, we divide the linear path β into $m + 1$ equidistant points $\{q^i\}_{i \in [0,...,m]}$, such that $q^0 = q_s$, $q^m = q$, and $\|q^i - q^{(i-1)}\| = \Delta > 0$. We refer to $\mathbf{q} = (q^1, \ldots, q^m)$ as the *multiscale SRNF* of an unknown multiscale surface $\mathbf{f} = (f^1, \ldots, f^m)$. Note that $f^0 = f_s$ and $q^0 = q_s$ are not included in the representation.

With this representation, the SRNF inversion problem can be reformulated as follows: given a multiscale SRNF $\mathbf{q}$, find a multiscale surface $\mathbf{f}$ such that for every i, $Q(f^i)$ is as close as possible to q^i, i.e., $E_0(f^i; q^i)$ is minimized. Gradient descent procedures are known to provide good results if the initialization is close to the solution. We thus use the following iterative procedure.

- In step 1, we find a surface f^1 that minimizes $E_0(f; q^1)$, initializing gradient descent with a sphere $f^0 = f_s$.

- Then, at step i, we find a surface f^i that minimizes $E_0(f; q^i)$, initializing gradient descent with $f^{(i-1)}$.

Since the optimization at each level i is initialized with the result of the previous level, and thus the initialization is close to the final solution, the gradient descent is more likely to converge to the correct solution.

Multiresolution Inversion Algorithm

While the multiscale approach allows us to invert a single SRNF, by allowing the gradient descent-based optimization procedure to converge to the desired solution, it can be computationally very expensive when dealing with high resolution surfaces. In practice, the computation time can be significantly reduced by adopting a *multiresolution* representation[14] of the elements of $\mathcal{F}$, and subsequently the elements of $L^2(D, \mathbb{R}^3)$. Specifically, given a surface $f \in \mathcal{F}$, we use spherical wavelet analysis to build a multiresolution representation $\mathbf{f} = (f^1, \ldots, f^m = f)$ of f. The surface f^i at level i is a smoothed, sub-sampled, and thus coarse version of the surface f^{i+1}. With a slight abuse of notation, we also define the multiresolution SRNF map sending $\mathbf{f} \mapsto Q(\mathbf{f}) = \mathbf{q} = (q^i)$, where $q^i = Q(f^i)$.

To build the multiresolution representation, an analysis filter $\tilde{h}_i$ is applied to the surface f via spherical convolution. The output is then convolved with another spherical filter h_i, called *a synthesis filter*, producing a coarse surface f^i that is an approximation of the surface f at scale i. By defining the analysis filters $\{\tilde{h}_i\}$ as dilated versions of a template filter ψ, i.e., $\tilde{h}_i = D_i\psi$, the reconstructed surfaces $\{f^i\}$ capture the original surface properties at multiple scales. For details of these filters, we refer the reader to Yeo et al. [2008]. In our implementation, the template wavelet ψ is chosen to be the Laplacian-of-Gaussian, and the wavelet decomposition of each coordinate function is computed using convolutions with the analysis-synthesis filters in the spherical harmonic domain. Since surfaces at large scales require a smaller number of samples, we can start with a spherical grid of resolution 128×128 and then, at each wavelet decomposition, subsample the obtained coarse surface by halving the spherical resolution. Four decomposition levels seem generally sufficient to achieve high inversion accuracy.

A multiresolution SRNF can be inverted using essentially the same procedure as the one described previously in this section. This time, the surface obtained at each iteration is first upsampled, and then used to initialize optimization at the next resolution. Figure 2.5c shows a reconstruction of the octopus surface given in Figure 2.5a from its SRNF using the proposed multiresolution inversion procedure. Figure 2.5b displays the inversion result when Equation (2.26) is solved using a single resolution representation. The latter results in a degenerate surface since the initialization is too far from the correct solution. The multiresolution procedure, on the other hand, converges to the correct solution since at each optimization step, the initialization is close to the correct solution.

Another important practical property of the multiresolution procedure is that it significantly reduces computational cost: although the optimizations at coarser scales require a large number of iterations, they operate on spherical grids of low resolution (e.g., 16×16) and are thus very fast. At the finest scale, although the resolution is high (128×128), gradient descent only requires a few iterations since the initialization is already very close to the solution.

---

[14]By a "multiscale representation," we mean a sequence of continuous objects with successively smaller amounts of high frequency information included. By "multiresolution," we mean a discretized version of the multiscale representation that exploits the decreasing dimensionality of the sequence by using increasingly coarse discretizations for its elements.

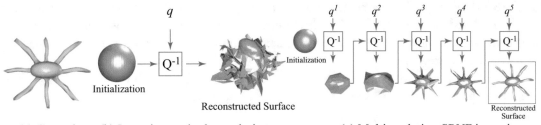

(a) Ground truth. (b) Inversion at single resolution. (c) Multiresolution SRNF inversion.

Figure 2.5: Comparison between the multiresolution approach (c) and the single resolution version (b). The latter fails to recover complex surfaces.

Notice that this all assumes that $\mathbf{q}$, the multiresolution representation of the SRNF q of an unknown surface f, is available, which seems like a restriction. However, this is not a restriction in practice, since usually we are interested in computing geodesics between known surfaces f_1 and f_2, deforming a given surface f_1 along a given geodesic direction, or computing summary statistics of a given set of surfaces. In the first application, for example, one can: (1) build a multiresolution representation of the surfaces f_1 and f_2, hereinafter denoted by $\mathbf{f}_1$ and $\mathbf{f}_2$, respectively, using the spherical wavelet decomposition described in this section; (2) compute their multiresolution SRNFs $\mathbf{q}_1$ and $\mathbf{q}_2$; and finally (3) invert the multiresolution SRNF $\mathbf{q} = (q^1, \dots, q^m)$ where $q^i = (1 - \tau)q_1^i + \tau q_2^i$, $\tau \in [0, 1]$. This point is illustrated in different contexts in Chapter 5.

Star-shaped Surfaces

Before moving on to how the optimization method works in practice, we pause here to consider a special subset of genus-0 surfaces, the "star-shaped" surfaces, which are of great relevance to many applications, e.g., the diagnosis of attention deficit hyperactivity disorder (ADHD) using magnetic resonance imaging (MRI) scans. Remarkably, in this case, an *analytic* solution to the inversion problem exists.

What is a "star-shaped" surface? A star-shaped surface is a parameterized surface $f \in \mathcal{F}$ that, up to a translation, can be written in the form:

$$f(u, v) = \rho(u, v)e(u, v) , \tag{2.32}$$

where $\rho(u, v) \in \mathbb{R}_{\geq 0}$, and $e(u, v) \in \mathbb{S}^2$ is the unit vector in $\mathbb{R}^3$ given in Euclidean coordinates by $e(u, v) = (\cos(u)\sin(v), \sin(u)\sin(v), \cos(v))$. It can be seen by inspection that in spherical coordinates,[15] f is given by $(r, \theta, \phi) = (\rho(u, v), u, v)$, i.e., the parameters correspond to the angular coordinates. This is only possible because, by design, the volume enclosed by a star-shaped surface is a "star domain," i.e., there exists a point (the "center") in the enclosed volume

---

[15]We use the ISO convention for spherical coordinates: $\theta \in [0, \pi]$ is inclination and $\phi \in [0, 2\pi)$ is azimuth.

such that the straight line segments from that point to every point on the surface all lie entirely in the enclosed volume. By choosing the center to be the origin, $r = 0$, we can parameterize a star domain as above. This particular parametrization of a star domain is the corresponding star-shaped surface.

For this type of surface, the SRNF map Q can be analytically inverted, as follows. The radial component of the normal vector n of a surface is, by definition, given by

$$n^r(u, v) = \langle n(u, v), e(\theta(u, v), \phi(u, v)) \rangle , \tag{2.33}$$

since $e(\theta, \phi)$ is the radial unit vector at any point in $\mathbb{R}^3$ with coordinates (θ, ϕ). Similarly, we have that

$$q^r(u, v) = \langle q(u, v), e(\theta(u, v), \phi(u, v)) \rangle , \tag{2.34}$$

and finally, from the definition of the SRNF, that

$$n^r = |q(u, v)| q^r(u, v) . \tag{2.35}$$

These equations are true for any surface, but they are not useful: they are simply a restatement of the inversion problem. However, if we knew the angular functions θ and ϕ, then we could calculate q^r from q using Equation (2.34), and hence n^r using Equation (2.35). We might then be able to use the expression for n^r in Equation (2.33), to recover information about f.

Of course, for star-shaped surfaces, i.e., star domains in the special parametrization, we *do* know the angular functions: $\theta(u, v) = u$ and $\phi(u, v) = v$. Not only that, but the expression for n^r, as derived from Equation (2.32) is very simple for star-shaped surfaces:

$$n^r(u, v) = \rho^2(u, v) . \tag{2.36}$$

We can thus recover the radial function of f very simply, and hence using Equation (2.32), the surface function f. More explicitly, given an SRNF q and a parameterization e, the star-shaped surface f corresponding to this q, i.e., such that $Q(f) = q$, takes the form:

$$f(u, v) = \left(\sqrt{|q(u, v)| q^r(u, v)} \right) e(u, v) , \tag{2.37}$$

where $q^r = \langle q, e \rangle$ is the radial component of q.

Note that f depends on both q and a fixed parameterization $e(u, v)$. If both are known, then q can be analytically inverted, as above. However, if a surface encloses a star domain, but is in a general parameterization, one could still choose to apply Equation (2.37). In this case, the resulting f would not in general be the original surface, but it might provide a good initialization for solving the reconstruction-by-optimization problem.

Reconstruction Examples

We return now to the general case of inversion of the SRNF of an arbitrary surface using the optimization approach. In this section, we demonstrate how well this method works in practice.

Figures 2.6 and 2.7 show some examples of the reconstruction of real objects. In each case, from the original surface f_o, we compute its multiresolution surface $\mathbf{f}_o$ and the multiresolution SRNF $\mathbf{q}_o = Q(\mathbf{f}_o)$, and then estimate f^* by SRNF inversion of $\mathbf{q}_o$. We display the original surface f_o, the reconstructed surface f^*, and the reconstruction errors $|f^*(s) - f_o(s)|$. All of these results were obtained using 3,642 spherical harmonic basis elements.

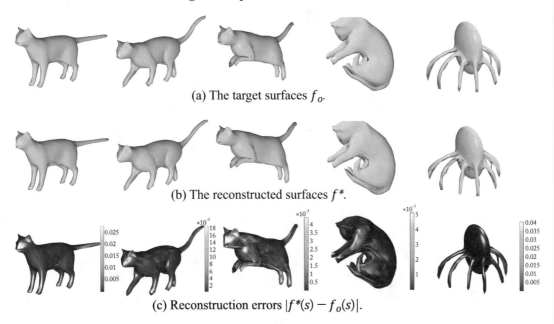

(a) The target surfaces f_o.

(b) The reconstructed surfaces f^*.

(c) Reconstruction errors $|f^*(s) - f_o(s)|$.

Figure 2.6: Reconstruction of surfaces from their SRNF representations, using 3,642 spherical harmonic basis elements.

An inspection of these results shows that the multiresolution inversion procedure is able to reconstruct the original surface to a very high accuracy. For the complex articulated surfaces in Figures 2.6 and 2.7, the iterative optimization procedure reduces the energy by three orders of magnitude. The plots of the reconstruction errors in row (c) of each figure show that most of the reconstruction errors occur at high curvature regions.

To quantify the impact of initialization on the convergence of the method, we tested it on 13 shape classes from the SHREC07 watertight dataset [Giorgi et al., 2007], with each class containing 20 models. For each model, we computed its SRNF, then re-estimated the original surface using the proposed inversion algorithm initialized with a unit sphere (a generic initialization). Finally, we measured the reconstruction error. Median reconstruction error was 0.0008 with a 25th percentile of 0.0003 and a 75th percentile of 0.0022. (All surfaces were rescaled to unit surface area.) Figure 2.8 shows the boxplots of the reconstruction errors for each class of shapes. As one can see, the proposed algorithm is able to recover the original surface with very high accuracy.

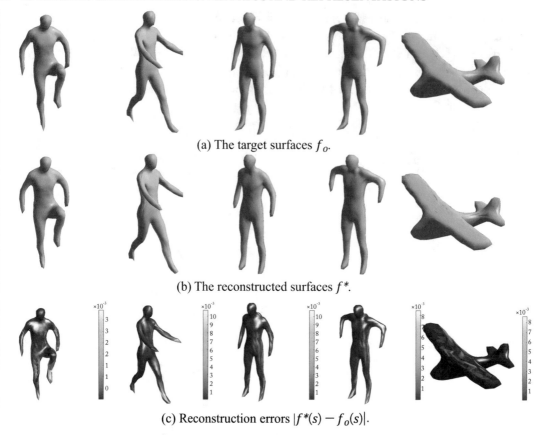

(a) The target surfaces f_0.

(b) The reconstructed surfaces f^*.

(c) Reconstruction errors $|f^*(s) - f_0(s)|$.

Figure 2.7: Other examples of the reconstruction of surfaces from their SRNF representations. In these examples we used 3,642 spherical harmonic basis elements.

Table 2.1 summarizes the average computational cost for inverting one SRNF on a 3.40Ghz i7-3770 CPU with 16GB RAM. In conjunction with Table 3.1, it underlines the dramatic improvements in computational effort that can be achieved by the inversion-as-optimization method when used for the statistical shape analysis tasks listed in Chapter 5.

Table 2.1: Computation time, in seconds, on an Intel i7-3770 CPU @ 3.40 Ghz with 16 GB of RAM

	3,642 Harmonic Basis	100 PCA Basis
Grids of 64 × 64	16.5 min	20.14 sec
Grids of 128 × 128	—	2.5 min

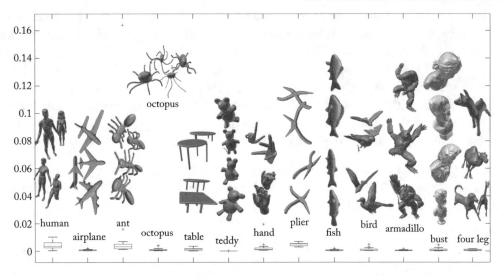

Figure 2.8: Boxplots of the average reconstruction error for each of the 13 shape classes in the SHREC07 dataset.

2.5   SUMMARY AND NEXT STEPS

We began this chapter by describing the framework for elastic shape analysis. We saw how a Riemannian Metric on a space of parameterized objects could be used to define a Euclidean invariant distance between unparameterized objects, while simultaneously providing their optimal registration, and an optimal deformation between them. We saw also how the distance could be rendered independent of the positions, orientations, and scales of the objects. We saw how this framework was implemented in the case of curves, using the elastic metric and the SRVF, and used this as a guide to constructing the ESA framework for surfaces.

We defined a generalized form of the elastic Metric that applies to curves, surfaces, and beyond, and laid out arguments for using the reduced elastic Metric as the Riemannian Metric of choice for surface ESA. However, we also saw that deep mathematical questions remain about the nature of the reduced Metric and the SRNF representation. We then outlined two possible ways of circumventing these questions, allowing the use of the reduced elastic Metric in practice, which we now recap.

- The first involves pulling the Metric back from the $(g, \hat{n})$ representation space to $\mathcal{F}$, subsequently performing all computations directly in $\mathcal{F}$. This has the advantage that it is "exact," up to numerical errors, but the disadvantage that it is computationally very expensive.

- The second involves performing computations in $L^2(D, \mathbb{R}^3)$ using the L^2 metric, and then transferring the results to $\mathcal{F}$. This requires a method for inverting the SRNF map. In the last section, we saw that despite the theoretical issues, a numerical inversion method based on optimization can be used to reconstruct surfaces reliably, and with high accuracy, thus opening the way to the use of the reduced elastic Metric and the SRNF representations for statistical shape analysis. The advantage of this approach is that both the computations in $L^2(D, \mathbb{R}^3)$ and the inversion technique are very efficient; the disadvantage is that the computations are approximate: for example, "geodesics" in $\mathcal{F}$ found by this method may not coincide with the exact geodesics computed by the pullback method because they may have resulted from paths in $L^2(D, \mathbb{R}^3)$ that did not lie entirely in $\mathcal{Q}$. The accuracy of the approximation is difficult to predict in advance, and its reliability is unknown.

In the next chapter, we show how the ESA framework is implemented by describing in detail how to compute optimal deformations, registrations, and geometrically invariant distances, using both of these approaches.

2.6   BIBLIOGRAPHIC NOTES

Elastic shape analysis of curves has been studied in a collection of papers [Joshi et al., 2007, Mio et al., 2007, Srivastava et al., 2011, Younes, 1998, Younes et al., 2008a]. Specifically, the SRVF representation for elastic shape analysis of Euclidean curves was introduced in Joshi et al. [2007] and Srivastava et al. [2011]. Statistical analysis of shapes and other properties of Euclidean curves has been studied in Kurtek et al. [2012b] and used in many applications such as the analysis of the shape of plant leaves [Laga et al., 2012, 2014]. For a comprehensive discussion on elastic shape analysis of curves, please refer to the textbook by Srivastava and Klassen [2016].

The SRM for shape analysis of surfaces was presented in Kurtek et al. [2010] and developed in a collection of papers [Kurtek et al., 2011b, 2012a]. A discussion on statistical analysis of surface shapes using SRMs can be found in Kurtek et al. [2011a]. The SRNF representation for performing elastic shape analysis of surfaces was introduced in Jermyn et al. [2012]. Since then, it has been used for shape analysis of 3D objects in Kurtek et al. [2016], Samir et al. [2014], and Xie et al. [2013]. The problem of inverting SRNF representations using numerical techniques has been discussed in Xie et al. [2014] and Laga et al. [2017].

CHAPTER 3

Computing Geometrical Quantities

In the previous chapter, we described a mathematical framework for representing and comparing the shapes of surfaces. We defined a representation of surfaces, called the SRNF, and showed that the L^2 Metric on the space $L^2(D, \mathbb{R}^3)$, which includes the space Q of SRNFs, was equivalent to a reduced form of the natural "elastic Metric" on the space $\mathcal{F}$ of surfaces, as described in terms of the induced metric and unit normal field of the surface.[1] We showed too that this reduced elastic metric satisfied our desiderata for use in the elastic shape analysis program, and, in particular, that it possessed the necessary invariance properties. We then described two ways in which these structures could be used to carry out statistical analysis: either directly in $\mathcal{F}$, using the pulled back reduced elastic metric; or in SRNF space, with the use of an approximate inversion method to move the results back from $L^2(D, \mathbb{R}^3)$ to $\mathcal{F}$.

According to the ESA program, given a Riemannian metric satisfying our desiderata, the building blocks of shape analysis, the optimal registration and deformation of two shapes, and the distance between them are computed in a unified fashion by finding the shortest path under the Riemannian metric ("geodesic") between all possible reparameterizations of the two shapes (see Section 2.2.2). In addition, we may wish to render the distance invariant to translations, rotations, and scalings of the two shapes via alignment (see Section 2.2.3). In this chapter, we describe the computational techniques needed to implement this program for both of the two strategies mentioned above: using the pullback metric, or working in SRNF space.

In Section 3.1, we first formalize the overall problem and then describe how the SRNF representation may be used to simplify significantly the computations involved by separating the problem of finding an optimal registration and alignment from the problem of finding a geodesic between two parameterized surfaces. We then tackle the problem of registration and alignment in Section 3.2, before moving on to the computation of geodesics. We start with an introduction to numerical techniques on general manifolds in Section 3.3, and then particularize the path-straightening approach to our context. Corresponding to the two strategies mentioned above, there are two possibilities for path-straightening; we examine them in Sections 3.4 and 3.5. We illustrate each technique with simple examples. Our main focus in this chapter is on the SRNF

---

[1] That is the last time we will have cause to mention the Riemannian metric induced on the surface, and so we will have no more need to distinguish between this and the Riemannian Metric on the space of surfaces or SRNFs: as a result, we henceforth drop the capital "M," and refer to the elastic metric.

representation of surfaces and corresponding computational tools; however, where appropriate, we outline these tools for the SRM representation briefly mentioned in the previous chapter.

3.1 COMPUTING IN SHAPE SPACE

In this section, we will formalize the problem of computing the optimal registration and deformation, and hence distance, between two surfaces, together with the alignment that will render the distance independent of the original positions, orientations, and scales of the surfaces.

Recall from Chapter 2 that translation invariance is already ensured because the (reduced) elastic metric is expressed entirely in terms of derivatives of the parameterized surface.[2] The resulting distance is therefore independent of the original positions of the surfaces. This independence means that the distance is, strictly speaking, not a metric at all, in the metric space sense, but a pseudometric. Although it is symmetric and satisfies the triangle inequality, it can be zero for non-identical points: two parameterized surfaces that are translated versions of each other will have zero distance. There is a mathematically elegant representation of this situation, as follows (further details may be found in Definition A.21). Any pseudometric defines an equivalence relation: two points are equivalent if they are at zero distance. One may take the quotient of the original space by this equivalence relation, whereupon the pseudometric becomes a semimetric on the quotient space. That is, it is zero if and only if the points are the same, and it is symmetric, but it may no longer satisfy the triangle inequality. We will see, however, that in the cases we deal with, the triangle inequality is satisfied, and thus the pseudometric becomes a true metric on the quotient space. We may thus think of the distance defined by the reduced elastic metric, either as a pseudometric on the space $\mathcal{F}$, or as a bona fide metric on the quotient of $\mathcal{F}$ by translations.[3]

Recall also that, if desired, scale invariance can be achieved by first scaling both surfaces to have unit area, and then calculating the distance between these scaled surfaces. The resulting distance is now independent of the original positions *and* scales of the surfaces; it is therefore zero whenever the two parameterized surfaces are translated, scaled versions of each other. Again there is a quotient space interpretation: we either have a pseudometric on $\mathcal{F}$, or a metric on the quotient of $\mathcal{F}$ by translations and scaling, which we will denote by $\mathcal{C}_f$ and call the "preshape space."

We assume from now on that this scaling has been performed. It remains to compute the optimal registration and deformation of two surfaces, and to render the distance independent of rotations.

---

[2]This is not true of the metric based upon the SRM representation; we will describe how translation invariance is achieved in that case at the appropriate point.

[3]Actually, this may not be true, since we are not sure that the reduced elastic metric measures all possible changes of a surface, but we will ignore this for the present discussion.

3.1.1 OPTIMAL REGISTRATION AND ALIGNMENT

Consider two parameterized surfaces, $f_i : D \to \mathbb{R}^3$, for $i \in \{1, 2\}$. Suppose that we can already compute the distance $d_{\mathcal{C}_f}(f_1, f_2)$ between the two surfaces in the space $\mathcal{C}_f$, by optimizing over all paths between them.[4] This distance is associated with a particular geodesic, $\alpha_f(f_1, f_2)$, which represents a particular deformation. To find the optimal registration, and hence the optimal deformation and distance, we must minimize this distance over all possible registrations of the parameterized surfaces. This process is greatly simplified by the fact that $d_{\mathcal{C}_f}$, because it is derived from the reduced elastic metric on $\mathcal{F}$, satisfies our second desideratum: if we act on both parameterized surfaces with an element $\gamma \in \Gamma$, we have

$$d_{\mathcal{C}_f}(f_1 \circ \gamma, f_2 \circ \gamma) = d_{\mathcal{C}_f}(f_1, f_2), \tag{3.1}$$

and similarly,

$$\alpha_f(f_1 \circ \gamma, f_2 \circ \gamma) = (\alpha_f(f_1, f_2), \gamma), \tag{3.2}$$

where the action of a reparameterization on a geodesic acts on each surface in that geodesic separately. Thus changes of parameterization that do not change the registration do not change the distance or the deformation.

This means that to find the optimal registration, we need only minimize the distance over all possible reparameterizations of *one* of the surfaces. We thus define a new distance

$$d_{\tilde{\mathcal{C}}_f}(f_1, f_2) = \min_{\gamma \in \Gamma} d_{\mathcal{C}_f}(f_1, f_2 \circ \gamma) = d_{\mathcal{C}_f}(f_1, f_2 \circ \gamma^*), \tag{3.3}$$

where the minimizing γ^* represents the optimal registration.[5] We use the subscript $\tilde{\mathcal{C}}_f$ because the distance can (again) be viewed as a metric on a quotient space, this time the quotient of $\mathcal{C}_f$ by the action of Γ, which we denote $\tilde{\mathcal{C}}_f$.

---

[4]We write $d_{\mathcal{C}_f}$ as a function of points f_1 and f_2 in $\mathcal{F}$, because it can be viewed as a pseudometric on this space. Equally, however, as we have said, it can be viewed as a metric on the space $\mathcal{C}_f$. The points in this space are equivalence classes of surfaces under translations and scalings, conventionally notated using square brackets around one member of the class, e.g., $[f_1]$ and $[f_2]$. We could therefore equally write $d_{\mathcal{C}_f}([f_1], [f_2])$, and we sometimes will.

[5]As claimed in Chapter 2, the fact that reparameterizations act by isometries is sufficient to guarantee the triangle inequality (this is a special case of the proof in Appendix A):

$$d_{\tilde{\mathcal{C}}_f}(f_1, f_2) + d_{\tilde{\mathcal{C}}_f}(f_2, f_3) = \min_{\gamma_1} d_{\mathcal{C}_f}(f_1, f_2 \circ \gamma_1) + \min_{\gamma_2} d_{\mathcal{C}_f}(f_2, f_3 \circ \gamma_2) \tag{3.4a}$$

$$= d_{\mathcal{C}_f}(f_1, f_2 \circ \gamma_1^*) + d_{\mathcal{C}_f}(f_2, f_3 \circ \gamma_2^*) \tag{3.4b}$$

$$= d_{\mathcal{C}_f}(f_1 \circ \gamma_1^{*-1}, f_2) + d_{\mathcal{C}_f}(f_2, f_3 \circ \gamma_2^*) \tag{3.4c}$$

$$\geq d_{\mathcal{C}_f}(f_1 \circ \gamma_1^{*-1}, f_3 \circ \gamma_2^*) \tag{3.4d}$$

$$\geq \min_{\gamma_1, \gamma_2} d_{\mathcal{C}_f}(f_1 \circ \gamma_1, f_3 \circ \gamma_2) \tag{3.4e}$$

$$= \min_{\gamma_1, \gamma_2} d_{\mathcal{C}_f}(f_1, f_3 \circ \gamma_2 \circ \gamma_1^{-1}) \tag{3.4f}$$

$$= \min_{\gamma} d_{\mathcal{C}_f}(f_1, f_3 \circ \gamma) \tag{3.4g}$$

$$= d_{\tilde{\mathcal{C}}_f}(f_1, f_3). \tag{3.4h}$$

Equations (3.4c) and (3.4f) both require the isometry property.

One step still remains. To render the distance independent of the initial orientations of the surfaces, we minimize over all possible rotations of one of the surfaces, as signaled in Chapter 2. Again, we can restrict ourselves to rotations of one surface only because, being derived from the reduced elastic metric, $d_{\tilde{C}_f}$ is preserved by equal rotations of both surfaces. We again define a new distance

$$d_{S_f}(f_1, f_2) = \min_{O \in SO(3)} d_{\tilde{C}_f}(f_1, Of_2) = d_{\tilde{C}_f}(f_1, O^* f_2), \qquad (3.5)$$

or, combining the two minimizations:

$$d_{S_f}(f_1, f_2) = \min_{(O, \gamma) \in SO(3) \times \Gamma} d_{C_f}(f_1, Of_2 \circ \gamma) = d_{C_f}(f_1, O^* f_2 \circ \gamma^*). \qquad (3.6)$$

Note that it does not matter in which order we perform these minimizations, since the actions of rotations and reparameterizations commute.

Here we have introduced yet another quotient space, denoted S_f. This is the quotient of $\tilde{C}_f$ by rotations; or, alternatively, the quotient of C_f by rotations and reparameterizations; or, alternatively, the quotient of $\mathcal{F}$ by translations, scalings, rotations, and reparameterizations.[6] Each point in S_f represents an unparameterized surface, up to translation, rotation, and scaling. It is known as "shape space," because one definition of "shape" is as the geometric properties that are left once translation, rotation, and scale have been removed [Kendall, 1977].

3.1.2 OPTIMAL DEFORMATION

So far, we have assumed that we know how to calculate d_{C_f} and the associated geodesic α_f. In this section, we discuss how to define d_{C_f} in terms of the reduced elastic metric, leaving the nitty-gritty of the computations to Sections 3.3, 3.4, and 3.5.

We denote the reduced elastic metric when restricted to C_f, by $\langle\langle \cdot, \cdot \rangle\rangle$. Thus, the size of a deformation δf of a parameterized surface f is given by $\langle\langle \delta f, \delta f \rangle\rangle_f$. Note that if δf corresponds to an infinitesimal translation or scaling, then its size will be zero; thus, $\langle\langle \cdot, \cdot \rangle\rangle$ becomes a well-defined Riemannian metric on C_f. The distance between two surfaces is then defined to be the length of the minimum-length path between those surfaces in this Riemannian metric. To begin with, then, we need to define the length of a path, and before that, a path.

A path in C_f is, by definition, a map $a_f : [0, 1] \to C_f$. The tangent vector at a point $t \in [0, 1]$ is then $\dfrac{da_f}{dt}(t)$, which we abbreviate for the moment to $\dot{a}_f(t)$. The length of the path is then given by

$$\mathcal{L}(a_f) = \int_0^1 dt \sqrt{\langle\langle \dot{a}_f(t), \dot{a}_f(t) \rangle\rangle_{a_f(t)}}, \qquad (3.7)$$

---

[6]For those who are somewhat familiar with these ideas, note that the quotient for scalings is defined with respect to the pseudometric induced by the restriction of the reduced elastic metric to $\mathcal{F}_1$, and not by the multiplicative group action of $\mathbb{R}_{>0}$.

or, in other words, the integral of the size of the infinitesimal deformations making up the path. We can thus define

$$d_{C_f}(f_1, f_2) = \min_{\substack{a_f:[0,1]\to C_f \\ a_f(0)=f_1 \\ a_f(1)=f_2}} \mathcal{L}(a_f) = \mathcal{L}(a_f^*) \,. \tag{3.8}$$

It turns out to be equivalent, and simpler, to replace $\mathcal{L}$ in this last equation with the "energy"

$$\mathcal{E}(a_f) = \int_0^1 dt \, \langle\langle \dot{a}_f(t), \dot{a}_f(t) \rangle\rangle_{a_f(t)} \,. \tag{3.9}$$

This results in the same distance function as before (except squared):

$$d_{C_f}(f_1, f_2)^2 = \min_{\substack{a_f:[0,1]\to C_f \\ a_f(0)=f_1 \\ a_f(1)=f_2}} \mathcal{E}(a_f) = \mathcal{E}(a_f^*) \,. \tag{3.10}$$

The only difference in the result is that the optimizing path, a_f^*, can have an arbitrary parameterization if the first definition is used, whereas its parameterization is fixed by the second definition to be proportional to arc length (the first equality in Equation (3.10) is precisely due to this fact). This makes no difference in practice. Computationally speaking, the second definition is much easier to deal with, due to the absence of the square-root.

3.1.3   PUTTING IT ALL TOGETHER

Combining the results of Sections 3.1.1 and 3.1.2, we find that the computation of geodesic paths and distances on $\mathcal{S}_f$ can be accomplished by solving the following joint optimization problem:

$$d_{C_f}(f_1, f_2)^2 = \min_{(O,\gamma)\in SO(3)\times\Gamma} \min_{\substack{a_f:[0,1]\to C_f \\ a_f(0)=f_1 \\ a_f(1)=Of_2\circ\gamma}} \mathcal{E}(a_f) = \mathcal{E}(\alpha_f(f_1, O^* f_2 \circ \gamma^*)) \,, \tag{3.11}$$

where $\alpha_f(f_1, O^* f_2 \circ \gamma^*)$ is the optimizing path, the geodesic in $\mathcal{S}_f$, between f_1 and the optimally rotated and reparameterized f_2. It represents the optimal deformation between the unparameterized surfaces, while γ^* represents the optimal registration. Figure 3.1 illustrates the joint optimization problem defined in Equation (3.11).

We thus see that we have succeeded in principle in calculating a distance between unparameterized surfaces, while simultaneously calculating an optimal registration and deformation between them, and rendering the distance invariant to translations, rotations, and scalings, all using the same, single structure: a Riemannian metric on the space of parameterized objects. This was the original promise of ESA.

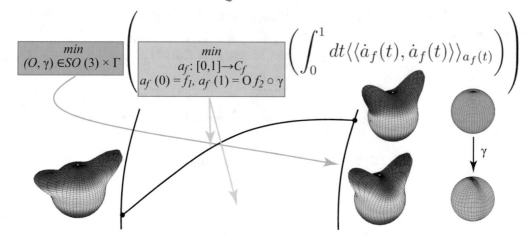

Figure 3.1: Pictorial description of the process of computing geodesics in the shape space of surfaces.

3.1.4   SIMPLIFYING THE COMPUTATIONS USING SRNFS

Our excitement may be short-lived, however, when we realize that, as it stands, we are faced with a very complex joint optimization problem, in which we must iterate between finding the best registration and alignment, and finding the geodesic between the resulting parameterized surfaces, the latter representing a formidable challenge even in isolation. (This complex optimization problem has been extensively studied in the past two decades; see van Kaick et al. [2011] and Tam et al. [2013] for a comprehensive survey.) In contrast, in Chapter 2 we saw that the very simple form of the reduced elastic metric in the SRNF representation means that we can write down the distance in $L^2(D, \mathbb{R}^3)$ in closed form. Can we leverage this to help us solve the problem?

The answer is yes, modulo a caveat we mention shortly. Given the distance in closed form, we can forget about finding the geodesic, and simply minimize the distance over $SO(3) \times \Gamma$ as in Equation (3.6), finding, once and for all, the optimal alignment and registration (γ^*, O^*) for the given endpoints f_1 and f_2. Since the actions of Γ on D and $SO(3)$ on $\mathbb{R}^3$ are the same for both $\mathcal{F}$ and $\mathcal{Q}$, the registration and alignment found in this way are the same, modulo the caveat, as those that would be found by performing the computations in $\mathcal{F}$.

The caveat is that the registration and alignment found in this way are necessarily only approximate. This is because, as we discussed at length in Chapter 2, the geodesic in $L^2(D, \mathbb{R}^3)$ may not lie entirely in $\mathcal{Q}$, and thus the map Q from $\mathcal{F}$ to $L^2(D, \mathbb{R}^3)$ may not be an isometry: the distance in $L^2(D, \mathbb{R}^3)$ may be less than the geodesic distance in $\mathcal{F}$. For the reasons discussed in Chapter 2, it is nevertheless expedient to ignore this possible complication, and simply proceed as if Q were an isometry.

CHECKPOINT

We have now seen how, in principle, we can approximate the joint optimal solution to the problem by first solving the registration and alignment problem in SRNF space, and then computing the geodesic path and distance between the aligned and registered surfaces. As we have already mentioned, this task can be tackled either by computing in SRNF space or by computing in $\mathcal{F}$ with the pullback metric, the advantage of the former being speed, and of the latter being lack of approximation.

We now dive into the details of the computations. We tackle the registration and alignment problem in SRNF space in Section 3.2, and then the computation of geodesics in Sections 3.3–3.5.

3.2   REGISTRATION AND ALIGNMENT USING SRNFS

We have seen how the actions of translations and scalings lead from $\mathcal{F}$ to the quotient space $\mathcal{C}_f$; and how the actions of rotations and reparameterizations lead from $\mathcal{C}_f$ to $\mathcal{S}_f$. We can follow the same sequence of quotients for SRNFs. The map $Q : \mathcal{F} \to L^2(D, \mathbb{R}^3)$ eliminates translations because it involves only derivatives. We can then restrict attention to the unit sphere $L^2_1(D, \mathbb{R}^3) \subset L^2(D, \mathbb{R}^3)$, which contains the SRNFs of unit area surfaces $\mathcal{Q}_1$. This defines the space $\mathcal{C}_q \equiv L^2_1(D, \mathbb{R}^3)$.

The distance $d_{\mathcal{C}_q}$ on $\mathcal{C}_q$ is given by the restriction of the L^2 distance $d_{\mathcal{Q}}(q_1, q_2) = \|q_1 - q_2\|$ on $L^2(D, \mathbb{R}^3)$ to the unit sphere. It can therefore be written in closed form:

$$d_{\mathcal{C}_q}(q_1, q_2) = \cos^{-1}(\langle q_1, q_2 \rangle_2) , \tag{3.12}$$

where $\langle \cdot, \cdot \rangle_2$ is the L^2 inner product. Rotations and diffeomorphisms then act on $\mathcal{C}_q$, taking q to $(q, (O, \gamma)) \equiv \sqrt{J[\gamma]}\,(Oq \circ \gamma)$. We can define a new distance by analogy with Equation (3.6), giving a pseudometric on $\mathcal{C}_q$:

$$d_{\mathcal{S}_q}(q_1, q_2) = \min_{(O, \gamma) \in SO(3) \times \Gamma} d_{\mathcal{C}_q}(q_1, (q_2, (O, \gamma))) = d_{\mathcal{C}_q}(q_1, (q_2, (O^*, \gamma^*))) , \tag{3.13}$$

with O^* and γ^* representing the optimal alignment and registration. It is easy to see that the product group $SO(3) \times \Gamma$ has $\mathcal{C}_q \equiv L^2_1(D, \mathbb{R}^3)$ as an invariant subset, and also preserves $d_{\mathcal{C}_q}$. Hence the pseudometric defines a true metric on the quotient space $\mathcal{S}_q$, the "shape space."

Note, however, that minimizing $d_{\mathcal{C}_q}$ with respect to the action of an isometry on one of its two arguments is equivalent to doing the same with the "chordal" L^2 distance $\|q_1 - q_2\|^2$, because

$$\|q_1 - (q_2, (O, \gamma))\|^2 = \|q_1\|^2 + \|(q_2, (O, \gamma))\|^2 - 2\langle q_1, (q_2, (O, \gamma)) \rangle_2 \tag{3.14a}$$
$$= \|q_1\|^2 + \|q_2\|^2 - 2\langle q_1, (q_2, (O, \gamma)) \rangle_2 , \tag{3.14b}$$

and the first two terms do not depend on the group elements. We can thus replace $d_{\mathcal{C}_q}$ by the L^2 norm in what follows, and this simplifies matters. The problem we have to solve in order to find the optimal registration and alignment is thus to minimize the cost function $E_{\text{reg}} : SO(3) \times \Gamma \to \mathbb{R}_{\geq 0}$:

$$E_{\text{reg}}(O, \gamma) = \|q_1 - (q_2, (O, \gamma))\|^2 = \|q_1 - \sqrt{J[\gamma]} \, (Oq_2 \circ \gamma)\|^2 \tag{3.15}$$

over $SO(3) \times \Gamma$.

3.2.1   OPTIMIZATION OVER THE ROTATION GROUP

For a fixed $\gamma \in \Gamma$, the minimization of E_{reg} over $SO(3)$ can be performed directly using Procrustes analysis. Let $\tilde{q}_2$ denote $(q_2, \gamma) \equiv \sqrt{J[\gamma]} \, (q_2 \circ \gamma)$ in Equation (3.15). The optimal rotation matrix

$$O^* = \arg \min_{O \in SO(3)} E_{\text{reg}}(O, \gamma) = \arg \min_{O \in SO(3)} \|q_1 - O\tilde{q}_2\|^2 \tag{3.16}$$

can then be obtained using Algorithm 3.1.

Algorithm 3.1 Optimal rotational alignment of two surfaces.

Input: Two surfaces $\{f_1, \ f_2\} \in \mathcal{F}$.

Output: Optimal rotation matrix O^* and optimally rotated surface f_2^*.

1: Compute the SRNFs $q_1 = Q(f_1)$ and $q_2 = Q(f_2)$.
2: Compute the 3×3 matrix $A = \int_D ds q_1(s) \tilde{q}_2(s)^T$.
3: Compute the singular value decomposition $A = U \Sigma V^T$.
4: Compute the optimal rotation as $O^* = U V^T$. (If the determinant of A is negative, the last column of V changes sign.)
5: Compute the optimally rotated surface $f_2^* = O^* f_2$.

3.2.2   OPTIMIZATION OVER THE REPARAMETERIZATION GROUP

In order to solve the optimization problem over Γ, we use a gradient descent approach. Although this approach has an obvious limitation of converging to a local solution, it is still general enough to be applicable to general surfaces. Note that the dynamic programming algorithm, which is commonly used for nonlinear registration of curves, does not apply here.

In order to specify the gradient, we focus on the current iteration, and define the reduced cost function $E_{\text{reg}} : \Gamma \to \mathbb{R}_{\geq 0}$:

$$E_{\text{reg}}(\gamma) = \|q_1 - (\tilde{q}_2, \gamma)\|^2 = \|q_1 - \phi(\gamma)\|^2, \tag{3.17}$$

where $\tilde{q}_2 = (q_2, \gamma_0)$, γ_0 and γ denote the current and the incremental reparameterizations respectively, and $\phi : \Gamma \to [q_2]$ is defined to be $\phi(\gamma) = (\tilde{q}_2, \gamma)$. Define b to be a unit vector in $T_{\gamma_{\text{id}}}(\Gamma)$ for $\gamma_{\text{id}}(s) = s$. Then, the directional derivative of E_{reg} at γ_{id}, in the direction of b, is given by $\langle q_1 - \phi(\gamma_{\text{id}}), d\phi(b) \rangle_2 b$, where $d\phi$ is the differential of ϕ. If we have an orthonormal basis for $T_{\gamma_{\text{id}}}(\Gamma)$, we can specify the full gradient of E_{reg} with respect to γ, which is an element of

$T_{\gamma_{\mathrm{id}}}(\Gamma)$ given by $\partial\gamma \simeq \sum_{b_i \in \mathcal{B}_I} \langle q_1 - \tilde{q}_2, d\phi(b_i) \rangle_2 b_i$. This linear combination of the orthonormal basis elements of $T_{\gamma_{\mathrm{id}}}(\Gamma)$ provides the incremental update of $\tilde{q}_2$ in the orbit $[q_2]$. This leaves two remaining issues: (1) the specification of an orthonormal basis of $T_{\gamma_{\mathrm{id}}}(\Gamma)$, and (2) an expression for $d\phi$.

Basis Construction

The tangent space of Γ at the identity element γ_{id} is defined as $T_{\gamma_{\mathrm{id}}}(\Gamma) = \{b : D \to T(D) \mid b$ is a smooth tangent vector field on $D\}$. In case $D = \mathbb{S}^2$, we are going to construct an orthonormal basis for $T_{\gamma_{\mathrm{id}}}(\Gamma)$ using the spherical harmonics basis. Spherical harmonics form a well-known basis for functions defined on a sphere, and thus provide a natural starting point in our setup. Let $Y_l^m : \mathbb{S}^2 \to \mathbb{C}$ denote the (complex) spherical harmonic function of degree l and order m, $m = 0, \ldots, l$. First, take the real and imaginary parts of Y_l^m, for all l and m, and label these individual functions as ψ_i, indexed by i in an arbitrary order. The set of these functions forms an orthonormal basis of the Hilbert space $L^2(\mathbb{S}^2, \mathbb{R})$. Since the imaginary part of Y_l^0 is always zero, we have $(l+1)^2$ distinct functions on $\mathbb{S}^2$ for the first l harmonics. For example, if $l = 2$, we will have $\psi_0 = Y_0^0, \psi_1 = Y_1^0, \psi_2 = \Re(Y_1^1), \psi_3 = \Im(Y_1^1), \psi_4 = Y_2^0, \psi_5 = \Re(Y_2^1), \psi_6 = \Im(Y_2^1), \psi_7 = \Re(Y_2^2), \psi_8 = \Im(Y_2^2)$ as nine basis elements of $L^2(\mathbb{S}^2, \mathbb{R})$.

By definition, the gradient of ψ_i, $\nabla\psi_i$, is a tangent vector field on $\mathbb{S}^2$. We will represent such vector fields with respect to a standard basis in the spherical coordinate system as follows. Let the elements of $\mathbb{S}^2$ be parameterized by (θ, ϕ) as before. In these coordinates, with $\left[\partial_\theta, \frac{1}{\sin(\theta)}\partial_\phi\right]$ as a basis, we can simply express the gradient as a 2-vector, $\nabla_{(\theta,\phi)}\psi = \left[\partial_\theta\psi, \frac{1}{\sin(\theta)}\partial_\phi\psi\right]$. Thus, the gradient of a function $\psi : \mathbb{S}^2 \to \mathbb{R}$ is given by $\nabla_{(\theta,\phi)}\psi = \left[\partial_\theta\psi\,\partial_\theta + \frac{1}{\sin(\theta)}\partial_\phi\psi\,\frac{1}{\sin(\theta)}\partial_\phi\right] \in T_{(\theta,\phi)}(\mathbb{S}^2)$. Note that $\nabla_{(\theta,\phi)}\psi_0$ is a zero vector field and thus will be excluded from the orthonormal basis. These vector fields provide half of the orthonormal basis elements of $T_{\gamma_{\mathrm{id}}}(\Gamma)$. The remaining half are obtained by a counterclockwise rotation of each vector in the vector field by $\pi/2$, when seen from outside of the sphere. Thus for $\nabla_{(\theta,\phi)}\psi = \left[\partial_\theta\psi, \frac{1}{\sin(\theta)}\partial_\phi\psi\right]$, its rotation $*\nabla_{(\theta,\phi)}\psi$ is simply the vector $\left[\frac{1}{\sin(\theta)}\partial_\phi\psi, -\partial_\theta\psi\right]$. For each $i = 1, 2, \ldots$, let $\tilde{b}_i = \frac{\nabla\psi_i}{\|\nabla\psi_i\|}$ and let $*\tilde{b}_i = \frac{*\nabla\psi_i}{\|*\nabla\psi_i\|}$. We can then define two sets as $B = \{\tilde{b}_i\}_{i=1,2,\ldots}$ and $*B = \{*\tilde{b}_i\}_{i=1,2,\ldots}$.

It turns out that the union of the sets B and $*B$ provides an orthonormal basis of the set of all smooth tangent vector fields on $\mathbb{S}^2$, i.e., $T_{\gamma_{\mathrm{id}}}(\Gamma)$. A complete proof of this proposition is given in Kurtek et al. [2011b]. We will denote the union of the two sets by $\mathcal{B}_I$ and will use $\{b_i, i = 1, \ldots, k = 2(l+1)^2 - 2\}$ to denote individual elements of $\mathcal{B}_I$. Figure 3.2 displays four examples of basis elements generated using this method.

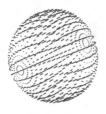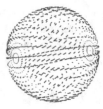

Figure 3.2: Four examples of basis elements of $T_{\gamma_{id}}(\Gamma)$ for $D = \mathbb{S}^2$.

Differential of Group Action

Next, we need to determine the differential of the group action mapping at the identity: $d\phi :$ $T_{\gamma_{id}}(\Gamma) \to T_{\tilde{q}_2}[q_2]$. Let b represent an arbitrary tangent vector field on $\mathbb{S}^2$, i.e., an element of $T_{\gamma_{id}}(\Gamma)$, and let $\tilde{q}_2 = (\tilde{q}_2^1, \tilde{q}_2^2, \tilde{q}_2^3)$, where each $\tilde{q}_2^j$ is a real-valued function on $\mathbb{S}^2$. Then $d\phi(b)$ also has three components $(d\phi^1, d\phi^2, d\phi^3)$, which are given by the formula [Kurtek et al., 2011b]:

$$d\phi^j(b) = \frac{1}{2}(\nabla \cdot b)\tilde{q}_2^j + \nabla\tilde{q}_2^j \cdot b. \tag{3.18}$$

In Equation (3.18) $\nabla \cdot b$ is the divergence of b, and $\nabla\tilde{q}_2^j$ is the gradient of $\tilde{q}_2^j$.

The formula for $d\phi(b)$ further simplifies when $D = \mathbb{S}^2$ and consequently $b = \dfrac{\nabla\psi_i}{\|\nabla\psi_i\|}$ or $\dfrac{*\nabla\psi_i}{\|*\nabla\psi_i\|}$ in the following manner. When $b = \dfrac{\nabla\psi_i}{\|\nabla\psi_i\|}$, its mapping under $d\phi$ is given by

$$d\phi^j\left(\frac{\nabla\psi_i}{\|\nabla\psi_i\|}\right) = \frac{1}{\|\nabla\psi_i\|}(-l_i(l_i + 1)\psi_i + (\nabla\tilde{q}_2^j \cdot \nabla\psi_i)), \tag{3.19}$$

since the Laplacian of a spherical harmonic Y_l^m is simply $-l(l + 1)$. Similarly when $b = \dfrac{*\nabla\psi_i}{\|*\nabla\psi_i\|}$, we obtain the simplification

$$d\phi^j\left(\frac{*\nabla\psi_i}{\|*\nabla\psi_i\|}\right) = \frac{1}{\|*\nabla\psi_i\|}(\nabla\tilde{q}_2^j \cdot *\nabla\psi_i), \tag{3.20}$$

since the divergence of $*\nabla\psi_i$ is zero. The full registration procedure is given as Algorithm 3.2.

Initialization of the Gradient

Since we are using a gradient-based approach to search for the optimal reparameterization, the problem of having a good initialization becomes an important one. In this section, we describe an efficient initialization approach for $D = \mathbb{S}^2$. In that case, the group Γ contains the compact rotation group $SO(3)$; this simply means that all rigid rotations of $\mathbb{S}^2$ are also reparameterizations of surfaces. While $SO(3)$ is much smaller than Γ, it still has an infinite number of elements.

Algorithm 3.2 Optimal registration of two surfaces.

Input: Two surfaces $\{f_1, f_2\} \in \mathcal{F}$ and small step size ϵ.
Output: Optimal registration γ^* and optimally registered surface f_2^*.
1: Generate basis $\mathcal{B}_I = \{b_i, \ i = 1, \ldots, N\}$ using procedure in Section 3.2.2.
2: Compute the SRNFs $q_1 = Q(f_1)$ and $q_2 = Q(f_2)$.
3: Initialize $\gamma_0 = \gamma_{\mathrm{id}}$, $q_2^0 = q_2$ and $j = 0$.
4: For each b_i, $i = 1, \ldots, N$, compute $d\phi(b_i)$ using Equation (3.18).
5: Compute the registration update $\partial\gamma = \sum_{b_i \in \mathcal{B}_I} \langle q_1 - q_2^j, d\phi(b_i) \rangle_2 b_i$.
6: Apply the registration update using $\gamma_{j+1} = \gamma_j \circ (\gamma_{\mathrm{id}} + \epsilon \partial\gamma)$.
7: Update $q_2^{j+1} = (q_2^0, \gamma_{j+1})$ and $j = j + 1$.
8: Iterate steps 4–7 until convergence.
9: Let $\gamma^* = \gamma_j$ and $f_2^* = f_2 \circ \gamma^*$.

Let K denote the largest (irreducible) finite subgroup of $SO(3)$; it is the group of symmetries of the dodecahedron, and has 60 elements. Shown on the left of Figure 3.3 is a picture of a dodecahedron and on the right is an illustration of the elements of K. In this figure, we show the points resulting from 60 rotations of the unit vector $[1, 0, 0]$, drawn over a unit sphere. We will use these 60 elements as the initial search space for the gradient search in Γ. Denote by $k_1, k_2, \ldots, k_{60}$ the elements of K; each of them acts on the space of SRNFs according to $(q, k_i) = q \circ k_i$ since the determinant of the Jacobian term $J[k_i]$ is always one, i.e., the elements of K are area-preserving transformations of $\mathbb{S}^2$.

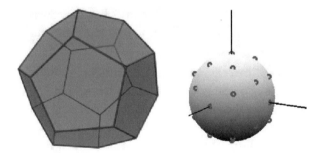

Figure 3.3: Left: Dodecahedron. Right: Points on $\mathbb{S}^2$ reached by multiplying $[1, 0, 0]$ by elements of the group of symmetries of a dodecahedron.

The initialization for optimization over Γ is a search over K by solving for $i^* = \arg\min_{i=1,\ldots,60} \|q_1 - (O_i^* \tilde{q}_2 \circ k_i)\|^2$. Here, O_i^* is the optimal rotation of $\tilde{q}_2 \circ k_i$ to best match q_1, obtained through Procrustes analysis as described earlier. The full algorithm is given in Algorithm 3.3.

Algorithm 3.3 Initialization of gradient search over Γ.

Input: Two surfaces $\{f_1,\ f_2\} \in \mathcal{F}$.

Output: Optimally initialized surface f_2^*.

1: Compute the SRNFs $q_1 = Q(f_1)$ and $q_2 = Q(f_2)$.
2: Generate the elements $k_1, \ldots, k_{60}$ of K.
3: For each $i = 1, \ldots, 60$, apply k_i to q_2 using $q_2^i = q_2 \circ k_i$ and compute $E_{\text{init}}(i) = \|q_1 - O^i q_2^i\|^2$, where O^i is computed via Algorithm 3.1.
4: Find the value of i for which E_{init} is smallest and call it $i*$.
5: Let $f_2^* = O^{i*}(f_2 \circ k_{i*})$.

Figure 3.4 shows an example of this initialization for two toy shapes. We start with two surfaces f_1 and f_2, mathematically represented by their SRNFs, q_1 and q_2, respectively. The k_i that minimizes the cost function becomes the initial parameterization for the gradient search over Γ.

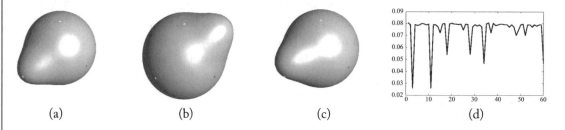

    (a)   (b)   (c)   (d)

Figure 3.4: Surface f_1 (a) and surface f_2 (b) before initialization. Surface 2 after initialization $(O_i^*(f_2 \circ k_{i*}))$ (c) and the values of the cost function over the elements of K (d).

The full algorithm for optimal alignment and registration of two surfaces is given in Algorithm 3.4. Figure 3.5 displays two examples of the complete alignment and registration procedure. In each example, we display the two surfaces before and after alignment and registration in panels (a)–(c). The optimal parameterization is given in panel (d) along with the energy at each iteration in panel (e). The matching of points across surfaces, i.e., registration, is displayed by mapping the color scheme on the first surface to the corresponding points on the second surface. Thus, if the registration is good, similar geometric features such as peaks should be shaded by similar colors. The first example considers the case where the two surfaces are within a reparameterization of each other: $f_2 = f_1 \circ \gamma$. The defined alignment and registration algorithm is able to recover the correct parameterization of the second surface, which is reflected in a final value of the energy being very close to zero (0.0582). The second example considers two surfaces with different numbers of peaks. With the given parameterizations (panels (a) and (b)), the peaks do not match well. The defined algorithm is able to drastically improve this matching as seen in panel (c). Furthermore, the alignment and registration of the two surfaces results in a more than 50% decrease in the energy.

Algorithm 3.4 Full alignment and registration procedure.

Input: Two surfaces $\{f_1, f_2\} \in \mathcal{F}$ and step size ϵ.

Output: Optimally aligned and registered surface f_2^*.

1: Initialize gradient search using Algorithm 3.3.
2: Find optimal alignment using Algorithm 3.1.
3: Find optimal registration using Algorithm 3.2.
4: Iterate steps 2–3 until convergence.

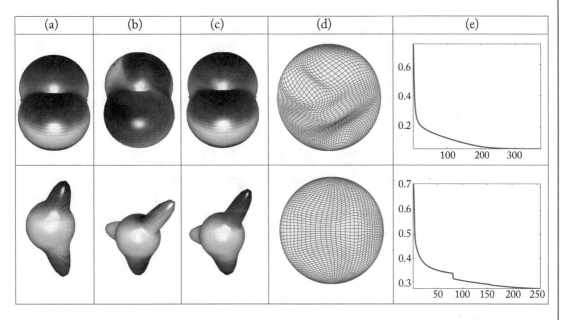

Figure 3.5: Two examples of alignment and registration of spherical surfaces. (a) Surface 1. (b) Surface 2 prior to alignment and registration. (c) Surface 2 after alignment and registration. (d) Optimal reparameterization. (e) Alignment and registration energy as a function of the number of iterations.

CHECKPOINT

In Sections 3.2.1 and 3.2.2, we have seen in detail how to compute the (approximate) optimal alignment O^* and registration γ^* of two surfaces. In order to complete our mission, we now have to show how to obtain the optimal deformation between the aligned and registered surfaces by computing the geodesic between them in the appropriate metric, i.e., how to implement Equation (3.10). As we have already pointed out, there are two ways to do this. We can compute in SRNF space and then use SRNF inversion to pull the result back to $\mathcal{F}$; or we can compute directly in $\mathcal{F}$ with the pullback of the L^2 metric, i.e., the reduced elastic metric.

We tackle the former in Section 3.5. In the next two sections, we show how to perform the latter computations. We first describe the computational techniques involved for a generic Riemannian manifold in Section 3.3, and then specialize to our case in Section 3.4.

3.3   GEODESIC COMPUTATION TECHNIQUES ON GENERAL MANIFOLDS

In this section, we consider the problem of computing geodesics between arbitrary points on a Riemannian manifold when analytical expressions are not available. This is precisely the case in our shape analysis setup. There are two main ideas for numerical construction of geodesic paths. In the first approach, called *path-straightening*, one initializes with an arbitrary path between the given two points on the manifold and then iteratively "straightens" it until a geodesic is reached. The second approach, called the *shooting method*, tries to "shoot" a geodesic from the first point, iteratively adjusting the shooting direction until the resulting geodesic passes through the second point.

3.3.1   GEODESIC COMPUTATION VIA PATH-STRAIGHTENING

The main numerical approach we consider for finding geodesic paths between points on a Riemannian manifold is based on a procedure called *path-straightening*. The main idea here is the following: initialize a path between two given points on the manifold and iteratively straighten it, using the gradient of an appropriate energy function, until it cannot be straightened any further. The resulting path will be a geodesic path. Relative to the shooting method there are several advantages to this method.

1. The solution is, by construction, guaranteed to start and end at the desired points in the manifold.

2. In case the gradient of the chosen energy can be written analytically, which is not the case in ESA of surfaces, the computational cost of implementing this approach is relatively low.

3. There is no need to approximate the tangent spaces (in case of infinite-dimensional manifolds) with finite-dimensional subspaces.

We briefly outline the theoretical setup for the path-straightening method in general terms and then pursue numerical implementations in the later sections. Now we pose the formal problem of finding geodesics on M. Say we are given two points $p_1, p_2 \in M$ that we want to join using a geodesic path in M. Let $\mathcal{A}$ be the set of all differentiable paths on M, whose first derivatives are L^2 functions, parameterized by $t \in [0, 1]$:

$$\mathcal{A} = \{a : [0, 1] \to M \mid a \text{ is differentiable and } \frac{da}{dt} \in L^2([0, 1], M)\}, \qquad (3.21)$$

and $\mathcal{A}_0$ be the subset of $\mathcal{A}$ consisting of those paths that start at p_1 and end at p_2:

$$\mathcal{A}_0 = \{a \in \mathcal{A} \mid a(0) = p_1, a(1) = p_2\}. \qquad (3.22)$$

The desired geodesic is an element of $\mathcal{A}_0$ and can be obtained by minimizing the energy given previously in Equation (3.9). That is, for elements of $\mathcal{A}$, define an energy function $E_{\text{path}} : \mathcal{A} \to \mathbb{R}_{\geq 0}$ by

$$E_{\text{path}}(a) = \int_0^1 dt \, \langle \dot{a}(t), \dot{a}(t) \rangle_{a(t)}, \qquad (3.23)$$

where $\dot{a}$ is the derivative of a as before. The inner product inside the integral comes of course from the Riemannian metric on M. We have some remarks about the definition of E_{path}.

- Note that for each t, $\dot{a}(t)$ is an element of $T_{a(t)}(M)$ and, by our assumption on $\mathcal{A}$, $\dot{a} : [0, 1] \to TM$ is an L^2 function.

- The critical points of E_{path} on the space $\mathcal{A}_0$ are precisely the constant-speed geodesic paths on M between p_1 and p_2. Therefore, one way to find a geodesic is to use the gradients of E_{path} to reach its critical points.

We will be using the gradient of E_{path} to find its critical points on $\mathcal{A}_0$. Thus we start with the differential structure of $\mathcal{A}_0$. The tangent spaces of $\mathcal{A}$ and $\mathcal{A}_0$ are:

$$T_a(\mathcal{A}) = \{\delta a : [0, 1] \to TM \mid \frac{D\delta a}{dt} \in L^2 \text{ and } \forall \, t \in [0, 1], \, \delta a(t) \in T_{a(t)}(M)\}, \qquad (3.24)$$

where $T_{a(t)}(M)$ is the tangent space of M at the point $a(t) \in M$, and

$$T_a(\mathcal{A}_0) = \{\delta a \in T_a(\mathcal{A}) \mid \delta a(0) = \delta a(1) = 0\}. $$

Note that the tangent space element δa is, by definition, a vector field along the path a tangent to M at each point of a.

3.3.2   GEODESIC COMPUTATION VIA SHOOTING

In order to specify an algorithm for computing geodesics using the shooting method, we require the definition of parallel transport on general Riemannian manifolds. Thus, we begin with this description.

For defining parallel transport on a Riemannian manifold M, there are two possible situations. The first is when M is a submanifold of a Hilbert space $\mathcal{H}$, either finite or infinite-dimensional, and the Riemannian metric on M is the one inherited from $\mathcal{H}$. A simple example is $M = \mathbb{S}^2$, a unit sphere in $\mathbb{R}^3$ with the Euclidean metric. The other situation is when M is actually a vector space but endowed with a Riemannian metric that is a non-standard one. An example is the hyperbolic upper-half plane $\mathbb{R}_+^2 = \{x = (x_1, x_2) \in \mathbb{R}^2 | x_2 > 0\}$ with the Riemannian metric $\langle v_1, v_2 \rangle_x = \dfrac{v_1 \cdot v_2}{x_2}$. Here, the underlying space is actually a vector space but its structure is not Euclidean. Consequently, geodesics are not straight lines in $\mathbb{R}_+^2$ and the parallel transports are not identity maps despite having $T_x(\mathbb{R}_+^2) = \mathbb{R}^2$ at every point x. In the first case, the description of parallel transport is relatively simple, both to define and to implement. Consider two nearby points p_1 and p_2 in M and we want to transport a vector v from p_1 to p_2. Since p_1, p_2 are also elements of $\mathcal{H}$, the larger Euclidean space, one can "transport" v in $\mathcal{H}$ and project it back into the tangent space at p_2. This provides a first-order approximation of the transport; the approximation improves as the distance between p_1 and p_2 decreases. However, this approach cannot be used in the second situation as the tangent space at p_2 is the full space with no projection possible.

In such cases, and other situations involving abstract manifolds, one relies on the use of Riemannian connections to define covariant derivatives and parallel transports. We state the important condition here and refer the reader to Boothby [1975] (Chapter VII) for details. Let E_k denote the local coordinate frame on M and, furthermore, let $g_{kh} = \langle E_k, E_h \rangle$ be the expression of the Riemannian metric in these local coordinates. For a path a and a vector field Y along that path, the covariant derivative of Y along a is given by $\dfrac{DY}{dt} = \nabla Y \left(\dfrac{da}{dt} \right)$, the directional derivative of Y along the direction of the velocity vector $\dfrac{da}{dt}$. The vector field Y is said to be constant or parallel if $\dfrac{DY}{dt} = 0$ for all t. Thus, if we express both $Y(t)$ in terms of the basis elements as $Y(t) = \sum_k y^k(t) E_k$ and $a(t)$ in the local coordinates as $a(t) = \{c^k(t), \ k = 1, 2, \dots\}$, then the condition $\dfrac{DY}{dt} = 0$ becomes (for all k) [Boothby, 1975]

$$\frac{dy^k}{dt} = -\sum_{i,j} \Gamma_{i,j}^k y^i(t) \frac{dc^j}{dt} . \tag{3.25}$$

Here, $\Gamma_{i,j}^k = \dfrac{1}{2} \sum_s g^{ks} \left(\partial_{x^j} g_{si} - \partial_{x^s} g_{ij} + \partial_{x^i} g_{js} \right)$ are the Christoffel symbols, and g^{ks} denotes elements of the inverse of the metric tensor g_{kh}. Now, in order to transport a vector $v \in T_{a(0)}(M)$ along a path a, we need to find a vector field Y along $a(t)$ satisfying Equation (3.25), such that $Y(0) = v$. Then, the vector $Y(t) \in T_{a(t)}(M)$ is called the parallel translation of v along a.

The second approach for finding geodesics on Riemannian manifolds is termed the shooting method. In this setting, our goal is to compute geodesics between any two points $p_1, p_2 \in M$, with respect to the given Riemannian metric. The basic approach is as follows.

1. Select one of the points, say p_1, as the starting point and the other, p_2, as the target point.

2. Construct a geodesic starting from p_1, in an arbitrary direction $v \in T_{p_1}(M)$, using the **exponential map**; denote it by $\alpha(t; p_1, v)$ where t is the time parameter for the geodesic flow. Note that this step usually requires parallel transport if the exponential map is not given analytically.

3. If this geodesic reaches p_2 in unit time, $\alpha(1; p_1, v) = p_2$, then we are done. If not, measure the amount of miss, i.e., the discrepancy between $\alpha(1; p_1, v)$ and p_2, using a simple measure. Call this discrepancy function E_{path}.

4. Iteratively update the shooting direction v to reduce the discrepancy E_{path} to zero. One can use the gradient of E_{path} to update v in the tangent space $T_{p_1}(M)$ but there are other ideas that are equally effective.

Implementation of this algorithm requires two important pieces. First, given a point $p_1 \in M$ and a direction $v \in T_{p_1}(M)$, we need to construct the geodesic path $\alpha(t; p_1, v)$ and we will do so in a general setting using numerical approximations based on parallel transport. Second, given two points p_1 and p_2, we will find a direction $v \in T_{p_1}(M)$ such that $\alpha(1; p_1, v) = p_2$. This ordering of the problem is important because the second piece uses the first piece. Actually, the solution of the first piece can be used to evaluate the exponential map and that of the second piece to evaluate the inverse exponential map. In the following, we particularize the path-straightening and shooting methods to find geodesics between surfaces under the reduced elastic metric.

3.4 ELASTIC GEODESIC PATHS BETWEEN SURFACES USING PULLBACK METRICS

In order to implement the shooting and path-straightening methods for computing geodesics between surfaces, we must first derive the appropriate pullback Riemannian metrics under the two representations of surfaces, i.e., SRNF and SRM. We begin with these derivations and then proceed to the definition of the two respective algorithms.

Pullback Metric under SRNF Representation

We remind the reader that the choice of the L^2 metric on the space of SRNFs is akin to the reduced elastic metric on the space of surfaces. One way to express this metric is in terms of perturbations of the surfaces themselves, which is different from the form given in Equation (2.20). Following this approach, in order to define the pullback metric on $\mathcal{F}$ we use the differential of the SRNF mapping given in Equation (2.30). This is a linear mapping between tangent spaces $T_f(\mathcal{F})$ and $T_{Q(f)}(\mathcal{Q})$. Using the differential dQ_f, we can equivalently define the reduced elastic metric on $\mathcal{F}$ for $\delta f_1, \delta f_2 \in T_f(\mathcal{F})$ as:

$$\langle\langle \delta f_1, \delta f_2 \rangle\rangle_f = \langle dQ_f(\delta f_1), dQ_f(\delta f_2) \rangle_2$$
$$= \int_D ds \frac{n_{\delta f_1}(s) \cdot n_{\delta f_2}(s)}{|n(s)|} - \frac{3}{4} \int_D ds \frac{(n(s) \cdot n_{\delta f_1}(s))(n(s) \cdot n_{\delta f_2}(s))}{|n(s)|^3} . \qquad (3.26)$$

The quantity $n_{\delta f}$ depends on both f and δf and is defined as $n_{\delta f} = f_u \times \delta f_v + \delta f_u \times f_v$ (subscripts indicate partial derivatives). Note that δf represents a vector field on the surface f.

Pullback Metric under SRM Representation

Here we derive the pullback metric under the SRM representation in similar manner. For a tangent vector $\delta f \in T_f(\mathcal{F})$, the mapping $dQ_{\text{SRM}f} : T_f(\mathcal{F}) \to T_{Q_{\text{SRM}}(f)}(Q_{\text{SRM}})$ is given by:

$$dQ_{\text{SRM}f}(\delta f) = \frac{1}{2|n|^{\frac{3}{2}}}(n \cdot n_{\delta f})f + \sqrt{|n|}\,\delta f \,. \tag{3.27}$$

The pullback metric on $\mathcal{F}$ is then defined using the differential as follows. For any $f \in \mathcal{F}$ and any $\delta f_1, \delta f_2 \in T_f(\mathcal{F})$ define the inner product:

$$
\begin{aligned}
\langle\langle \delta f_1, \delta f_2 \rangle\rangle_f &= \langle dQ_{\text{SRM}f}(\delta f_1), dQ_{\text{SRM}f}(\delta f_2)\rangle_2 \\
&= \langle \frac{1}{2|n|^{\frac{3}{2}}}(n \cdot n_{\delta f_1})f + \sqrt{|n|}\,\delta f_1, \frac{1}{2|n|^{\frac{3}{2}}}(n \cdot n_{\delta f_2})f + \sqrt{|n|}\,\delta f_2\rangle_2 \\
&= \langle \frac{1}{4|n|^3}(n \cdot n_{\delta f_1})f, (n \cdot n_{\delta f_2})f\rangle_2 + \langle \frac{1}{2|n|}\left[(n \cdot n_{\delta f_2})\delta f_1 + (n \cdot n_{\delta f_1})\delta f_2\right], f\rangle_2 \\
&\quad + \langle |n|\delta f_1, \delta f_2\rangle_2.
\end{aligned}
\tag{3.28}
$$

As discussed in Chapter 2, the action of Γ on Q_{SRM} is by isometries under the L^2 metric, and consequently this pullback metric.

3.4.1   PATH-STRAIGHTENING UNDER PULLBACK METRICS

Recall that in order to compute a geodesic path between two given surfaces $f_1, f_2 \in \mathcal{F}$, we are tasked with minimizing the energy $E_{\text{path}}(a_f) = \int_0^1 dt \langle\langle \dot{a}_f(t), \dot{a}_f(t)\rangle\rangle_{a_f(t)}$. We will compute the solution to this problem using a gradient descent approach. In order to approximate the full gradient of E_{path}, we will use a finite number of basis elements $\delta a_{f\,i} \in T_{a_f}(\mathcal{A}_0)$, $i = 1, \ldots, B$: $\nabla E_{\text{path}} \approx \sum_{i=1}^B \nabla E_{\text{path}}(\delta a_{f\,i})\delta a_{f\,i}$. Here, each $\delta a_{f\,i}$ is a perturbation of the path a_f, and $T_{a_f}(\mathcal{A}_0)$ denotes the set of all possible perturbations of a_f that vanish at $t = 0$ and $t = 1$. We will update the current estimate of the geodesic path according to $a_f = a_f - \epsilon \nabla E_{\text{path}}$, where $\epsilon > 0$ is a small step size. Once the algorithm has converged, it results in the geodesic path (α_f) as well as the unique shooting vector field $(\frac{d\alpha_f}{dt}(0))$, which can be used to optimally deform f_1 to f_2. Note that at this stage we require two additional tools to specify the full algorithm: (1) the expression for the gradient of the energy E_{path}, and (2) the basis $\{\delta a_{f\,i}, i = 1, \ldots, B\}$. We address these two problems in the following sections.

Figure 3.6 is a depiction of this approach. We start with an initial path a_f and iteratively update it in the direction of ∇E_{path} until we arrive at the critical point α_f, which is the desired geodesic.

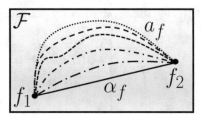

Figure 3.6: Computation of geodesic paths using the path-straightening algorithm.

Directional Derivatives of E_{path}

When the pullback metric comes from the SRM representation of surfaces, the expression for energy E_{path} is

$$E_{\text{path}}(a_f) = \int_0^1 dt \int_D ds \left[\frac{1}{4|N|^3} \left(N \cdot \frac{dN}{dt} \right)^2 (a_f \cdot a_f) \right.$$
$$\left. + \frac{1}{|N|} \left(N \cdot \frac{dN}{dt} \right) \left(\frac{da_f}{dt} \cdot a_f \right) + |N| \left(\frac{da_f}{dt} \cdot \frac{da_f}{dt} \right) \right],$$
(3.29)

where $N(t)$ implies $n(a_f(t))$, and all of the spatial and temporal arguments have been suppressed for brevity. We will approximate the gradient of this energy ∇E_{path} using directional derivatives $\nabla E_{\text{path}}(\delta a_f)$ where δa_f is an element of an orthonormal basis that spans all possible perturbations of a path a_f. The final expression of the directional derivative $\nabla E_{\text{path}}(\delta a_f)$ is given by

$$\nabla E_{\text{path}}(\delta a_f) = \frac{d}{d\epsilon}|_{\epsilon=0} E_{\text{path}}(a_f + \epsilon \delta a_f) = \int_0^1 dt \int_D ds \left[\frac{-3(N \cdot \delta N(\delta a_f))}{4|N|^5} (N \cdot \frac{dN}{dt})^2 (a_f \cdot a_f) \right.$$
$$+ \frac{1}{2|N|^3} (N \cdot \frac{dN}{dt})(N\delta\frac{dN}{dt}(\delta a_f)) + \frac{dN}{dt} \cdot \delta N(\delta a_f))(a_f \cdot a_f) + \frac{1}{2|N|^3}(N \cdot \frac{dN}{dt})^2 (a_f \cdot \delta a_f)$$
$$+ \frac{-(N \cdot \delta N(\delta a_f))}{|N|^3}(N \cdot \frac{dN}{dt})(\frac{da_f}{dt} \cdot a_f) + \frac{1}{|N|}(N \cdot \delta\frac{dN}{dt}(\delta a_f) + \frac{dN}{dt} \cdot \delta N(\delta a_f))(\frac{da_f}{dt} \cdot a_f)$$
$$+ \frac{1}{|N|}(N \cdot \frac{dN}{dt})(\frac{da_f}{dt} \cdot \delta a_f + a_f \cdot \frac{d\delta a_f}{dt}) + \frac{(N \cdot \delta N(\delta a_f))}{|N|}(\frac{da_f}{dt} \cdot \frac{da_f}{dt}) + 2|N|(\frac{da_f}{dt} \cdot \frac{d\delta a_f}{dt}) \right],$$

where $\delta N(\delta a_f) = \partial_u \delta a_f \times \partial_v a_f + \partial_u a_f \times \partial_v \delta a_f$ and $\delta\frac{dN}{dt}(\delta a_f) = \partial_u \frac{d\delta a_f}{dt} \times \partial_v a_f + \partial_u \frac{da_f}{dt} \times \partial_v \delta a_f + \partial_u \delta a_f \times \partial_v \frac{da_f}{dt} + \partial_u a_f \times \partial_v \frac{d\delta a_f}{dt}$. A detailed derivation of this directional derivative can be found in Kurtek et al. [2012a].

Similarly, in the case of SRNFs, the expression for the energy E_{path} is given by

$$E_{\text{path}}(a_f) = \int_0^1 dt \int_D ds \left[\frac{-3(N \cdot \frac{dN}{dt})^2}{4|N|^3} + \frac{\left|\frac{dN}{dt}\right|^2}{|N|} \right]. \tag{3.30}$$

The final expression of the directional derivative $\nabla E_{\text{path}}(\delta a_f)$ is [Samir et al., 2014]

$$\nabla E_{\text{path}}(\delta a_f) = \frac{d}{d\epsilon}|_{\epsilon=0} E_{\text{path}}(a_f + \epsilon \delta a_f)$$

$$= \int_0^1 dt \int_D ds \left[\frac{-3(N \cdot \delta \frac{dN}{dt}(\delta a_f) + \frac{dN}{dt} \cdot \delta N(\delta a_f))(N \cdot \frac{dN}{dt})}{2|N|^3} \right.$$

$$\left. - \frac{2\left|\frac{dN}{dt}\right|^2 (N \cdot \delta N(\delta a_f))}{2|N|^3} + \frac{9(N \cdot \delta N(\delta a_f))(N \cdot \frac{dN}{dt})^2}{4|N|^5} + \frac{2(\frac{dN}{dt} \cdot \delta \frac{dN}{dt}(\delta a_f))}{|N|} \right].$$

The expressions for the two directional derivatives look daunting and this is not surprising due to the complex nature of the pullback metrics. However they still allow us to implement a numerical approach for finding geodesics. The simplification of the alignment and registration problems via SRNFs is key as it allows us to compute the geodesic only once per each pair of surfaces.

Basis for Path-straightening

The basis set $\{\delta a_{f_i}, \ i = 1, \ldots, B\}$ for the case $D = \mathbb{S}^2$ used in the path-straightening algorithm is created using a combination of spherical hamornics and a modified Fourier basis as follows. Each element $\delta a_f : \mathbb{S}^2 \times [0, 1] \to \mathbb{R}^3$ has three arguments $\theta, \ \phi, \ t$ where (θ, ϕ) are the spatial coordinates on $\mathbb{S}^2$ as before and t is the time index along the path. We form bases for the spatial coordinates (θ, ϕ) and the temporal component t separately; the spatial basis is defined using the spherical harmonics introduced earlier. Now, we focus on defining the temporal basis with an additional restriction that preserves the starting and end points of the path a: the temporal basis is defined using a modification of the Fourier basis as $\{\sin(2\pi it), \cos(2\pi it) - 1 | i \in \mathbb{Z}_+\}$. We use all possible products of the spatial and temporal basis functions to form the final path-straightening basis, and orthonormalize using the Gram-Schmidt procedure.

Algorithm 3.5 outlines the path-straightening approach for computing a geodesic path and distance between two given surfaces.

To demonstrate the effectiveness of the path-straightening approach, we consider a special example where $f_1 = f_2 = f$ and initialize the algorithm with a path where $a_f(t) \neq f$ for t in the interior of the path. Here, we use the SRM-based pullback metric. Of course, we expect the geodesic path to be $\alpha_f(t) = f$, a constant path. The results are displayed in Figure 3.7.

Algorithm 3.5 Geodesic computation using path-straightening.

Input: Two surfaces $\{f_1, f_2\} \in \mathcal{F}$ and step size ϵ.

Output: Geodesic path α_f and geodesic distance $\mathcal{L}(\alpha_f)$.

1: Generate basis for path-straightening $\{\delta a_{f_i}, \ i = 1, \ldots, B\}$ using the procedure given in Section 3.4.1.

2: Initialize a path $a_f{}^0$ in $\mathcal{F}$ such that $a_f{}^0(0) = f_1$ and $a_f{}^0(1) = f_2$. Set $j = 0$.

3: For each $i = 1, \ldots, B$, calculate $\nabla E_{\text{path}}(\delta a_{f_i})$.

4: Update the path using $a_f{}^{j+1} = a_f{}^j - \epsilon(\sum_{i=1}^{B} \nabla E_{\text{path}}(\delta a_{f_i})\delta a_{f_i})$ and set $j = j + 1$.

5: Iterate steps 3–4 until convergence.

6: Let $\alpha_f = a_f{}^j$ and calculate $\mathcal{L}(\alpha_f)$ using Equation (3.7).

Using path-straightening, we obtain a 91.4% decrease in the energy E_{path} (right panel), and the resulting path is visibly the same surface. When we increase the number of basis elements used to approximate ∇E_{path}, we find the energy decrease to be even greater. The given paths are computed and displayed by discretizing at times $t_i = (i - 1)/6, \ i = 1, 2, \ldots, 7$.

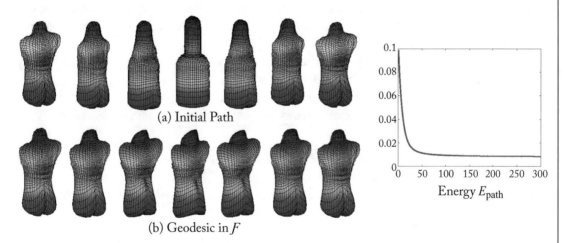

(a) Initial Path

(b) Geodesic in $\mathcal{F}$

Figure 3.7: An example of geodesic computation in $\mathcal{F}$ using the path-straightening approach.

3.4.2 SHOOTING GEODESICS UNDER SRNF PULLBACK METRIC

Next, we particularize the general shooting method for finding geodesics to the space of surfaces under the reduced elastic metric. Let $\{b_1, b_2, \ldots\}$ denote an orthonormal basis of $\mathcal{F}$. Any surface can be expressed with respect to these basis elements such that $f(s) = \sum_k c_k b_k(s)$. Then, $f \cong (c_1, c_2, \ldots) \in \mathbb{R}^\infty$ forms an alternative representation of the surface f. Using such a basis expansion, we begin by providing tools for parallel transport of vectors on $\mathcal{F}$ under the reduced elastic metric, which will be subsequently used to define an algorithm for computing shooting geodesics on $\mathcal{F}$. The choice of basis here can be the same as the one described in Chapter 2 for SRNF inversion.

Parallel Transport under Reduced Elastic Metric

To apply the general definition of parallel transport to the case at hand, suppose we want to parallel transport a deformation vector field $\delta f \in T_{a_f(0)}(\mathcal{F})$ along a path of surfaces a_f. Since we can express $a_f(t)$ and δf as $a_f(t) = \sum_k c_k(t)b_k$ and $\delta f = \sum_k y_k(0)b_k$, we want to define a vector field $Y(t) = \sum_k y_k(t)b_k$ along $a_f(t)$ such that $Y(0) = \delta f$ and $\dfrac{DY}{dt} = 0$. The coefficients of the tangent vector must satisfy the differential Equation (3.25) with the initial condition $\sum_k y_k(0)b_k = Y(0)$. The transported vector at time t is then $Y(t) = \sum_k y_k(t)b_k$. Discretizing Equation (3.25) with time step δt, we can transport incrementally from time t to $t + \delta t$ using, for each k,

$$y_k(t + \delta t) = y_k(t) - \delta t \sum_{i,j} \Gamma_{ij}^k y_i(t) \frac{dc^j}{dt}, \qquad (3.31)$$

and the transported vector becomes $Y(t + \delta t) = \sum_k y_k(t + \delta t)b_k$. In order to implement this equation, we need expressions for the Christoffel symbols Γ_{ij}^k which, in turn, depend on the Riemannian metric and its derivatives.

First, we evaluate the metric tensor using the basis set as $g_{kh} = \langle\langle b_k, b_h\rangle\rangle_{a_f(t)}$. For any $f(s) = \sum_k c_k b_k(s)$, $s \in D$, $f_u = \sum_k c_k \partial_u b_k$, $f_v = \sum_k c_k \partial_v b_k$, $n = \sum_k c_k \partial_u b_k \times \sum_k c_k \partial_v b_k$ and $n_{b_h} = \partial_u b_h \times \sum_k c_k \partial_v b_k + \sum_k c_k \partial_u b_k \times \partial_v b_h$. Defining $T_{kh} = n_{b_k} \cdot n_{b_h}$, $R_k = n \cdot n_{b_k}$ and $S = n \cdot n$, the notation for the metric tensor g_{kh} at a surface f can be simplified to

$$g_{kh} = \int_D ds \left(\frac{T_{kh}}{S^{1/2}} - \frac{3}{4} \frac{R_k R_h}{S^{3/2}} \right). \qquad (3.32)$$

All arguments have been suppressed here for brevity. Then, the partial derivatives of the metric tensor $g_{kl,m} = \partial_{c_m} g_{kl}$ (note: $g_{kl,m} = g_{lk,m}$) are given by

$$g_{kh,m} = \int_D ds \left(\frac{T_{kh,m}}{S^{1/2}} - \frac{T_{kh} R_m}{S^{3/2}} - \frac{3}{4} \frac{R_{k,m} R_h + R_{h,m} R_k}{S^{3/2}} + \frac{9}{4} \frac{R_k R_h R_m}{S^{5/2}} \right), \qquad (3.33)$$

where $T_{kh,m} = n_{b_h} \cdot (w_{km} + w_{mk}) + n_{b_k} \cdot (w_{hm} + w_{mh})$, $R_{k,m} = n_{b_m} \cdot n_{b_k} + n \cdot (w_{km} + w_{mk})$, $S_m = 2n \cdot n_{b_m}$ and $w_{ij} = \partial_u b_i \times \partial_v b_j$. Given these derivatives of the tensor matrix, we can compute $\Gamma_{ijk} = \frac{1}{2}(g_{ik,j} + g_{jk,i} - g_{ij,k})$. At this stage we need the inverse of the metric tensor matrix and will obtain it by truncating the basis set to a finite number N. Thus, the tensor matrix g_{ij} is of size $N \times N$ and we can compute its inverse $g^{ij} \in \mathbb{R}^{N \times N}$ in a straightforward manner. As a last step, the desired Christoffel symbols can be computed using $\Gamma_{ij}^k = \sum_m g^{km} \Gamma_{ijm}$, where g^{km} denotes the corresponding entry in the matrix g_{ij}^{-1}.

Exponential Map and Shooting Geodesics using Parallel Transport

Parallel transport can be used to evaluate the exponential map under the nonstandard reduced elastic metric. Given a surface $f \in \mathcal{F}$ and a deformation (tangent vector) δf_0 of f, we can evaluate the exponential map $\exp_f(t\delta f_0) = \alpha_f(t)$, $t \in [0, 1]$ using n discrete segments. First, we initialize the geodesic path as $\alpha_f(0) = f$ and the initial velocity as $\delta f(0) = \delta f_0$. For the tth segment, given $\delta f\left(\frac{t-1}{n}\right)$ and $\alpha_f\left(\frac{t-1}{n}\right)$, perform the following steps for $t = 2, 3, \ldots, n$.

1. Compute the parallel transport $\delta f\left(\frac{t-1}{n}\right)$ to $\alpha_f\left(\frac{t}{n}\right)$ and name it $\delta f\left(\frac{t}{n}\right)$.

2. Set $\alpha_f\left(\frac{t}{n}\right) = \alpha_f\left(\frac{t-1}{n}\right) + \frac{1}{n}\delta f\left(\frac{t}{n}\right)$.

This results in the evaluation of the exponential map of δf_0 at f. The following algorithm provides a procedure for computing a geodesic between two surfaces f_1 and f_2 in $\mathcal{F}$ using the shooting method.

Algorithm 3.6 Geodesic computation using the shooting method.

Input: Two surfaces $\{f_1, f_2\} \in \mathcal{F}$ and step size ϵ.

Output: Geodesic path α_f and geodesic distance $\mathcal{L}(\alpha_f)$.

1: Initialize the shooting direction as δf_0 and set $j = 0$.
2: Shoot a geodesic $\alpha_f{}^j(t) = \exp_{f_1}(t\delta f_j)$ for $t \in [0, 1]$.
3: Compute $r = f_2 - \alpha_f{}^j(1)$ and parallel transport r from $t = 1$ to $t = 0$ along $\alpha_f{}^j$. Call it $r^{\|}$.
4: If $\|r^{\|}\|$ is small, stop and set $\alpha_f = \alpha_f{}^j$ and compute $\mathcal{L}(\alpha_f)$ using Equation (3.7). Otherwise, update the shooting direction $\delta f_{j+1} = \delta f_j + \epsilon r^{\|}$ and return to step 2.

To evaluate this numerical method for computing geodesics between surfaces, we consider a synthetic example in Figure 3.8. In the top panel, we show the initial path and the evolution of the shooting method energy E_{path} as a function of the number of iterations. In the bottom panel, we show the final geodesic path and the difference between the given surface f_2 and the surface reached by the computed geodesic path $\exp_{f_1}(\delta f)$. In the given example, this difference quickly converges to the ideal value of zero.

3.5   ELASTIC GEODESIC PATHS BETWEEN SURFACES USING SRNF INVERSION

The ability to numerically invert the mapping Q greatly simplifies some of the tasks at hand. In contrast to the pullback metric approaches, the idea here is to perform the shape comparison directly in the space of SRNFs, and transform only the end results to $\mathcal{F}$. We provide a detailed description of this procedure next.

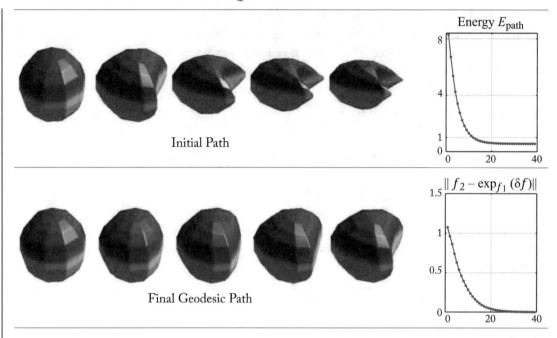

Figure 3.8: Geodesic path between synthetic surfaces computed using the shooting method.

3.5.1   GEODESICS USING SRNF INVERSION

Given two surfaces f_1 and f_2 and their corresponding SRNFs q_1 and q_2, the task at hand is to construct a geodesic path α indexed by t that connects their two shapes. To do so, we first optimally align and register f_2 to f_1 using the SRNF framework described in Section 3.1. That is, we find the optimal rotation O^* and optimal reparameterization γ^* such that Equation (3.13) is minimized. Let $q_2^* = (O^* q_2, \gamma^*)$ and $f_2^* = O^*(f_2 \circ \gamma^*)$. Let $\beta : [0, 1] \rightarrow L^2(\mathbb{S}^2, \mathbb{R}^3)$ denote the straight line connecting q_1 and q_2^*. Then, for any arbitrary point $\beta(t) \in L^2(\mathbb{S}^2, \mathbb{R}^3)$, we want to find a surface $\alpha(t)$ such that $\| Q(\alpha(t)) - \beta(t) \|$ is minimized. We will accomplish this using the following multiresolution analysis.

- Let $\mathbf{f}_1$ and $\mathbf{f}_2^*$ be the multiresolution representations of f_1 and f_2^*, respectively.

- We compute the multiresolution SRNFs of $\mathbf{f}_1$ and $\mathbf{f}_2^*$, which we denote by $\mathbf{q}_1$ and $\mathbf{q}_2^*$, respectively. Recall that $\mathbf{q}_i = (q_i^1, \ldots, q_i^m)$ where $q_i^j = Q(f_i^j)$.

- To compute the point $\alpha(t)$ on the geodesic path α, we compute $\alpha^j(t)$, for $j = 1, \ldots, m$, by SRNF inversion of $\beta^j(t) = (1 - t)q_1^j + tq_2^{*j}$, using $\alpha^{j-1}(t)$ as an initialization for the optimization procedure.

- The final solution $\alpha(t)$ is set to be $\alpha^m(t)$.

For the first iteration, one can set $\alpha^0(t)$ to be either a unit sphere or f_1^1. Note that, using this approach, one can compute $\alpha(t)$ for any arbitrary $t \in [0, 1]$ without computing the entire geodesic. This is not the case for the pullback metric-based approaches of path-straightening and shooting. The above procedure also applies to computation of geodesics on the preshape sphere with minor adjustments to ensure scale invariance. Additionally, in case the given surfaces are star-shaped, one can use the analytic solution described in Section 2.4.6 together with numerical inversion to construct the geodesic path α more efficiently.

3.5.2   PARALLEL TRANSPORT IN SRNF SPACE

As mentioned earlier, parallel transport is an important tool in many statistical shape analysis tasks. We describe the approach to parallel transport using the SRNF inversion in the context of deformation transfer. Given surfaces f_1, h_1, $f_2 \in \mathcal{F}$, we are interested in estimating the shape deformation from f_1 to h_1, and then applying this deformation to f_2. We first optimally align and register h_1 and f_2 to f_1. To simplify the notation, we also use f_1, h_1, and f_2 to denote the optimally registered surfaces. The deformation transfer task can be decomposed into three steps.

- Compute the deformation vector field v from f_1 to h_1 by computing a geodesic path between their shapes.

- Transfer v at f_1 to f_2 using parallel transport resulting in $v^{\|}$.

- Deform f_2 into h_2 using the exponential map of $v^{\|}$.

Note that the first and third steps require the computation of geodesics and this can be done via SRNF inversion using methods described in the previous section.

Under the proposed framework, h_2 can be computed by inversion of $Q(f_2) + (Q(h_1) - Q(f_1))$. Figure 3.9 shows an example of transferring a deformation from one surface to another using the SRNF inversion approach. Again, in case the surfaces are constrained to be of unit area, i.e., invariant to scale, this approach works as given with minor adjustements.

The computational cost advantages of parallel transport and deformation transfer using SRNF inversion are listed in Table 3.1. The comparsion is made to the pullback metric approaches described earlier in this chapter. The computationally intensive steps are underlined, and the computational complexity is indicated in boxes.

3.6   ELASTIC GEODESIC PATH EXAMPLES

In this section, we present several examples that validate all of the computational approaches presented in this chapter. In particular, we show multiple geodesic paths between shapes computed using path-straightening, the shooting method, and SRNF inversion. Before we proceed with the results, we provide a short description on the discretization of the functional surface representations, which is performed at the implementation stage.

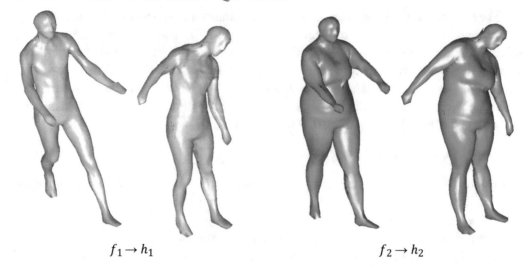

$$f_1 \rightarrow h_1 \qquad\qquad f_2 \rightarrow h_2$$

Figure 3.9: Deformation transfer. Surfaces f_1, h_1, and f_2 are given. Deformation from f_1 to h_1 is learned from the data (left) and used to deform f_2 to result in the new surface h_2 (right).

3.6.1   DISCRETIZATION

The described surface representations are functional in nature, i.e., infinite-dimensional. Thus, at the implemenation stage, we are required to discretize the given data. Each given surface is resampled to a regular grid of size $N \times N$ (the choice of N varies across applications). This is performed via spline interpolation. To approximate derivatives, we use finite differencing methods (forward and backward for boundary points, and central for interior points). The integrals are approximated using the trapezoidal rule. Furthermore, all geodesics are sampled using several equally spaced points (again, the number of points sampled along the geodesic depends on the application of interest).

3.6.2   PATH-STRAIGHTENING

Figure 3.10 displays several examples of geodesic comparisons for complex surfaces with many articulated parts. These geodesics were computed using the path-straightening approach under the pullback Riemannian metric based on the SRM. We note the clear benefit of finding optimal alignment and registration (second column of the figure): the geodesics in the shape space are much more natural than those in the preshape space. Furthermore, the decrease in the distance due to this process is significant in all of the presented examples.

In Figure 3.11, we again provide a comparison of geodesics computed in the preshape space and shape space under the reduced elastic metric using path-straightening. We use the same examples as in Figure 3.10 for comparison. As previously, the geodesics in the shape space have much lower distances than their preshape counterparts. The geodesic paths are also much

Preshape Geodesic	Shape Geodesic
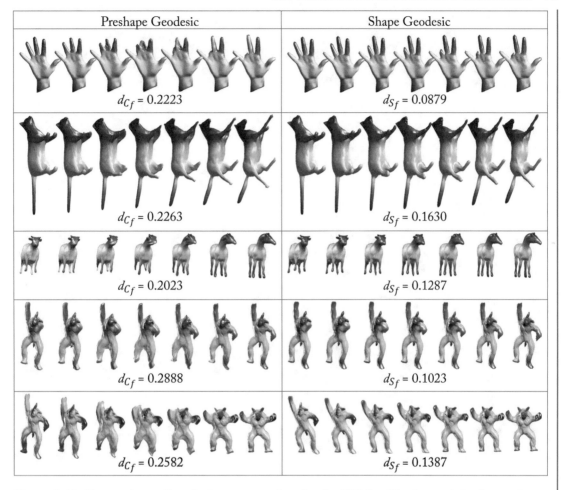	
$d_{C_f} = 0.2223$	$d_{S_f} = 0.0879$
$d_{C_f} = 0.2263$	$d_{S_f} = 0.1630$
$d_{C_f} = 0.2023$	$d_{S_f} = 0.1287$
$d_{C_f} = 0.2888$	$d_{S_f} = 0.1023$
$d_{C_f} = 0.2582$	$d_{S_f} = 0.1387$

Figure 3.10: Comparison of geodesics computed under the SRM pullback metric in the preshape space (left) and shape space (right).

more natural due to improved correspondence of geometric features across surfaces during the registration. Take for example, the hand shape deformations shown in the first column. The geodesic in the preshape space deforms all three of the middle fingers. On the other hand, the shape space geodesic simply grows the missing finger, which is more intuitive and visually pleasing. Similar improvements can be seen in all of the other examples as well.

When comparing the shape space results in Figure 3.11 to those in Figure 3.10, we notice that the reduced elastic metric provides improved results over the SRM pullback metric. This is expected due to the nice interpretation and invariance properties of the elastic metric as described in detail in Chapter 2. This improvement in geometric correspondences across surfaces

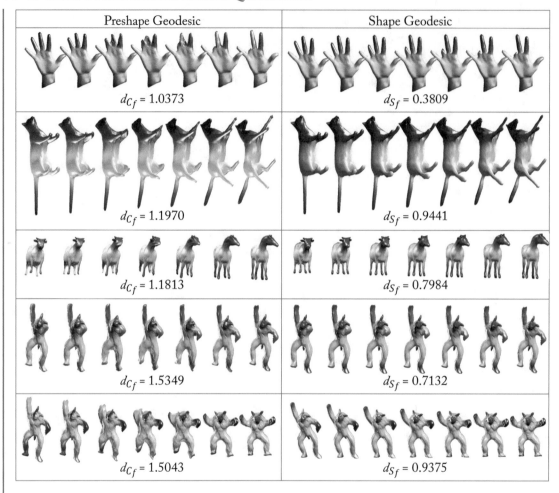

Preshape Geodesic	Shape Geodesic
$d_{C_f} = 1.0373$	$d_{S_f} = 0.3809$
$d_{C_f} = 1.1970$	$d_{S_f} = 0.9441$
$d_{C_f} = 1.1813$	$d_{S_f} = 0.7984$
$d_{C_f} = 1.5349$	$d_{S_f} = 0.7132$
$d_{C_f} = 1.5043$	$d_{S_f} = 0.9375$

Figure 3.11: Comparison of geodesics computed under the reduced elastic metric in the preshape space (left) and shape space (right).

additionally leads to more natural shape statistics, including averages and principal modes of variability, and more parsimonious shape models as will be seen in the next chapter.

3.6.3   SHOOTING METHOD

Next, we show several examples of geodesic paths between shapes of surfaces computed using the shooting method under the reduced elastic metric. As before, these examples consider highly articulated shapes including human hands and animals (cats and horses). The results are shown in Figure 3.12. As previously, the surfaces are first optimally aligned and registered to each other resulting in $f_2^* = O^*(f_2 \circ \gamma^*)$, where O^* is the optimal rotation and γ^* is the optimal reparameterization. The resulting geodesics represent intuitive and natural deformations between the given shapes.

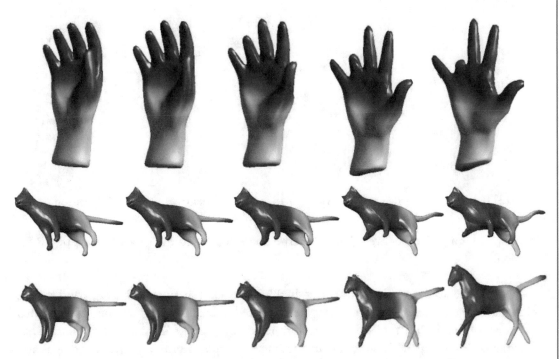

Figure 3.12: Shooting method shape geodesics between highly articulated surfaces.

3.6.4   SRNF INVERSION

In this final section, we show geodesic examples computed using the SRNF inversion approach. Prior to geodesic computation, the surfaces f_1 and f_2 are optimally aligned and registered. We again use the notation $f_2^* = O^*(f_2 \circ \gamma^*)$ to denote the surface f_2 after alignment and registration. Figure 3.13 shows two examples of deformation paths between surfaces f_1 and f_2^*, where f_1 is a straight cylinder and f_2 is a bent cylinder. Figure 3.13a shows a linear path between f_1 and f_2^* in $\mathcal{S}_f$ (i.e., each pair of corresponding points is connected by a straight line); note that this linear path was computed in $\mathcal{S}_f$ and not $\mathcal{S}_q$, and thus is not a geodesic. The intermediate shapes along this path shrink unnaturally. Figure 3.13b shows the geodesic path computed by SRNF inversion. That is, we first compute the linear path $\beta(t) = tQ(f_1) + (1 - t)Q(f_2^*)$, $t \in [0, 1]$ and then estimate, using the SRNF inversion algorithm, the geodesic path α such that $Q(\alpha(t)) = \beta(t)$ for all t. Here, the inversion procedure uses a spherical harmonics basis and is initialized with a sphere. Observe that, in both examples, the geodesic path smoothly deforms one cylinder into the other without shrinking the intermediate shapes as is the case when using linear interpolation in $\mathcal{S}_f$.

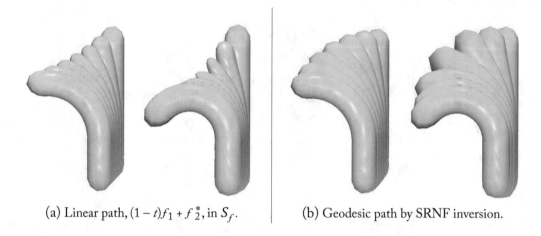

(a) Linear path, $(1 - t)f_1 + f_2^*$, in $\mathcal{S}_f$.　　(b) Geodesic path by SRNF inversion.

Figure 3.13: Comparison between linear interpolation in $\mathcal{S}_f$ and the geodesic path by SRNF inversion.

Next, we consider geodesics involving highly articulated surfaces such as cats and horses, which undergo complex motion involving bending and stretching. In the examples presented in Figures 3.14 and 3.15, the SRNF inversion procedure uses 3,642 spherical harmonics basis elements. We compare these results to the linear interpolation in $\mathcal{S}_f$ after alignment and registration. In all examples, the approach based on SRNF inversion produces improved deformations between these complex shapes, despite the fact that the surfaces are optimally aligned and registered in both cases; linear interpolation in $\mathcal{S}_f$ leads to unnatural deformations as shown in Figure 3.14a. In particular, the intermediate shapes produced by linear interpolation contain self-intersections and unnatural shrinkage of the parts that bend.

Finally, Table 3.1 summarizes the parallel transport and deformation transfer algorithms presented in this chapter and compares their complexity and computational times. While the SRNF inversion method approximates the underlying geodesics (due to the technical issues described in Section 2.4.6), it is much more efficient than the pullback metric approaches.

3.7 SUMMARY AND NEXT STEPS

In this chapter, we provided a set of tools for computing geometric quantities under the elastic metric, including alignment, registration and geodesic paths and distances, and parallel transport. We described multiple approaches to computing geodesics, including path-straightening, the shooting method, and SRNF inversion. The methods were evaluated using several examples,

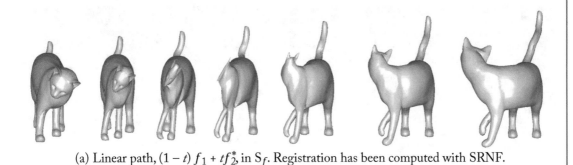

(a) Linear path, $(1 - t)f_1 + tf_2^*$, in S_f. Registration has been computed with SRNF.

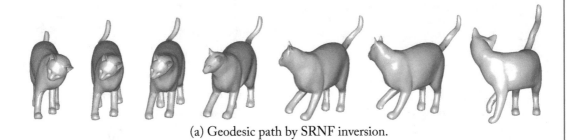

(a) Geodesic path by SRNF inversion.

Figure 3.14: Comparison of linear interpolation in $\mathcal{S}_f$ (a) and a formal shape geodesic computed using SRNF inversion (b).

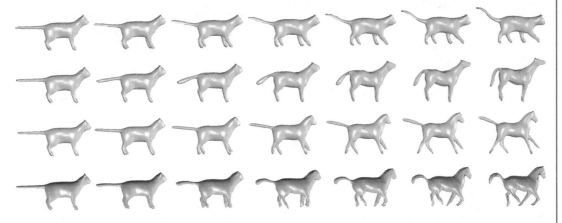

Figure 3.15: Additional geodesics between highly articulated 3D shapes obtained by SRNF inversion.

Table 3.1: Comparison of algorithms in terms of complexity and computational time

	Analysis Using the Pullback of the Elastic Metric (spherical grids of 32 × 32)	Analysis by SRNF Inversion (spherical grids of 64 × 64)
Parallel Transport	**Algorithm 1** *Find a <u>geodesic</u> $\alpha(t)$ connecting f_1 to f_2. For $t = 1, \ldots, m$, do the following.* 　1. *<u>Parallel transport</u> $V\left(\frac{t-1}{m}\right)$ from $\alpha(\frac{t-1}{m})$ to $\alpha(\frac{t}{m})$ and name it $V(\frac{t}{m})$.* *Set $v^{\parallel} = V(1)$.* Computational Task Summary: 1 geodesic + m parallel transports, 2 hours per geodesic.	**Algorithm 2** *Parallel transport on L^2 remains constant.* 　1. *Compute $w = dQ_{f_1}(v)$ (differential of Q).* 　2. *Find f by <u>inversion</u> s.t. $Q(f) = Q(f_2) + \epsilon w$, ϵ is small.* 　3. *Evaluate $\frac{f-f_2}{\epsilon}$ and set it to be $v^{\parallel}$.* Computational Task Summary: 1 inversion, 16.5 min (with harmonic basis) or 20.14 sec (with PCA basis).
Deformation Transfer	**Algorithm 3** 　1. *Find a <u>geodesic</u> $\beta(t)$ connecting f_1 to h_1 and evaluate $v = exp_{f_1}^{-1}(h_1)$.* 　2. *Find a <u>geodesic</u> $\alpha(t)$ connecting f_1 to f_2. Set $V(0) = v$. For $t = 1, \ldots, m$, do the following.* 　　(a) *<u>Parallel transport</u> $V\left(\frac{t-1}{m}\right)$ from $\alpha(\frac{t-1}{m})$ to $\alpha(\frac{t}{m})$ and name it $V(\frac{t}{m})$.* 　3. *Find a <u>geodesic</u> $\beta'(t)$ from f_2 with velocity $v^{\parallel} = V(1)$ and set $h_2 = \beta'(1)$.* Computational Task Summary: 3 geodesics + m parallel transports, 2 hrs per geodesic.	**Algorithm 4** *Parallel transport on L^2 remains constant.* 　1. *Compute $v = Q(h_1) - Q(f_1)$.* 　2. *Find h_2 by <u>inversion</u> s.t. $Q(h_2) = Q(f_2) + v$.* Computational Task Summary: 1 inversion, 16.5 min (with harmonic basis) or 20.14 sec (with PCA basis).

and we discussed the advantages and disadvantages of each approach, including computational complexity. The tasks described in this chapter are fundamental to providing a comprehensive framework for the statistical shape analysis of 3D objects under the elastic metric, to which we now turn.

3.8   BIBLIOGRAPHIC NOTES

The problem of registration of points across surfaces using the reparameterization group, albeit based on square-root maps, was introduced in the papers Kurtek et al. [2010, 2011b]. The same tool was applied to SRNF representations later in several other papers, including Jermyn et al. [2012] and Samir et al. [2014].

For a discussion on shooting and path-straightening techniques for computing geodesics on general manifolds, please refer to the textbook by Srivastava and Klassen [2016]. The path-straightening approach for computing geodesic paths in the preshape space of Euclidean curves was presented in Klassen and Srivastava [2006]. Later, it was applied to computing geodesics in the preshape space of surfaces, with the SRM representation in Kurtek et al. [2012a]. The path-straightening approach for computing geodesics using the SRNF representation was applied in Kurtek et al. [2016] and Samir et al. [2014].

The use of parallel transport using a finite-dimensional representation of surfaces was developed in the paper Xie et al. [2013]. A more comprehensive set of tools for elastic shape analysis of surfaces using SRNF inversion has been proposed recently in Laga et al. [2017].

CHAPTER 4

Statistical Analysis of Shapes

In this chapter, we present tools for performing four fundamental tasks in statistical shape analysis:

1. summarization of shape data using an average or template shape;

2. dimension reduction using Principal Component Analysis on the shape space;

3. definition of a generative shape model that is easy to sample from; and

4. classification and clustering of 3D models based on their shape.

To the best of our knowledge, there is no natural embedding of the shape space $\mathcal{S}_f$ inside a Hilbert space. Thus, we do not pursue the idea of computing extrinsic shape statistics in this book. Instead, we focus on the development of intrinsic statistics using the tools for surface registration and geodesic computation that were outlined in Chapter 3.

Most modern applications, including computer vision, graphics, biometrics, and medical imaging, require efficient statistical tools for analyzing shapes. An important area of special interest in this book is diagnosis and monitoring of medical pathology, based on shape data obtained from various medical imaging modalities. In this setting, it is crucial to develop statistical models of shape, which are able to capture variability within and across healthy and disease populations. This enables model-based classification tools, which can be used for developing accurate disease diagnostics. See Chapter 5 for more details.

4.1   STATISTICAL SUMMARIES OF 3D SHAPES

We start this section by presenting two distinct approaches for computing statistical summaries of 3D shapes. The first approach relies on pulling back the Riemannian metric from the SRNF or SRM space to the space of surfaces and performing the full analysis there. The second approach is based on the SRNF inversion technique described in detail in Section 2.4.6.

4.1.1   PULLBACK METRIC APPROACH

We begin by defining an intrinsic shape mean, called the Karcher mean. Let $\{f_1, f_2, \ldots, f_n\} \in \mathcal{F}$ denote a sample of surfaces. Then, the sample Karcher mean shape is given by:

$$[\bar{f}] = \underset{[f] \in \mathcal{S}_f}{\operatorname{argmin}} \sum_{i=1}^{n} d_{\mathcal{S}_f}([f], [f_i])^2. \tag{4.1}$$

That is, the Karcher mean is the minimizer of the Karcher variance defined as $\frac{1}{n} \sum_{i=1}^{n} d_{S_f}([f], [f_i])^2$. Note that the resulting average is actually an entire equivalence class. For the purposes of visualization and subsequent analysis, we select one representative element from this class, i.e., $\bar{f} \in [\bar{f}]$.

A gradient-based approach for finding the Karcher mean by solving the optimization problem of Equation (4.1) is given in multiple places, including Dryden and Mardia [1998] and Le [2001], and is repeated here for convenience as Algorithm 4.1.

Figure 4.1 shows an example of computing the mean shape for a toy dataset. The data in this example was simulated in such a way that one of the peaks on each surface was already matched perfectly, while the position of the second peak was slightly perturbed. All surfaces in this dataset are displayed in the left panel of Figure 4.1. We computed three averages in this example: simple pointwise average in the preshape space (right-top of Figure 4.1), Karcher mean under the SRM pullback metric (right-center of Figure 4.1), and Karcher mean under the reduced elastic metric (right-bottom of Figure 4.1). One can clearly see that in the preshape mean, one of the peaks is sharp while the other is averaged out due to lack of surface registration. Thus, the preshape mean is not a very good summary of the given data. The Karcher mean under the SRM pullback metric is much better, although it also shows slight averaging out of the second peak. The best representative shape is given by the Karcher mean computed under the SRNF pullback metric (reduced elastic metric) where the two peaks are sharp as in the original data.

Algorithm 4.1 Sample Karcher mean using the pullback metric.

Input: Set of surfaces $\{f_1, \ldots, f_n\} \in \mathcal{F}$ and small step size ϵ.
Output: Karcher mean surface $\bar{f}$.

1: Set $j = 1$ and initialize the mean shape as $\bar{f}_j$.
2: For each $i = 1, \ldots, n$, normalize the translation and scale of f_i.
3: For each $i = 1, \ldots, n$, register f_i to $\bar{f}_j$ resulting in $f_i^* = O^*(f_i \circ \gamma^*)$, where O^* and γ^* are the optimal rotation and reparameterization, respectively.
4: For each $i = 1, \ldots, n$, compute the shape space geodesic path α_{f_i} between $\bar{f}_j$ and f_i^*.
5: Compute the average shooting direction as $v = \frac{1}{n} \sum_{i=1}^{n} \frac{d\alpha_{f_i}}{dt}|_{t=0}$.
6: If $\|v\|$ is small, stop and return $\bar{f} = \bar{f}_j$. Otherwise, update the mean using $\bar{f}_{j+1} = \bar{f}_j + \epsilon v$ and normalize $\bar{f}_{j+1}$ with respect to scale and translation.
7: Set $j = j + 1$ and return to step 3.

> Computational Task Summary: n geodesics per iteration, 2 hours per geodesic on spherical grids of size 32×32.

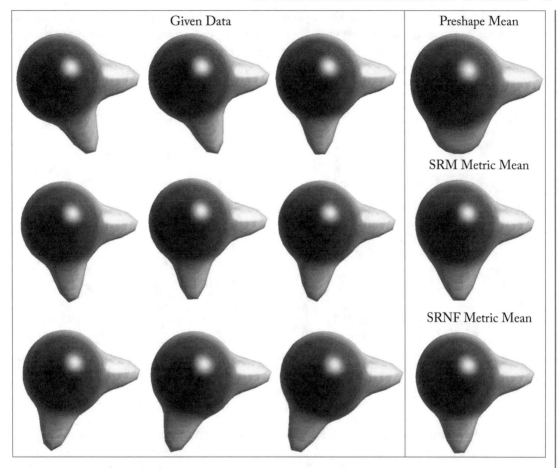

Figure 4.1: Left: Given data. Right: Shape means computed in the preshape space (top), under the SRM pullback metric (center), and under the reduced elastic metric (bottom).

In Figure 4.2 we present four additional Karcher mean results. For each example, we compare the preshape mean to the shape mean computed using the reduced elastic metric. In the first row, we display the sample surfaces that were used in computing the sample means. It is clear from this figure that the averages computed in the shape space are much better representatives of the given data. The preshape space sample averages are often distorted, and lose most of the structure present in the given samples. On the other hand, the shape space sample averages exhibit similar structure to those present in the given data. This is due to improved registration of geometric features across surfaces in the shape space. Consider Example 4 in Figure 4.2. The sample surfaces are three cats and one horse. Note that the surfaces are in very different poses. As a result, the average of these surfaces in the preshape space has distorted extremities (legs and tail) due to severe misalignment of those parts across all sample surfaces. In the SRNF-based shape space, the average surface has well-defined legs and tail, which results in a more natural representative of the given data. Such shape averages are very important in subsequent tasks such as estimating the covariance and summarizing variability in given data using PCA. We shift our focus to those tasks next.

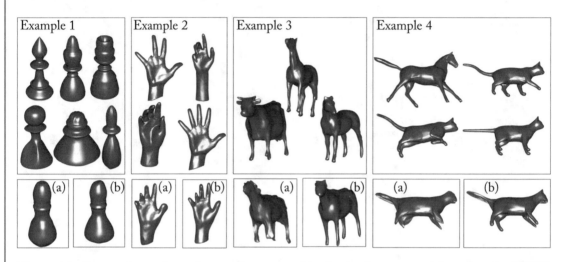

Figure 4.2: Comparison of sample means computed in the preshape space (a), and in the SRNF shape space (b).

Karcher covariance. Once the sample Karcher mean has been computed, the evaluation of the Karcher covariance is performed using shooting vectors from the mean to individual shapes. We compute the shooting vectors from the estimated Karcher mean $\bar{f} \in [\bar{f}]$, to each of the surface shapes in the sample, according to $v_i = \dfrac{d\alpha_{f_i}}{dt}|_{t=0}$, where $i = 1, 2, \ldots, n$, and α_f denotes a geodesic path in $\mathcal{S}_f$ between $\bar{f}$ and $f_i^* = O^*(f_i \circ \gamma^*)$. Here O^* and γ^* are the optimal rotation and reparameterization, respectively. This computation is akin to computing the inverse exponential map. Then, we perform PCA of the shooting vectors: we perform the Gram-Schmidt procedure (under the chosen pullback metric), to generate an orthonormal basis $\{B_j \mid j = 1, \ldots, k\}$, $k \leq n$, of the observed shooting vectors $\{v_i, i = 1, \ldots, n\}$. Then, we project each of the vectors v_i onto this orthonormal basis using $v_i \approx \sum_{j=1}^{k} c_{ij} B_j$, where $c_{ij} = \langle\langle v_i, B_j \rangle\rangle_{\bar{f}}$ and $\langle\langle \cdot, \cdot \rangle\rangle$ denotes the pullback metric. Now, each original shape can simply be represented using the reduced coefficient vector $c_i = \{c_{ij}\}$.

Given this representation, the sample covariance matrix of the given shapes can be computed in the coefficient space as $K = \dfrac{1}{n-1} \sum_{i=1}^{n} c_i c_i^T \in \mathbb{R}^{k \times k}$. One can use the singular value decomposition of K, i.e., $K = U \Sigma U^T$, to determine the principal directions of variation in the given data. For example, if $u \in \mathbb{R}^k$ corresponds to a principal singular vector of K, then the corresponding tangent vector in the shape space is given by $v = \sum_{j=1}^{k} u_j B_j$. One can then map this vector to a surface f using the exponential map: $f = \exp_{\bar{f}}(v)$. In Chapter 3, we provided the derivation of the exponential map for the SRNF pullback metric. For simplicity, we approximate the exponential map for both pullback metrics using a linear mapping in subsequent results.

In Figure 4.3, we display the two principal directions of variation in the data given in Figure 4.1. We show the same set of results for three cases: (1) preshape space variation, (2) shape space variation under SRM pullback metric, and (3) shape space variation under SRNF pullback metric (reduced elastic metric). The result computed in the preshape space does not reflect the true variability in the given data. In fact, as one goes in the positive second principal direction, the resulting shapes have three peaks. This result is again improved under the SRM pullback metric. But there is still some misalignment, which can be seen in the second principal direction where a wide peak evolves into a thin peak. The best result is observed in the case of the reduced elastic metric. Here, all of the variability is contained in the first principal direction of variation where the peak naturally moves without any distortion. Based on the given data, this is the most intuitive summary of variability.

Figure 4.4 displays the first principal direction of variation (preshape space in left panel and SRNF shape space in right panel) for Examples 1, 2, and 4 of Figure 4.2. The variation around the mean shape is more natural in the SRNF-based shape space than in the preshape space. The improvement is especially evident in Example 4. In the preshape space, the tail, head, and legs are severely distorted along the principal direction of variability. These issues mostly disappear when considering the same direction but in the SRNF shape space.

4.1.2   SRNF INVERSION APPROACH

We are again given a sample of observed surfaces $f_1, \ldots, f_n$ with the goal of estimating a mean shape and principal directions of variation in the data. To compute the mean, one can simplify the iterative procedure given in Algorithm 4.1 by first mapping all surfaces to the SRNF space, resulting in $\{q_1, \ldots, q_n\}$. Then, the mean shape in SRNF space, denoted by $\bar{q}$, is computed by iterating between registering all q_i to $\bar{q}$, and subsequently updating $\bar{q}$. Finally, at the last step, the mean shape $\bar{f} \in [\bar{f}]$ is computed by SRNF inversion, i.e., such that $Q(\bar{f}) = \bar{q}$. This procedure is summarized in Algorithm 4.2.

Next, let $\bar{q}$ represent the SRNF of the final average shape and q_i^*, $i = 1, \ldots, n$ denote the SRNFs of the surfaces in the sample optimally registered to this average. Then, due to the linearity of the SRNF space under the L^2 metric, the covariance matrix can be computed in a standard way. Using the singular value decomposition of the covariance matrix, one can extract the principal directions of variability in the SRNF space in a similar manner as described in the previous section. Let u_q^k denote the kth principal direction. Then, one can explore the variability in this direction around the mean using $\bar{q} \pm \lambda u_q^k$, where $\lambda \in \mathbb{R}_+$. To visualize the principal

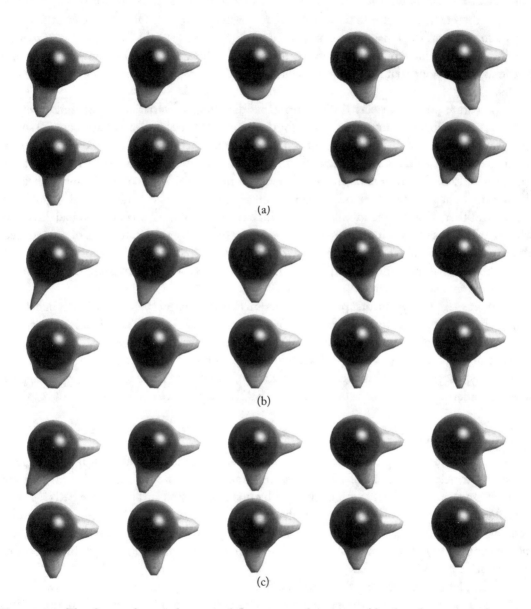

Figure 4.3: The first and second principal directions of variation (displayed as a path from −2 standard deviations to +2 standard deviations) for the preshape space (a), the shape space under the SRM pullback metric (b), and the shape space under the reduced elastic metric (c).

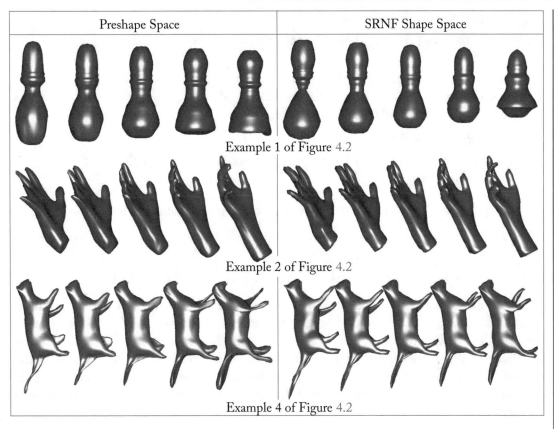

Preshape Space	SRNF Shape Space

Example 1 of Figure 4.2

Example 2 of Figure 4.2

Example 4 of Figure 4.2

Figure 4.4: Principal direction of variation within ±1 standard deviation of the mean for Examples 1, 2, and 4 from Figure 4.2.

directions of variation in $\mathcal{S}_f$, we need to find f^k such that $Q(f_\lambda^k) = \bar{q} \pm \lambda u_q^k$. This is a geodesic shooting problem, which requires one SRNF inversion for each λ.

Figure 4.5 shows an example of a mean shape computed using the SRNF inversion procedure. In this example, we take the human body shapes of four males and four females who have significant body shape differences, map them into the SRNF space, jointly register them, compute their mean in the SRNF space, and finally map the computed mean back to the shape space of surfaces using the SRNF inversion procedure. This is computationally very efficient since all statistics are computed using the standard L^2 metric. One has to only compute one SRNF inversion. Chapter 5 shows more examples of shape statistics computed using this procedure.

Algorithm 4.2 Sample Karcher mean by SRNF inversion.

Input: Set of surfaces $\{f_1, \ldots, f_n\}$ and their corresponding SNRFs $\{q_1, \ldots, q_n\}$.
Output: Karcher mean surface $\bar{f}$.

1: Let $\bar{q} = Q(\bar{f}^0)$ with $\bar{f}^0$ as an initial estimate of the Karcher mean. Set $j = 0$.
2: For each $i = 1, \ldots, n$, register q_i to $\bar{q}$ resulting in $q_i^* = O^*(q_i, \gamma^*)$, where O^* and γ^* are the optimal rotation and reparameterization, respectively. Set $q_i \leftarrow q_i^*$.
3: Update the average $\bar{q} = \dfrac{1}{n}\sum_{i=1}^{n} q_i$.
4: If change in $\bar{q}$ is small, stop. Else, set $j = j + 1$ and return to step 2.
5: Find $\bar{f}$ by <u>inversion</u> s.t. $Q(\bar{f}) = \bar{q}$.

> Computational Task Summary: 1 inversion, 16.5 min with harmonic basis, or 20.14 seconds with PCA basis.

4.2   STATISTICAL MODELS ON SHAPE SPACES

Statistical models on shape spaces provide useful tools for simulation, classification, and other inferential procedures. The goal of this section is to estimate a probability model based on a sample of observed surfaces $f_1, \ldots, f_n$. A main requirement of such models is to be able to generate random samples efficiently. Estimating probability models on nonlinear spaces such as $\mathcal{C}_f$ is difficult: classical statistical approaches, developed for vector spaces, do not apply directly. Instead, we propose two solutions: (1) using the tangent space approximation and the pullback metric; and (2) using the SRNF inversion procedure. We describe these two methods in the following subsections.

4.2.1   TANGENT SPACE AND PULLBACK METRIC APPROACH

In case our main goal is to sample from a probability model and we do not need an explicit density function, we can do so using the Gaussian distribution on the linear tangent space and the exponential map. In particular, given the Karcher mean and covariance, we can impose a Gaussian model in the tangent space (i.e., a distribution on the shooting vectors) centered at the mean shape with the specified covariance structure. Then, to sample a random tangent shooting vector v from such a probability model, we first draw k independent and identically distributed standard normals: $z_j \overset{iid}{\sim} N(0, 1)$, $j = 1, \ldots, k$. A random tangent vector can be sampled from the Gaussian distribution using $v = \sum_{j=1}^{k} z_j \sqrt{\Sigma_{jj}} u_j B_j$, where Σ_{jj} is the variance of the jth principal component, u_j is the corresponding principal singular vector, and B_j is a basis element as defined previously. One can then map this element of the tangent space to a 3D shape using the exponential map under the appropriate pullback metric. This procedure results in a random shape from the wrapped Gaussian distribution (wrapped from the tangent space onto the shape space): $f_{rand} = \exp_{\bar{f}}(v)$.

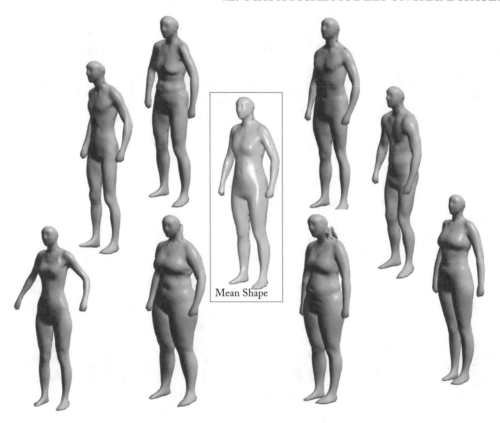

Mean Shape

Figure 4.5: Example of a mean shape of a set composed of eight male and female subjects with different body shapes. The mean, highlighted in the figure, was computed using the SRNF inversion procedure.

In Figure 4.6, we show two random samples from the wrapped Gaussian distribution defined in (1) the preshape space, (2) the shape space under the SRM pullback metric, and (3) the shape space under the reduced elastic metric. The data used to generate these results is displayed in Figure 4.1. The two random samples in the preshape space do not resemble the given data as they both have three peaks. While the SRM-based method produces random samples with two peaks, one can see that in both cases the shape of one of the peaks is inconsistent (either too thin or too wide). The SRNF-based approach produces better random shapes, in terms of matching the structures present in the given data.

Figure 4.7 displays some additional examples for the SRNF pullback metric. In each case, we display three random samples from the wrapped Gaussian model in the preshape space, and in the SRNF shape space. Note that in most cases, the random samples in the shape space have much better structure than those generated in the preshape space. This is especially evident in

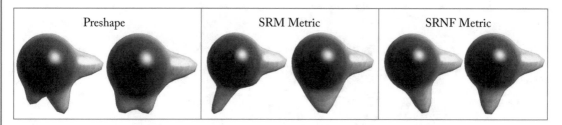

Figure 4.6: Random samples from a wrapped Gaussian model computed in the preshape space (left), under the SRM pullback metric (center), and under the reduced elastic metric (right). The original data for this experiment is shown in Figure 4.1.

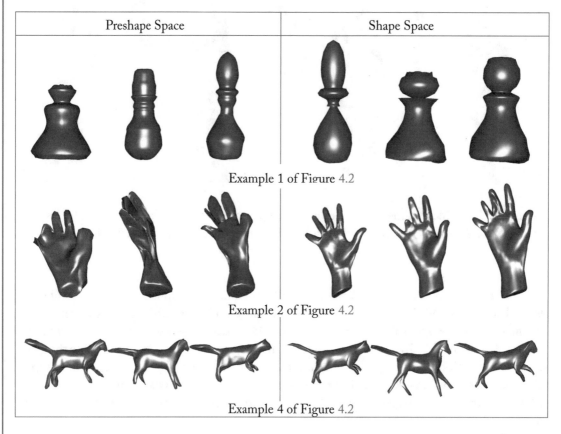

Figure 4.7: Three random samples from a generative-wrapped Gaussian model in the preshape space (left panel) and the SRNF shape space (right panel) for Examples 1, 2, and 4 in Figure 4.2.

Example 2. The randomly sampled hands in the preshape space have multiple distorted fingers, which is not the case in the shape space.

4.2.2   SRNF INVERSION APPROACH

By first computing the SRNF representations of the given surfaces, one can use all of the usual statistical tools in the vector space $\mathcal{Q}$ (after removing the variability due to rotation and reparameterization), and then map the results to $\mathcal{C}_f$ using the SRNF inversion algorithm. In particular, as seen earlier, one can easily estimate the mean and covariance structure in the SRNF shape space. Then, given these two statistics, a Gaussian generative shape model is easily imposed on $\mathcal{Q}$ due to its linear structure under the L^2 metric. Other models, including nonparametric ones, are also available. We provide more details next.

Let $q_1^*, \ldots, q_n^*$ be the SRNFs of the surfaces $f_1^*, \ldots, f_n^*$ aligned and registered to the mean $\bar{f}$. Also, let $G(q)$ denote the probability model fitted to $\{q_1^*, \ldots, q_n^*\}$. Recall that registration and alignment are performed using the SRNF framework described in Chapter 3. Then, a random sample q_s can be generated from G and mapped back to the space of surfaces by finding f_s such that $Q(f_s) = q_s$. Note that G can be any distribution on $\mathcal{Q}$, parametric or nonparametric. In subsequent chapters, we use a Gaussian-type distribution, whose parameters are learned using the Karcher mean and covariance on $\mathcal{S}_q$. Chapter 5 shows a few examples of 3D shapes synthesized by randomly sampling from the Gaussian distribution fitted to a collection of 3D human body shapes in the SRNF space.

We caution the reader that the distribution is defined and analyzed in the SRNF space; a distribution on $\mathcal{Q}$ induces a distribution on $\mathcal{F}$, but we have not derived it explicitly. We compute f_s for the purposes of display and validation only.

4.3   CLUSTERING AND CLASSIFICATION

In this section, we demonstrate how to use the outlined statistical shape analysis framework for clustering and classification of 3D models based on their shape. For this purpose, we use the SHREC07 watertight 3D model benchmark [Giorgi et al., 2007], which is composed of 400 watertight 3D models evenly divided into 20 shape classes. We only consider the 13 classes that are composed of genus-0, triangulated surfaces. First, we compute their spherical parameterizations, and then normalize all of the surfaces according to translation and scale. Thus, these surfaces become elements of the preshape space $\mathcal{C}_f$. Finally, we map the surfaces to the space of SRNFs; since the surfaces have been scale-normalized, their SRNFs are elements of $\mathcal{C}_q$. Let $\{f_i \in \mathcal{C}_f, \ i = 1 \ldots, n\}$ be the set of normalized surfaces, and $\{q_i \in \mathcal{C}_q, \ i = 1 \ldots, n\}$ their corresponding SRNF representations.

Below, we consider three examples. In the first one, we present the problem of unsupervised clustering using the reduced elastic metric. In the second and third examples, we apply the statistical framework to the important problem of classifying generic 3D shapes. In addition to the choice of shape metric, there is also an issue of choosing a specific classifier in these experiments. Here, we test two classification approaches. One example uses the nearest-neighbor distance-based classifier, while the other uses the Gaussian-type likelihood classifier in the space of SRNFs.

Example 4.1 Unsupervised clustering.   In order to cluster the shapes of the given set of genus-0 surfaces $\{f_i \in \mathcal{C}_f, i = 1 \ldots, n\}$, we first compute the pairwise distances in $\mathcal{S}_q$ between every pair of surfaces, using Equation (3.13), and then apply a standard non-supervised clustering algorithm on the resulting pairwise distance matrix. In this example, and for illustrative purposes, we hierarchically cluster the shapes by applying the average linkage function on the computed pairwise distance matrix. The clustering results are shown in Figure 4.8. As one can see, surfaces belonging to the same category of shapes are grouped together. The only false positive observed in this experiment is in Cluster 9 where one table is mis-clustered as an armadillo shape.

Example 4.2 Classification using the nearest-neighbor (NN) classifier.   In this example, we use a distance-based NN classifier, and we compare performances for methods that use different distances defined in different spaces. Specifically, we choose Euclidean distances in five different spaces, as defined below.

- **Case 1: Euclidean distance in the preshape space $\mathcal{C}_f$.** This is the baseline method. It defines the (extrinsic) distance between a pair of surfaces $f_1, f_2 \in \mathcal{C}_f$ as $\|f_1 - f_2\|$ where $\|\cdot\|$ refers to the standard L^2 norm. Note that the surfaces are used as given. They can potentially be quite misaligned and unregistered.

- **Case 2: Euclidean distance in the preshape space $\mathcal{C}_f$ after rigid registration.** Here, we use the Iterative Closest Point (ICP) algorithm of Besl and McKay [1992] to register the two surfaces with respect to rigid transformations (translation, rotation, and scale). Once the surfaces have been registered, we use the Euclidean distance defined in Case 1 to compute shape differences.

- **Case 3: Euclidean distance in the shape space $\mathcal{S}_f$.** The surfaces are first aligned and registered using SRNFs as described in Chapter 3. Then, for their classification, we use the Euclidean distance between the aligned and registered surfaces.

- **Case 4: Euclidean distance in the preshape space $\mathcal{C}_q$.** Here, the surfaces are first mapped to the SRNF preshape space $\mathcal{C}_q$. We then use the Euclidean distance in $\mathcal{C}_q$ for their classification. Note that this distance corresponds to the reduced elastic metric in $\mathcal{C}_f$.

- **Case 5: Euclidean distance in the shape space $\mathcal{S}_q$.** For this last case, we use the metric defined by Equation (3.13). This means that the surfaces are first aligned and registered using SRNFs. Then, to perform their classification, we use the Euclidean distance between the aligned and registered SRNFs.

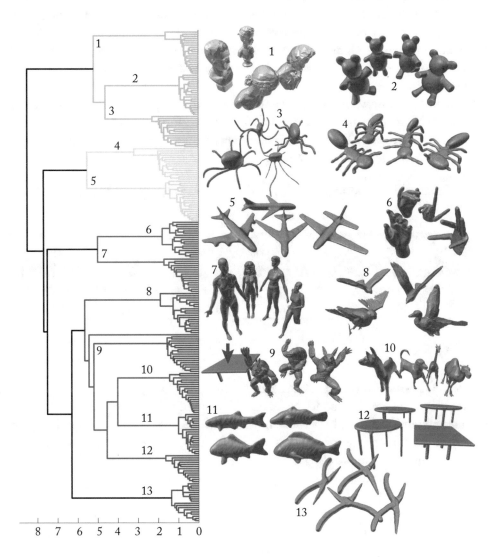

Figure 4.8: Illustration of the unsupervised hierarchical clustering performance on the SHREC07 dataset. For each cluster, we show four sample shapes. Observe that the approach results in only one false classification in Cluster 9 (highlighted with a red arrow), where a table is clustered with the armadillos.

To evaluate the performance of each of the five classification strategies, we use the leave-one-out approach. That is, for each shape in the collection, we compute its distance to the other shapes based on one of the above five cases, and classify it to the class of its nearest neighbor. The classification performance of each of the five cases is reported in the first row of Table 4.1. The best-performing method is highlighted in bold. As one can see, classification using the reduced elastic metric, computed as the L^2 distance in the shape space S_q, significantly outperforms all of the other classifiers.

An important observation is that the methods which optimally align and register the surfaces prior to computing the distance (Cases 3 and 5), perform much better than the methods which do not use such a step. The rigid-only alignment method provides a classification rate that falls somewhere in between. This additionally highlights the need for non-rigid registration.

Table 4.1: Classification performance, in %, on the genus-0 watertight 3D models in SHREC07 [Giorgi et al., 2007]

	C_f (Case 1)	C_f + ICP (Case 2)	S_f (Case 3)	C_q (Case 4)	S_q (Case 5)
Euclidean NN	56.38	82.81	96.91	52.86	**100**
Gauss	44.49	–	91.18	52.42	**96.47**

Example 4.3   Classification using a Gaussian likelihood.   Using the same data as in Example 4.2, we perform a Gaussian model-based classification of shapes represented in the different spaces considered in Cases 1–5. In particular, we first fit a Gaussian model to a training dataset, represented in the appropriate space, and then use the trained Gaussian model to classify test data via the likelihood. Here, we also refer to the different spaces as Case 1 to Case 5. Note that we ignore the metric structure of C_f and S_f in Cases 1 and 3, and simply use the L^2 metric to define the Gaussian likelihood.

To evaluate the performance of each of the five cases, we use 5-fold cross-validation: we randomly select 80% of the dataset for training and evaluate the classification performance on the remaining 20%. We repeat the experiment five times and average the classification performance over the five runs. The corresponding classification results are reported in the second row of Table 4.1.

As in the previous example, classification in the SRNF shape space, S_q, significantly outperforms the other approaches (with the extrinsic Gaussian model in S_f also providing good performance). These results suggest that the parametrization-invariant metric and intrinsic probability model in the SRNF shape space, S_q, greatly improve surface registration, resulting in better 3D shape classification. For reference, we additionally provide classification performance of other state-of-the-art techniques in Table 4.2. As one can see, the analysis in $\mathcal{S}_q$ achieves the best results.

Table 4.2: Classification performance, in %, of (1) BoC [Tabia and Laga, 2015, Tabia et al., 2014], (2) spatial BoC [Tabia and Laga, 2015], (3) hybrid BoW [Lavoué, 2012], and (4) curve-based approach [Tabia et al., 2011]

Other Methods	BoC	Spatial BoC	Hybrid BoW	Curve-Based
NN	93.25	92.5	91.8	85.3

4.4   BIBLIOGRAPHIC NOTES

Statistical analysis and modeling of shapes using landmark representations is covered thoroughly in the literature, including the textbooks Dryden and Mardia [1998], Kendall et al. [1999] and Small [1996]. Similar ideas for shape analysis of Euclidean curves have been discussed using nonelastic [Srivastava et al., 2005] and elastic representations [Kurtek et al., 2012b, Srivastava and Klassen, 2016, Srivastava et al., 2011]. The use of elastic shape analysis of surfaces for statistical summaries and modeling was first covered in Kurtek et al. [2010, 2011a,b, 2012a, 2013]. These earlier solutions were based on SRMs for representing surfaces and the pullback metric approach. Later works, including Laga et al. [2017] and Xie et al. [2014], were based on SRNF representations and their inversion using numerical techniques. The problems of clustering and classification have been studied in these and other papers throughout the literature. The latter set is too large to cover here.

CHAPTER 5

Case Studies Using Human Body and Anatomical Shapes

In the previous chapters, we developed both theory and algorithms for a comprehensive statistical shape analysis of surfaces. In this chapter, we show how to use this framework to complete five fundamental tasks, namely:

- shape clustering and classification;

- geodesic interpolation;

- deformation transfer;

- computation of statistical summaries of 3D shapes; and

- reflection symmetry analysis and symmetrization of 3D shapes.

We apply these concepts to the analysis of two types of datasets: 3D subcortical structures in the human brain and 3D human body shapes.

Shape analysis of anatomical structures in the brain: In the past two decades, there has been immense improvement in non-invasive medical imaging technology, which has enabled researchers in various fields to study the variabilities of different anatomical structures. In brain imaging, shape changes of subcortical structures are often associated with progression of cognitive disabilities, and thus, statistical analysis of the shapes of these structures plays an important role in diagnosis, rehabilitation, and monitoring. Currently, standard practice in the medical field is to use clinical symptoms, such as behavioral tests, to detect and quantify these abnormalities. However, such tests are often subjective and mainly qualitative. Statistical shape analysis of 3D anatomical structures provides an opportunity for a quantitative assessment of disease types. Additionally, alterations of anatomical shapes can potentially be detected much earlier, before clinical symptoms become obvious, thus providing a new avenue for developing possible treatments.

Shape analysis of the human body: Accurate 3D human body shape modeling is useful for many applications ranging from graphics/animation to fashion and medicine. Despite significant advances in digitizing technologies, creating and animating 3D models of human shapes still remain formidable challenges, mainly due to the complexity of the geometry and vast deformations of body shapes under different poses. Here we will demonstrate how to use the computational tools presented in this book for a comprehensive shape analysis of human bodies. Specifically, we will illustrate examples of computing optimal registrations and deformations between pairs of human body shapes, transferring deformations from one shape to another, and automatically generating new instances of 3D human body shapes with no interaction from the user. These tasks depend on identifying one-to-one matches between the 3D shapes being analyzed. Establishing such registrations is particularly difficult for articulated shapes such as the human body that possess highly varied geometries and poses.

5.1   CLUSTERING AND CLASSIFICATION

We start this chapter by describing two problems, namely classification and clustering, which are very important in analyzing morphological differences between anatomical structures and the 3D shapes of the human body.

5.1.1 ATTENTION DEFICIT HYPERACTIVITY DISORDER (ADHD) CLASSIFICATION

We apply the elastic shape analysis framework to shape-based diagnosis of Attention Deficit Hyperactivity Disorder (ADHD). The surfaces of brain subcortical structures used here for classification were extracted from T1-weighted Magnetic Resonance Images (MRIs) of young adults aged between 18 and 21. These subjects were recruited from the Detroit Fetal Alcohol and Drug Exposure Cohort. Among the 34 subjects studied, 19 were diagnosed with ADHD and the remaining 15 were controls (non-ADHD). Some examples of the left subcortical structures used in this work are shown in Figure 5.1.

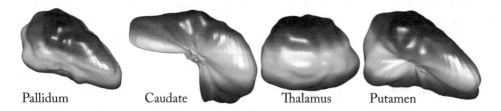

Pallidum   Caudate   Thalamus   Putamen

Figure 5.1: Left subcortical structures in the brain.

To perform our analysis, we first normalize the surfaces with respect to scale and translation, and compute their SRNF (or SRM) representations. We then align and register all of the surfaces as described in Chapter 3 and use the nearest neighbor (NN) and Gaussian classifiers, as described in Chapter 4, to characterize the healthy and non-healthy populations. These are very basic classifiers. The purpose of using them, instead of more advanced and complex ones such as deep-learning based classifiers [Tabia and Laga, 2017, Yi et al., 2016], is to show the strength of the elastic metric and the impact of elastic registration on classification performance.

Table 5.1 reports the leave-one-out nearest neighbor (LOO-NN) classification rates using the SRNF and SRM-based models compared to three other state-of-the-art techniques.

- The Iterative Closest Point (ICP) algorithm of Besl and McKay [1992]. Surfaces are first rigidly registered using ICP. Then, a surface f is assigned the class of its first nearest neighbor under the L^2 metric in $\mathcal{C}_f$.

- The SPHARM-PDM framework of Styner et al. [2006] under the LOO-NN classifier.

- The Harmonic approach using a fixed surface parametrization (SPHARM) [Kelemen et al., 1999] and the L^2 distance between the surfaces in $\mathcal{C}_f$, under the LOO-NN classifier.

The best performances are attained using the SRNF and SRM Gaussian classifiers on the left putamen shapes. These results suggest that the parametrization-invariant elastic metric and probability models based on it provide improved matching and modeling of the subcortical shapes, resulting in a superior ADHD classification performance. The SRNF framework has an additional advantage over the SRM in that, in addition to being more discriminative, it is also more efficient computationally; the computational cost is an order of magnitude smaller than the SRM-based framework since all computations are performed using the L^2 metric in the space of SRNFs.

Table 5.1: Classification performance, in %, for six different techniques, namely the Gaussian classifier on the (1) SRNF and (2) SRM spaces, and the Nearest Neighbor (NN) classifier using the (3) SRM space, (4) Harmonic method, (5) ICP algorithm, and (6) SPHARM-PDM

	SRNF Gauss	SRM Gauss	SRM NN	SPHARM	ICP	SPHARM-PDM
L. Caudate	**67.7**	–	41.2	64.7	32.4	61.8
L. Pallidus	85.3	**88.2**	76.5	79.4	67.7	44.1
L. Putamen	**94.1**	82.4	82.4	70.6	61.8	50.0
L. Thalamus	**67.7**	–	58.8	**67.7**	35.5	52.9
R. Caudate	55.9	–	50.0	44.1	50.0	**70.6**
R. Pallidus	**76.5**	67.6	61.8	67.7	55.9	52.9
R. Putamen	67.7	**82.4**	67.7	55.9	47.2	55.9
R. Thalamus	**67.7**	–	58.8	52.9	64.7	64.7

5.1.2   CLUSTERING OF IDENTITY AND POSE OF HUMAN BODY SHAPES

In this experiment, we consider a dataset of 550 human body shapes provided by Hasler et al. [2009b]. The dataset consists of human body shapes in various complex poses and belonging to 115 different male and female subjects. We use the SRNF representation to perform two types of clustering tasks. In the first task, we consider only the surfaces that are in neutral poses and run a binary hierarchical clustering using the inner squared distance (minimum variance algorithm) implemented in the linkage function of Matlab. As shown in Figure 5.2, the approach produces two distinct clusters corresponding, respectively, to male and female subjects.

In the second task, we consider the entire dataset and, similar to the first task, we perform a hierarchical binary classification. As shown in Figure 5.3, the approach is able to efficiently cluster subjects based on their pose. The procedure produces only two false positives where two shapes (highlighted with red arrows in Figure 5.3) from Pose 3 have been assigned to the cluster corresponding to Pose 7.

5.2   GEODESIC DEFORMATION

In this section we present examples of geodesics between human body shapes that undergo complex elastic deformations, including large bending and stretching in different parts (Section 5.2.1). We then discuss two applications, deformation transfer (Section 5.2.2) and symmetry analysis (Section 5.2.3), which can both be formulated as the problem of computing and shooting geodesics.

5.2.1   GEODESICS

We present and analyze some examples of shape registration and construction of geodesics, using the SRNF inversion procedure, between human body shapes under different poses. The shapes differ in both isometric (i.e., bending) and elastic deformations. In these experiments, SRNFs are inverted using only 100 PCA basis elements computed from a collection of 398 human shapes. The results are shown in Figures 5.4–5.9. In each example, we compare the geodesics obtained by SRNF inversion with linear paths obtained before and after registration.

As shown in Figure 5.4a, the original registration may be far from optimal; the shapes that lie along this path are heavily deformed. These shapes contain many artifacts and degenerate patches. In fact, the visual quality of the intermediate shapes is often an indication of the quality of the registration between the source and target shapes. Figure 5.4b, on the other hand, shows that linear interpolation between a pair of shapes, even when they are in optimal registration, may not produce natural deformations particularly when the 3D models undergo large deformations. This is surely the case of human shapes that exhibit large articulations under various poses. In this example, one can clearly see that the highly articulated parts unnaturally shrink along the linear path. When we compare this result to the geodesic shown in Figure 5.4c, the geodesic

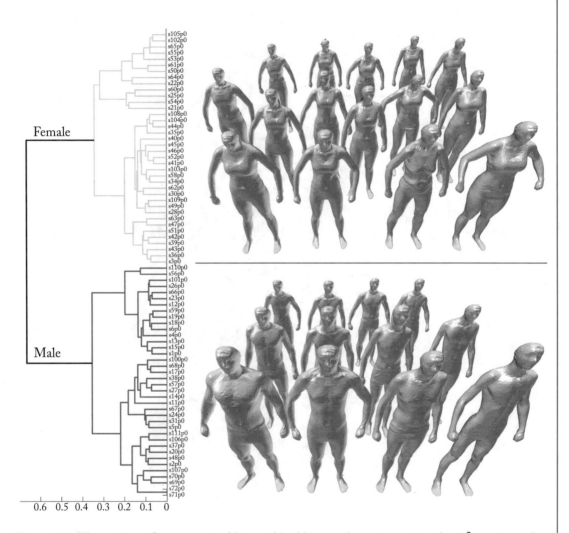

Figure 5.2: Illustration of unsupervised hierarchical binary clustering, using the L^2 metric in the space of SRNFs, of human body shapes in neutral poses. The approach is able to discover two main clusters, which correspond to male and female 3D body shapes. The clustering is obtained using the inner squared distance (minimum variance algorithm) implemented in the linkage function of Matlab. Each shape is labeled as sXXXpYY, where XXX corresponds to the identity of the subject and YY to the pose.

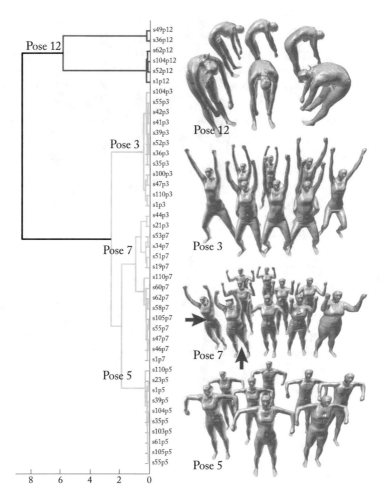

Figure 5.3: Illustration of unsupervised hierarchical binary clustering, using the L^2 metric in the space of SRNFs, of human body shapes in different poses. The framework is able to cluster body shapes based on their pose. The two missclassified shapes are highlighted with red arrows. The clustering is obtained using the inner squared distance (minimum variance algorithm) implemented in the linkage function of Matlab.

(a) Linear path $(1 - t)f_1 + tf_2$, before computing the optimal registration.

(b) Linear path, $(1 - t)f_1 + tf_2^*$, i.e., after computing optimal registration using SRNFs.

(c) Geodesic path after registration using SRNF inversion.

Figure 5.4: Illustration of geodesics computed using (a) linear interpolation in $\mathcal{C}_f$, i.e., before registration, (b) linear interpolation in $\mathcal{S}_f$ after optimal registration of f_2 to f_1 using the SRNF framework, and (c) linear interpolation in the SRNF space $\mathcal{S}_q$, i.e., after optimal registration and SRNF inversion. Observe that, first, the in-between shapes in (a) are noisy due to sub-optimal registration, and second, the highly articulated parts in (b) unnaturally shrink when deformations are computed using linear interpolation in $\mathcal{S}_f$.

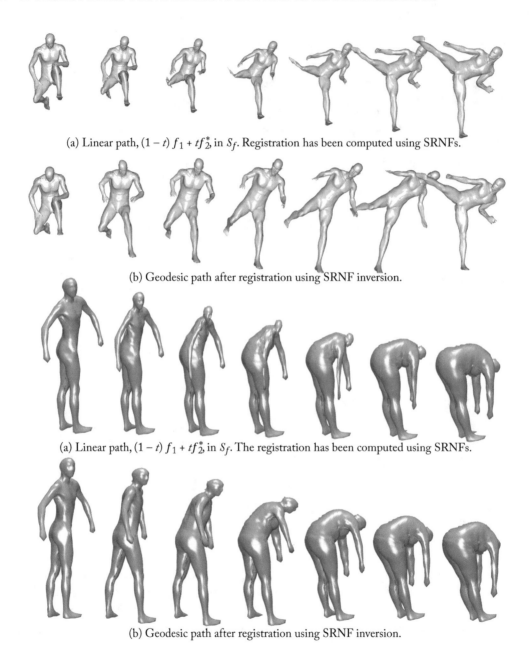

(a) Linear path, $(1-t)f_1 + tf_2^*$, in $\mathcal{S}_f$. Registration has been computed using SRNFs.

(b) Geodesic path after registration using SRNF inversion.

(a) Linear path, $(1-t)f_1 + tf_2^*$, in $\mathcal{S}_f$. The registration has been computed using SRNFs.

(b) Geodesic path after registration using SRNF inversion.

Figure 5.5: Comparison between linear interpolations in $\mathcal{S}_f$ and geodesic paths by SRNF inversion. Here, f_2^* refers to the version of f_2 that is optimally registered to f_1.

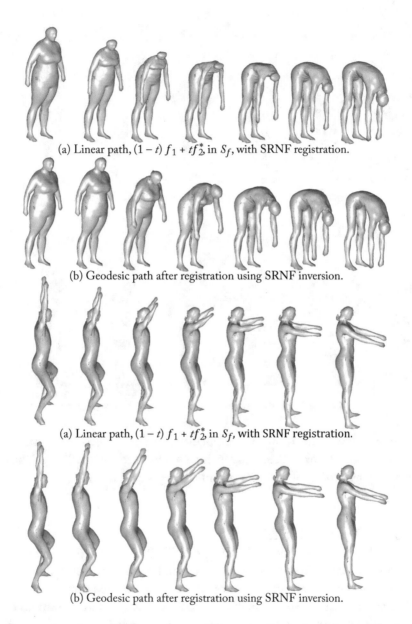

(a) Linear path, $(1 - t) f_1 + t f_2^*$, in $\mathcal{S}_f$, with SRNF registration.

(b) Geodesic path after registration using SRNF inversion.

(a) Linear path, $(1 - t) f_1 + t f_2^*$, in $\mathcal{S}_f$, with SRNF registration.

(b) Geodesic path after registration using SRNF inversion.

Figure 5.6: Comparison between linear interpolations in $\mathcal{S}_f$ and geodesic paths by SRNF inversion (obtained using 100 PCA basis elements). Here, f_2^* refers to the version of f_2 that is optimally registered to f_1.

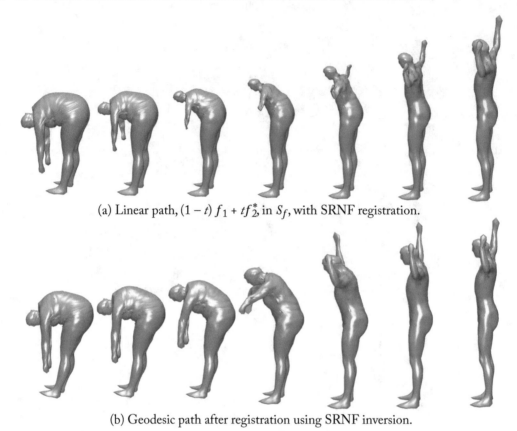

(a) Linear path, $(1 - t) f_1 + t f_2^*$, in $\mathcal{S}_f$, with SRNF registration.

(b) Geodesic path after registration using SRNF inversion.

Figure 5.7: Comparison between linear interpolations in $\mathcal{S}_f$ and geodesic paths by SRNF inversion. The SRNF inversions in these examples were obtained using 100 PCA basis elements. Here, f_2^* refers to the version of f_2 that is optimally registered to f_1.

path seems to provide a more natural deformation. This geodesic is computed by mapping the linear path in the SRNF space back to $\mathcal{C}_f$ using the SRNF inversion procedure.

Figures 5.5, 5.6, and 5.7 show a few more examples where the deformation between the source and target shapes is very large. Figures 5.8 and 5.9, on the other hand, show examples where the deformations are relatively small. In the latter case, and as one would expect, linear paths in $\mathcal{S}_f$ already provide a good approximation of the geodesics. In fact, there is no significant visual difference between geodesics computed by linear interpolation in $\mathcal{S}_f$ and by SRNF inversion of linear paths in $\mathcal{S}_q$.

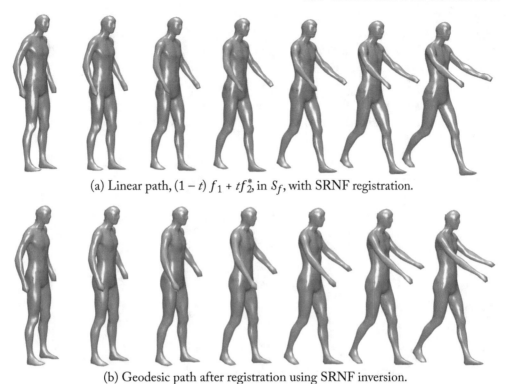

(a) Linear path, $(1 - t) f_1 + t f_2^*$, in $\mathcal{S}_f$, with SRNF registration.

(b) Geodesic path after registration using SRNF inversion.

Figure 5.8: Comparison between linear interpolations in $\mathcal{S}_f$ and geodesic paths by SRNF inversion. The SRNF inversion in this example has been obtained using 100 PCA basis elements. Here, f_2^* refers to the version of f_2 that is optimally registered to f_1.

5.2.2 DEFORMATION TRANSFER

As another application of the elastic shape analysis framework, we consider human body surfaces of different subjects in arbitrary complex poses, and demonstrate how previously developed tools can be used to transfer a deformation from one subject to another. Specifically, we will use the computational tools for geodesic shooting and for computing parallel transport of tangent vectors in the shape space of interest. The basic approach for transferring deformations has already been described in Section 3.5.2. Here we present a number of examples relating to pose-related deformations of human bodies.

In the examples in Figure 5.10, the source deformations, i.e., the surfaces f_1 and h_1, are shown in Figure 5.10a while Figure 5.10c shows these deformations transferred onto another subject using geodesics obtained by SRNF inversion. For comparison, we also show, in Figure 5.10b, the deformations transferred by linear extrapolation in $\mathcal{S}_f$. Observe that, unlike the deformations obtained by linear extrapolation, the deformations transferred by SRNF inver-

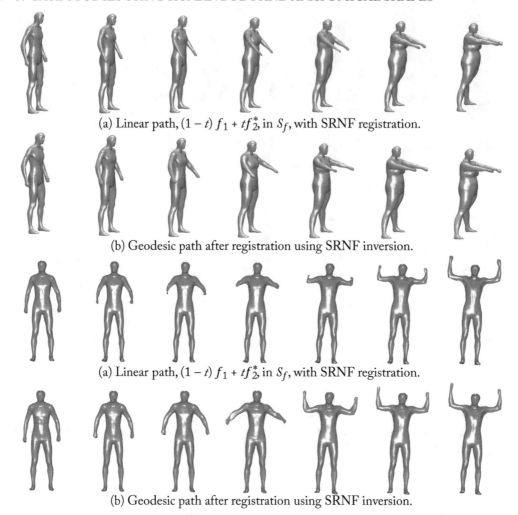

(a) Linear path, $(1-t)f_1 + tf_2^*$, in $\mathcal{S}_f$, with SRNF registration.

(b) Geodesic path after registration using SRNF inversion.

(a) Linear path, $(1-t)f_1 + tf_2^*$, in $\mathcal{S}_f$, with SRNF registration.

(b) Geodesic path after registration using SRNF inversion.

Figure 5.9: Comparison between linear interpolations in $\mathcal{S}_f$ and geodesic paths by SRNF inversion. The SRNF inversions in these examples have been obtained using 100 PCA basis elements. Here, f_2^* refers to the version of f_2 that is optimally registered to f_1.

sion look very natural and are free of artifacts, self-intersections, and unnatural elongations and shrinkage.

The transfer of deformations associated with articulations of human bodies is a very powerful tool, with lots of potential in computer graphics, animation, and video synthesis. We believe that the use of elastic shape analysis enhances the quality of deformation transfer and leads to more natural solutions.

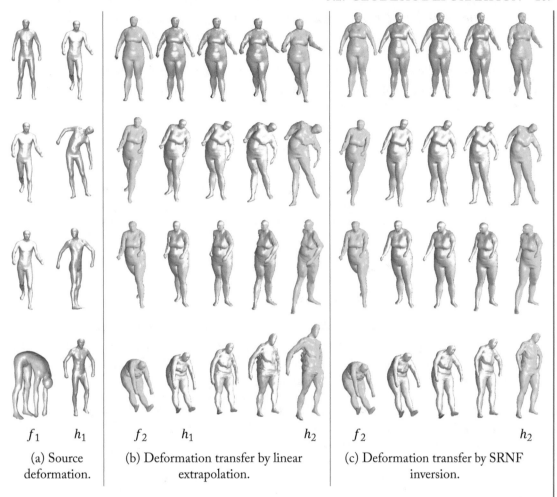

f_1 h_1 f_2 h_1 h_2 f_2 h_2

(a) Source   (b) Deformation transfer by linear   (c) Deformation transfer by SRNF
deformation.   extrapolation.   inversion.

Figure 5.10: Examples of deformation transfer using geodesic shooting in the space of SRNFs. The middle shapes, in gray, are intermediate shapes along the deformation paths.

5.2.3   REFLECTION SYMMETRY ANALYSIS AND SYMMETRIZATION

An interesting use of elastic shape analysis is in quantifying reflection symmetry of 3D objects. Symmetry is an important feature of an object and can be useful in many different applications. Detection and analysis of symmetry has been studied in the literature from different perspectives; see Mitra et al. [2012] for a detailed survey on the topic. Most of the previous works take a 3D model, and then identify and extract pairs of regions such that each pair of regions, under an appropriate distance measure, is similar when the respective regions are aligned using an allowable transformation. These methods often rely on segmenting shapes into regions and matching them using descriptors and appropriate measures of dissimilarity [Mitra et al., 2012].

In this section, we focus on reflection symmetry, and show that detecting such symmetry is a by-product of the process of computing elastic geodesics. That is, to analyze the level of reflection symmetry of a surface f, we first obtain its reflection with respect to an arbitrary plane. Let $v \in \mathbb{R}^3$ be a vector orthogonal to this plane. Then:

$$\tilde{f} = H(v)f, \text{ where } H(v) = \left(I - 2\frac{vv^T}{v^T v} \right). \tag{5.1}$$

$H(v)$ is the reflection matrix for the plane perpendicular to the vector v. f is the original surface and $\tilde{f}$ is its reflection under the chosen plane. Let $\alpha_f : [0, 1] \mapsto \mathcal{S}_f$ be the elastic geodesic path between f and $\tilde{f}$ in the shape space of surfaces. α_f provides valuable information relating to the symmetry of f.

- First, its length gives a formal measure of asymmetry of f.

- Second, the halfway point along this geodesic, i.e., $\alpha_f(0.5)$, is symmetric.

- Lastly, if this geodesic path is unique, then amongst all symmetric shapes, $\alpha_f(0.5)$ is the nearest to f in $\mathcal{S}_f$ under the shape metric. The path from $\alpha_f(0)$ to $\alpha_f(0.5)$ is precisely the smallest deformation needed to symmetrize f. Thus, as already stated, half of the length of this path is also a measure of asymmetry of the shape.

Figure 5.11 shows several examples of symmetrizing highly articulated surfaces. Note that the highlighted midpoints of the presented geodesics are symmetric. Thus, these paths provide natural symmetrizations of the given surfaces.

5.3 STATISTICAL SUMMARIES OF SHAPES

Next, we present some results for computing statistical summaries of complex human body shapes based on the SRNF inversion method. The detailed methods have already been covered previously in Sections 4.1 and 4.2. Here we simply apply those ideas to shape data associated with human body shapes.

5.3.1 MEANS AND MODES OF VARIATION

We consider a collection of 398 human shapes, composed of multiple subjects in different poses. The first subject has 35 different poses including a neutral one. The other subjects include instances that are in a neutral pose and in a few other poses. We first compute the SRNF representations of these surfaces, perform statistical analysis in the quotient space, $\mathcal{S}_q$, using standard linear statistics such as PCA, and finally map the results to the surface shape space, $\mathcal{S}_f$, using the SRNF inversion algorithm.

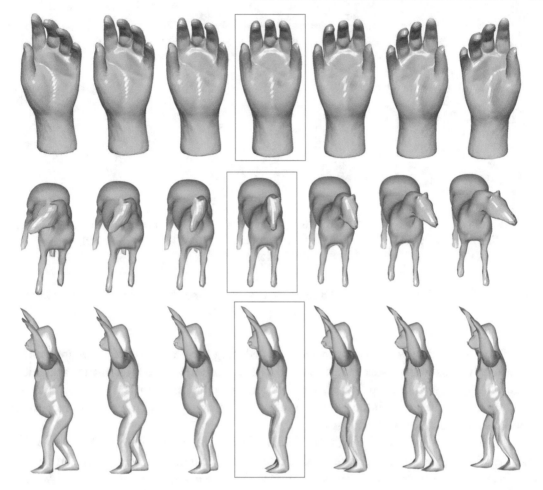

Figure 5.11: Symmetrizing complex surfaces. Each example shows the geodesic between a surface and its reflection. The highlighted midpoint of the geodesic is the nearest symmetric shape.

Figure 5.12a shows the mean shape and the first three modes of variation computed using all of the instances that are in a neutral pose. We refer to this statistical model as *pose-independent*. Similarly, we consider the 35 different poses of the first subject and compute their mean shape and modes of variation (Figure 5.12b). We call the resulting model the *pose shape model*.

5.3.2 RANDOM SAMPLING FROM SHAPE MODELS

Now that we have mean and principal modes of variability in body shapes, associated with the pose-independent and the pose shape model, we consider the problem of imposing statistical models on the shape space of surfaces. These summaries—mean and principal modes of

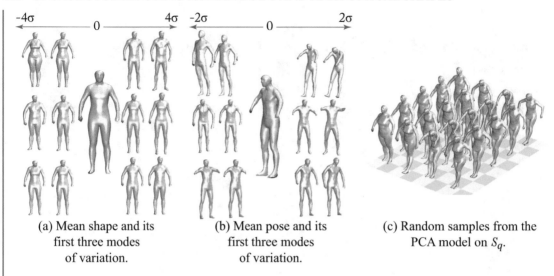

(a) Mean shape and its first three modes of variation.

(b) Mean pose and its first three modes of variation.

(c) Random samples from the PCA model on S_q.

Figure 5.12: Statistical analysis of 3D human body shapes using the SRNF inversion procedure.

variability—effectively provide a mechanism for reducing the dimension of the representation space. One way to evaluate such statistical models is to synthesize random human shapes and to analyze the quality of these random shapes. We generate random coefficients from a multivariate normal distribution (with the estimated mean and covariance) and use them to reconstruct random shapes as described previously.

There are several ways to synthesize random human shapes, under different poses, and we take the following two-step approach. First, we randomly generate a surface f_2 that is in a neutral pose using the pose-independent statistical model. We then generate an arbitrary pose h_1 using the pose shape model. Let f_1 be the neutral pose in the 35 models that we used to learn the pose shape model. Finally, we use the deformation transfer procedure (Section 5.2.2) to deform f_2 in the same way that f_1 deforms into h_1. This results in a new random human shape h_2 in an arbitrary pose. Figure 5.12c shows 20 arbitrary 3D human body shapes generated using this method. Note that this approach uses two separate models to capture inter- and intra-subject variability. Used in conjunction with the deformation transfer mechanism, it provides greater control over the generation of different subjects and poses.

Another approach to modeling human shapes is to consider all of the human shapes together, irrespective of their pose and body variability, and learn a single statistical model from which random instances can be sampled. Figure 5.13 shows ten arbitrary 3D human body shapes automatically synthesized by sampling from a Gaussian distribution fitted to the entire collection of human body shapes. Note that, usually, subject-specific deformations, i.e., those due to variations in pose, are significantly larger than those due to inter-subject differences. Thus, the leading modes in the statistical model capture these large-scale deformations. We conclude that a mixture model for human shapes found by learning two different statistical models, one for shapes in neutral poses (inter-subject variability) and another for pose (within-subject variability), may be more appropriate in this situation.

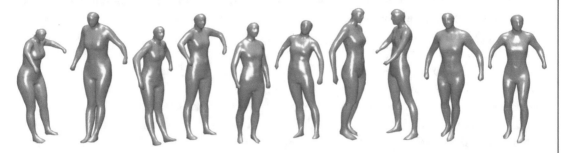

Figure 5.13: Ten arbitrary 3D human body shapes automatically synthesized by sampling from a Gaussian distribution fitted, in the SRNF shape space $\mathcal{S}_q$, to a collection of human body shapes belonging to different subjects in different poses.

5.4   BIBLIOGRAPHIC NOTES

In this chapter, we have analyzed the clustering and classification performance of the L^2 metric in the space of SRNFs, which is equivalent to the reduced elastic metric in the space of shapes. Since our goal is to show the capabilities of the metric, we have used it in combination with basic nearest neighbor and Gaussian classifiers, and compared the performance with basic techniques such as ICP [Besl and McKay, 1992], which performs rigid alignment only, and with SPHARM-PDM [Styner et al., 2006], which fixes parameterizations to arc-length type. The results in Section 5.1 clearly show that elastic deformations are better captured with parameterization-invariant elastic metrics. Note that the goal here is to show the capability of the elastic metric, compared to other metrics, rather than the capability of the classifiers, which can be built on the top of any metric. In fact, since the SRNF space is equipped with a proper metric, one can use it with more sophisticated classification and clustering algorithms, e.g., Support Vector Machines (SVM), spectral clustering, or even deep learning techniques, which have proven to be very effective in large-scale 3D shape analysis, as demonstrated in recent articles [Tabia and Laga, 2017, Yi et al., 2016].

    We have shown various applications of elastic shape analysis in the space of SRNFs using 3D data of human body shapes. We have demonstrated that, with the same framework, one can compute accurate one-to-one registrations, and geodesic deformations. One can transfer deformations, compute summary statistics, and synthesize random instances of human body shapes of different subjects in different poses. The analysis of 3D human body shapes has been extensively studied in the literature; see, for example, Allen et al. [2002, 2003, 2006] and Anguelov et al. [2005] and the series of work by M. Black's group, e.g., Freifeld and Black [2012], Loper et al. [2015], Pons-Moll et al. [2015] among others. These works, however, take as input a set of registered 3D models and learn mathematical models for synthesizing the geometry and dynamics of the human body shape. For instance, Loper et al. [2015] required thousands of registered scans. Registration is often performed either semi-automatically or automatically using a different method and an optimality criterion, or metric, that is different from the one used for statistical analysis. Other techniques, e.g., Pons-Moll et al. [2015], require a subject-specific template in a predefined pose. The advantage of the framework described here is that elastic registration and geodesic computation are performed jointly under the same metric. The framework does not require subject-specific templates. Note also that other works for computing geodesics between generic 3D models require pre-registered surfaces [Berkels et al., 2013, Heeren et al., 2012, 2014, Kilian et al., 2007]. Other applications of the proposed framework include the analysis of the shape of planar objects that undergo topological deformations [Kurtek et al., 2014].

The two main application areas (and associated case studies) discussed in this chapter have been partially presented in the following papers. The work on anatomical shapes has been presented in the papers Kurtek et al. [2011a,b, 2012a] and Xie et al. [2013]. The application of elastic shape analysis to human shapes was first covered in Laga et al. [2017].

The idea of using geodesics in the shape space for symmetry analysis was first introduced in Samir et al. [2009], in the case of 2D shapes, and extended to 3D shapes in Kurtek and Srivastava [2012] and Kurtek et al. [2013]. We also refer the reader to the paper by Mitra et al. [2012] for a detailed survey of work on symmetry analysis.

The use of parallel transport to transfer deformations across shapes has been discussed in a number of papers including Lorenzi et al. [2011], Pennec and Lorenzi [2011], Younes et al. [2008b]. This idea was first applied to elastic shape analysis of surfaces in Xie et al. [2013]. Results obtained using SRNF inversion appeared in Laga et al. [2017].

The brain subcortical structures used in Section 5.1.1 were extracted from T1-weighted Magnetic Resonance Images (MRIs) of young adults aged between 18 and 21. These subjects were recruited from the Detroit Fetal Alcohol and Drug Exposure Cohort [Burden et al., 2010, Jacobson et al., 2004]. The generic 3D models used are from the SHREC07 benchmark [Giorgi et al., 2007] and the TOSCA database [Bronstein et al., 2008]. The 3D human body models are courtesy of Hasler et al. [2009b]. All models were provided as triangulated meshes, which we parameterized using the procedure described in Appendix C.

CHAPTER 6

Landmark-driven Elastic Shape Analysis

In this chapter, we explore the use of auxiliary information, specifically the presence of sparse landmark points, as additional knowledge for guiding registration and shape analysis. In general, the landmarks can be points, curves, or regions on the surfaces being analyzed. The motivation behind using landmarks is two-fold.

1. First, in many applications, particularly those involving datasets where semantic correspondences are required, the solutions described in the previous chapters of this book may not give satisfactory results. This is because registering complex surfaces that share semantic similarities but are geometrically very different, and discovering sophisticated shape deformations between such surfaces, are challenging problems. Thus, it is reasonable that an automated algorithm is unable to produce registrations that perform as well as an expert, without additional prior knowledge. This prior knowledge can come in the form of registered landmarks, generated automatically or manually, that help in dealing with complex shapes.

2. In many medical and biological applications, datasets are often annotated using domain-specific knowledge. It is imperative to use such annotations to enforce global registration, and in the computation of geodesics and statistical summaries.

We focus on the situation where a sparse set of (labeled) point landmarks, in addition to the surface data, are available for shape analysis, and develop a framework that performs the following tasks.

1. **Registration**: We incorporate landmark information in elastic shape registration, by formulating it as a constrained optimization problem over a subset of reparameterizations that preserve the given landmark matching.

2. **Geodesic-based Deformations**: We compute geodesic paths between surfaces using both shape and landmark information.

3. **Summary Shapes**: We provide summary statistics of shapes of annotated surfaces obtained as samples from a given population.

We will also discuss possible extensions to other types of landmarks, e.g., curves and surface regions. Figure 6.1 shows a few examples of complex shapes with automatically detected landmarks.

Figure 6.1: Examples of automatically detected and matched landmarks using Heat Kernel Signatures (HKS) and Möbius voting.

6.1   PROBLEM STATEMENT

We are given a collection of surfaces $f_i \in \mathcal{C}_f, i = 1, \dots, n$. Each parameterized surface f_i is annotated with a set of m labeled point landmarks. For each f_i, let $\{f_i(s_1^i), \dots, f_i(s_m^i)\}$ be the locations of these landmarks on f_i, i.e., the corresponding locations on $\mathbb{S}^2$ under the current parameterization are $\{s_1^i, \dots, s_m^i\}$. Also, let q_i denote a square-root representation (either an SRM or SRNF) of f_i. We can restate the three problems of interest as follows.

- **Pairwise Registration**: Given any pair of annotated surfaces f_i and f_j, with square-root representations q_i and q_j, we seek the optimal rotation $O \in SO(3)$ and optimal diffeomorphism $\gamma \in \Gamma$ that register f_i and f_j while preserving the landmark matching. That is, we seek to solve the following optimization problem:

$$(O^*, \gamma^*) = \arg \min_{SO(3) \times \Gamma} \|q_i - (Oq_j, \gamma)\|^2,$$
$$\text{subject to: } \gamma(s_k^j) = s_k^i, \text{ for } k = 1, \dots, m. \tag{6.1}$$

We will refer to this problem as *landmark-guided surface registration*.

- **Geodesic Computation**: In the same setting, we want to compute a geodesic path $\alpha_f : [0, 1] \rightarrow \mathcal{C}_f$, between f_i and f_j in $\mathcal{C}_f$, under the elastic metric, such that all surfaces along the path preserve the landmark-registration. We will call this the *landmark-guided elastic geodesic*.

- **Multiple Registration and Shape Averaging**: More generally, we seek to compute the mean shape $\bar{f}$ and jointly co-register the set of surfaces $\{f_1, \ldots, f_n\}$ while preserving the landmark matching. Formally, we seek to find a surface $\bar{f}$, whose square-root representation is denoted by $\bar{q}$, and the optimal rotations O_i and reparameterizations γ_i that minimize

$$\sum_{i=1}^{n} \|\bar{q} - (O_i q_i, \gamma_i)\|^2 \text{ subject to: } \forall i, j, \ \gamma_i(s_k^i) = \gamma_j(s_k^j) \text{ for } k = 1, \ldots, m. \quad (6.2)$$

We will refer to this problem as *landmark-constrained atlas generation.*

In what follows, we will first discuss solutions to landmark-constrained pairwise registration and geodesic computation (Sections 6.2 and 6.3). We will then show that a solution to the landmark-constrained atlas generation problem follows in a straightforward fashion (Section 6.4).

6.2   LANDMARK-GUIDED REGISTRATION

The landmark-guided registration problem in Equation (6.1) can be efficiently solved in two steps. In the first step, we find an initial rotation O_0 and reparameterization γ_0 that together map the landmarks of one surface onto their corresponding counterpart on the other surface (Section 6.2.1). This initial registration is not optimal but has the benefit of constraining possible solutions for full registration onto only a subgroup Γ_0 of the group of all possible diffeomorphisms Γ. We define Γ_0 as the subgroup of diffeomorphisms that do not change the location of the landmarks. Thus, in the second stage of the algorithm, we seek a diffeomorphism $\gamma \in \Gamma_0$ that fully registers the two surfaces while preserving the location of landmarks (Section 6.2.2). Figure 6.2 summarizes this process.

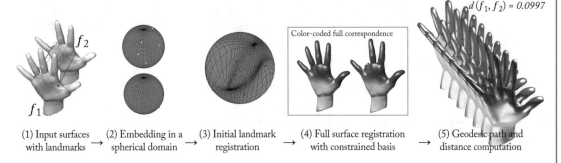

(1) Input surfaces with landmarks $\rightarrow$ (2) Embedding in a spherical domain $\rightarrow$ (3) Initial landmark registration $\rightarrow$ (4) Full surface registration with constrained basis $\rightarrow$ (5) Geodesic path and distance computation

Figure 6.2: Pipeline of the landmark-guided elastic shape analysis framework for spherically parameterized surfaces.

6.2.1 INITIAL REGISTRATION USING LANDMARKS

We are given a set of reference landmarks $(s_1, \ldots, s_m \in \mathbb{S}^2)$, and a surface $f_i \in C_f$ annotated with m landmarks $s_1^i, \ldots, s_m^i$. Note that, here, surfaces of interest are elements of C_f and thus they have been already normalized according to translation and scale.

We seek a diffeomorphism γ_0 that maps the landmarks on f_i to the given reference landmarks. Although we do not require any optimal property to be associated with γ_0, it does make sense to seek a diffeomorphism that is optimal in the sense of a quadratic deformation energy, similar to splines on Euclidean spaces. For this purpose, we use the approach of Glaunès et al. [2004]. We provide some details next.

Let $v_j \in T_{s_j^i}(\mathbb{S}^2)$ be the tangent vector to the shortest arc on $\mathbb{S}^2$ that connects s_j^i to s_j. We seek a smooth vector field $v : T(\mathbb{S}^2) \to \mathbb{R}^3$ that will deform every point on the sphere and will match the landmarks to each other, i.e., $\forall\ j \in \{1, \ldots, m\}$, $v(s_j^i) = v_j$. This can be solved by defining v using a reproducing kernel K on $\mathbb{S}^2$:

$$\forall\ s \in \mathbb{S}^2,\ v(s) = \sum_{j=1}^m K(s_j^i, s) u_j\,, \tag{6.3}$$

$$\text{subject to: } v(s_j^i) = v_j\,.$$

The tangent vectors $u_j \in T_{s_j^i}(\mathbb{S}^2)$ are solutions to the following system of $m \times 3$ linear equations:

$$\sum_{k=1}^m K(s_k^i, s_j^i) u_k = v_j,\ \text{for } j = 1, \ldots, m. \tag{6.4}$$

Geometrically, this formulation can be interpreted as follows: each landmark s_j^i serves as a deformation handle for the spherical grid. The amount of deformation that is applied to a point $s \in \mathbb{S}^2$ is the weighted sum of all deformations induced by the landmarks. The influence of a landmark s_j^i on s is a decreasing function of its distance to s and this is controlled by the kernel K. In other words, K defines a region of influence for each landmark. Finally, the tangent vector field v induces a diffeomorphism $\gamma_0 : \mathbb{S}^2 \to \mathbb{S}^2$ such that $\gamma_0(s) = \exp_s(v(s))$, where $\exp_s$ refers to the exponential map that takes elements on $T_s(\mathbb{S}^2)$ onto $\mathbb{S}^2$.

Defining the reproducing kernel K. The performance of this formulation depends on the choice of the kernel K and its parameters. For the spherical domain, we found experimentally that a Gaussian kernel of radius $\sigma \in [0.2, 0.4]$ provides satisfactory results. All of the results shown in this chapter have been obtained using $\sigma = 0.4$.

Large deformations. The approach described above is suitable when the distance between every pair of corresponding landmarks is small. In practice, however, deformations can be very large, and thus one cannot directly construct the deformation maps by integration of velocity fields that minimize a quadratic smoothness energy under the specified landmark constraints (as done in Glaunès et al. [2004]). Instead, we take an iterative approach. We divide the problem into k smaller deformation steps and proceed as follows.

- First, connect each pair of matched landmarks on $\mathbb{S}^2$ with a great circle and sample it uniformly using k steps.

- Then, using the approach described above, solve for a small deformation that matches the $(k-1)$st point to the kth point on this circle for all landmarks.

- Finally, the desired deformation mapping γ_0 is obtained by composition of these k small deformations.

Figure 6.3 shows an example of this process. The left panel shows five pairs of matched landmarks on $\mathbb{S}^2$; each pair is connected by a great circle sampled into $k = 5$ steps. The middle panel shows the cumulative deformation resulting from computing and composing five smaller diffeomorphisms as described above. The rightmost panel shows the magnitude of the total deformation vector field where areas of large deformation are highlighted in red.

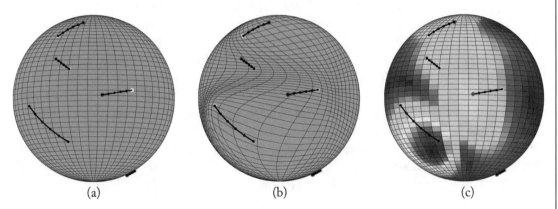

(a) (b) (c)

Figure 6.3: Landmark-constrained initial deformation. (a) Five pairs of matched landmarks on $\mathbb{S}^2$. (b) The cumulative deformation resulting from computing and composing five smaller diffeomorphisms. (c) The magnitude of the total deformation vector field to highlight areas of large deformation (in red).

6.2.2 REGISTRATION USING LANDMARK-CONSTRAINED DIFFEOMORPHISMS

Given that the landmarks across the two surfaces f_i and f_j are now matched, and that the surfaces have been normalized according to translation and scale, we seek to find an optimal rotation $O \in SO(3)$ and a reparameterization $\gamma \in \Gamma$ that fully align and register the surfaces. These are dealt with by removing them algebraically from the representation space as described in

Chapter 3. Importantly, since the landmarks are now matched, the search for γ will be restricted to a subgroup $\Gamma_0 \subset \Gamma$, the subset of diffeomorphisms that preserve the landmark matching.

Definition 6.1   Landmark-constrained diffeomorphisms.   Define the set of landmark-constrained diffeomorphisms as $\Gamma_0 = \{\gamma_0 : \mathbb{S}^2 \to \mathbb{S}^2 \mid \gamma_0$ is a diffeomorphism and $\gamma_0(y_j) = x_j, \forall j = 1, \ldots, m\}$, where x_j is a parameter for a landmark of one surface and y_j is the parameter of the landmark on the target surface such that x_j is in correspondence with y_j.

Note that specifying fixed landmarks on a surface does not change the optimization over the rotation group, but it constrains the reparameterization group to a subgroup that fixes the landmarks. Thus, the equivalence class of a surface f is given by:

$$[f] = \{O(f \circ \gamma_0)|O \in SO(3), \gamma_0 \in \Gamma_0\}. \tag{6.5}$$

It represents a shape with fixed landmarks uniquely. The set of all such equivalence classes is defined to be $\mathcal{S}_f^c$, the *landmark-constrained shape space*. Because $SO(3) \times \Gamma_0$ acts on $\mathcal{C}_f$ by isometries, the metric descends to the quotient space $\mathcal{S}_f^c$, making it a metric space.

With this formulation, the registration of two surfaces becomes a search for the optimal rotation O and reparameterization $\gamma_0 \in \Gamma_0$. The shape space $\mathcal{S}_f^c$, however, is different from the previous formulation, which does not use landmarks, in that the subgroup Γ_0 is being considered here instead of the full Γ. This poses additional difficulties when exploring the space Γ_0. In particular, the search space becomes disconnected and the search for the global optimum with gradient descent-like techniques may require multiple initializations. Assuming that the initial diffeomoprhic registration of surfaces, obtained using landmarks as described in Section 6.2.1, is in the optimal subset, we can restrict the search for optimal incremental diffeomorphisms to only the subset that contains the identity map. Since this subset is connected, a gradient-based search is sufficient for producing satisfactory results.

6.2.3   LANDMARK-CONSTRAINED BASIS FOR REGISTRATION

Before detailing the procedure for geodesic computation under landmark constraints, we first define an orthonormal basis for $T_{\gamma_{id}}(\Gamma_0)$, i.e., the tangent space of Γ_0 at the identity γ_{id}. (Recall that $\gamma_{id}(s) = s, \forall s \in \mathbb{S}^2$.) This basis is a set of tangent, smooth vector fields that vanish at the landmarks $s_j \in \mathbb{S}^2$. The basis is required in order to apply the registration algorithm presented in Section 3.2.2. We begin by providing a construction for an orthonormal basis that vanishes at only one point, say s_1.

1. Generate the full basis for $T_{\gamma_{id}}(\Gamma)$, denoted by $\mathcal{B}_I$ with elements $b_1, \ldots, b_n$, using gradients of spherical harmonics as described in Chapter 3.

2. Among the basis elements in $\mathcal{B}_I$, choose two of them, say b_1 and b_2, such that $\{b_1(s_1), b_2(s_1)\}$ form a basis of $T_{s_1}(\mathbb{S}^2)$.

3. For each basis element b_i other than b_1 and b_2, replace it by $b_i - (z_1 b_1 + z_2 b_2)$, where scalars z_1 and z_2 are chosen such that $b_i(s_1) = z_1 b_1(s_1) + z_2 b_2(s_1)$.

4. Remove b_1 and b_2 from the basis set.

5. The altered vector fields form a basis of the smooth vector fields that vanish at s_1.

6. Orthonormalize the remaining basis elements using the Gram-Schmidt procedure under the L^2 metric.

Now, consider that instead of a single point s_1, one has m landmark points where the vector fields must vanish. In this case, in Step 2, choose $2m$ basis elements with the property that together, their values at the m points form a basis for the direct sum of the tangent spaces at the m landmark points. The rest of the procedure remains unchanged.

To improve the efficiency of the registration algorithm, we use a multiscale approach with respect to the landmark-constrained basis. Because the basis is based on gradients of spherical harmonics, we first solve for the optimal reparameterization using the lower order spherical harmonics ($b_1, \ldots, b_k$ for a smaller k) and continue updating the solution by systematically adding the higher order harmonics (increasing k). This allows us to capture more global deformations initially using the lower order harmonics and then update the solution with smaller local changes using the higher order harmonics. We have found that this provides better registration results, and significantly improves the computational time.

6.3 ELASTIC GEODESICS UNDER LANDMARK CONSTRAINTS

We start with two spherically parameterized surfaces f_1 and f_2, such that $f_i(s_j)$, $j = 1, \ldots, m$, and $i = 1, 2$, denote the landmark annotations. We define the geodesic distance in $\mathcal{S}_f^c$ between f_1 and f_2, denoted by $d_{\mathcal{S}_f^c}([f_1], [f_2])$, as follows:

$$\min_{\gamma_0 \in \Gamma_0, O \in SO(3)} \left(\min_{\substack{a_f : [0,1] \to \mathcal{C}_f \\ a_f(0) = f_1,\, a_f(1) = O(f_2 \circ \gamma_0)}} \left(\int_0^1 \langle\langle \dot{a}_f(t), \dot{a}_f(t) \rangle\rangle_{a_f(t)}^{(1/2)} \, dt \right) \right), \quad (6.6)$$

where $a_f(t)$ is a parameterized path in $\mathcal{C}_f$ with $t \in [0, 1]$. This expression is very similar to the one presented in Chapter 3, and the inside optimization problem can be solved using the same path-straightening algorithm. The outer optimization problem is also solved using the same procedure but replacing the spherical harmonic basis with the landmark-constrained basis defined in the previous subsection. We omit the details for brevity. In subsequent descriptions, we use α_f^* to denote the geodesic path between two optimally registered landmark annotated shapes, and $L(\alpha_f^*)$ to denote the geodesic distance in the landmark-constrained shape space.

6.3.1 ILLUSTRATION OF GEODESIC PATHS

We present examples of computing landmark-constrained registrations, geodesic paths, and geodesic distances between complex 3D shapes that have been annotated with a sparse set of landmarks. We display the registration along the computed geodesic by rendering corresponding points with the same color. The visual quality of the geodesic is an important evaluation criterion of the quality of the dense correspondences. Small registration errors will result in significant artifacts and distortions in the intermediate shapes.

The 3D models used in these examples are part of the TOSCA and SHREC2007 datasets. They have been provided as watertight genus-0 triangulated meshes. Their spherical parameterizations have been computed using the approach described in Appendix C. Results are obtaind using five to ten landmarks.

Example 6.2 Shapes with missing parts. Figure 6.4 shows three examples of geodesics between 3D shapes with missing parts. In row (a), the source and target shapes are similar but the target has a missing finger. In rows (b) and (c), in addition to stretching, the legs and tails of the horse and centaur also bend.

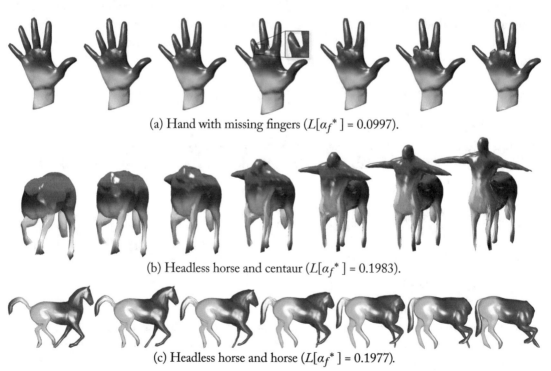

(a) Hand with missing fingers ($L[\alpha_f^*] = 0.0997$).

(b) Headless horse and centaur ($L[\alpha_f^*] = 0.1983$).

(c) Headless horse and horse ($L[\alpha_f^*] = 0.1977$).

Figure 6.4: Results on surfaces with missing parts. We show the geodesic between given surfaces and the geodesic distance.

Using only a sparse set of landmarks, the approach described in this chapter is able to obtain natural geodesics that match human intuition. Observe the quality of the intermediate shapes, where the quality of the geodesic depends on the quality of the registration. This observation demonstrates that the approach described here is able to find good full correspondences between surfaces with missing parts.

Example 6.3   Isometric deformations.   Figure 6.5 shows geodesic paths and distances between surfaces that undergo nearly isometric deformations. Here, the landmarks and initial sparse correspondences are automatically computed and matched as described in Appendix D. The elastic shape analysis framework then simultaneously finds the registration and the geodesic that deforms one shape into the other. The figure shows, for each example, the computed geodesic and its length, which measures the dissimilarity between the two shapes. Again, the quality of the intermediate shapes generated by this approach is very good.

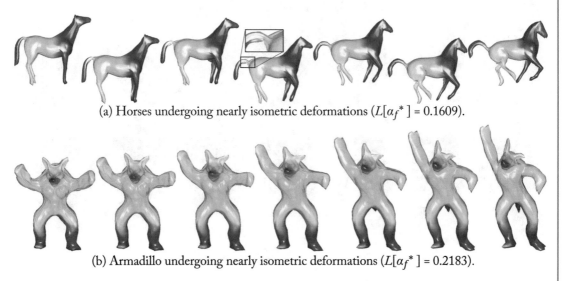

(a) Horses undergoing nearly isometric deformations ($L[\alpha_f^*] = 0.1609$).

(b) Armadillo undergoing nearly isometric deformations ($L[\alpha_f^*] = 0.2183$).

Figure 6.5: Results on surfaces with nearly isometric deformations.

Example 6.4   Elastic deformations.   Figure 6.6a considers two hands that significantly bend and stretch. The geodesic computed using the landmark-constrained approach efficiently handles this large elastic deformation. The shapes in Figure 6.6b differ considerably; the horse is missing its tail, the cow has horns in addition to ears, and the heads are in different poses. Yet, the geodesic computed using the approach described in this chapter handles all of these transformations very well and provides a natural geodesic deformation.

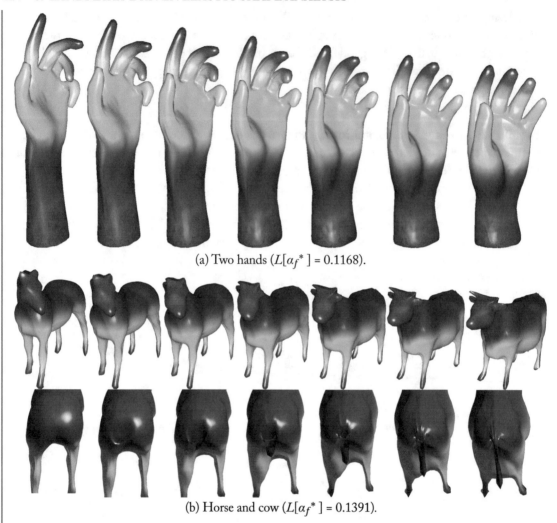

(a) Two hands ($L[\alpha_f^*] = 0.1168$).

(b) Horse and cow ($L[\alpha_f^*] = 0.1391$).

Figure 6.6: Examples of geodesics between surfaces undergoing both elastic (stretching) and isometric (bending) deformations.

6.3.2   EVALUATION OF PERFORMANCE AND COMPUTATIONAL COST

We quantitatively evaluate the performance of the computed correspondences and compare them to Blended Intrinsic Maps (BIM) [Kim et al., 2011], Möbius Voting (MV) [Lipman and Funkhouser, 2009], and Generalized Multidimensional Scaling (MDS) [Bronstein et al., 2008]. For the evaluation, we use all of the centaurs, four cats, two gorillas, and six ant models arbitrarily chosen from the TOSCA and SHREC07 datasets. The ground truth correspondences are kindly made publicly available by the authors of Kim et al. [2011].

To evaluate the performance of the different algorithms, we compute the average correspondence error. For each pair of surfaces f_1 and f_2, we are given a set of ground-truth point correspondence pairs (s_i, s_i^g), where $f_2(s_i^g)$ is the point on f_2 that matches $f_1(s_i)$. If γ_0^* is the optimal landmark-constrained reparameterization, then the correspondence error is defined as

$$E = \frac{1}{n} \sum_{i=1}^{n} d_g(f_2(s_i^g), f_2(\gamma_0^*(s_i))), \tag{6.7}$$

where d_g is the distance along the surface f_2, and n is the number of ground truth correspondence pairs. Table 6.1 summarizes the average correspondence error per shape class for each method. We observe that the framework described in this chapter performs as well as MV on cats and gorillas, which undergo isometric deformations, and outperforms BM on the centaur and ant classes. The elastic shape analysis framework has the advantage that it can handle large elastic deformations, and simultaneously computes geodesics, which enable one to compute shape statistics (see Section 6.4).

Table 6.1: Average correspondence errors on four classes of shapes that undergo isometric deformations

	# Models	Ours	BIM	MV	GMDS
Centaur	6	0.046	0.058	0.043	0.089
Cat	4	0.056	0.034	0.083	0.149
Gorilla	2	0.050	0.019	0.021	0.091
Ant	6	0.053	0.278	–	–

One of the advantages of the framework described in this book is that it finds a diffeomorphic mapping between surfaces. To illustrate the importance of this property, we compute correspondences between two 3D models of ants using the BIM approach [Kim et al., 2011] and using the approach described in this chapter. Next, we linearly interpolate the registered surfaces and show the results in Figure 6.4a and Figure 6.4b, respectively. Observe that when the mapping is not diffeomophic the intermediate shapes contain many artifacts, as one would expect.

The processing time for solving the joint minimization problem in Equation (6.6) between two spherically parameterized surfaces with 100^2 vertices each is approximately 580 sec.

6.4   LANDMARK-CONSTRAINED 3D SHAPE ATLAS

The methods for computing statistical summaries as described in Chapter 4 extend in a straightforward fashion to the landmark-constrained case, which seeks to compute the mean shape $\bar{f}$

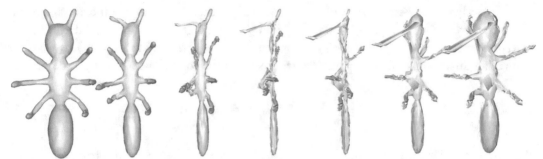

(a) Linear morphing of two ants after computing correspondences using Kim et al. [2011].

(b) Linear morphing between two ants after computing correspondences with the framework described in this chapter.

Figure 6.7: Linear interpolation paths between surfaces whose correspondence was computed using Blended Intrinsic Maps [Kim et al., 2011] (a) and the method described in this chapter (b).

and jointly co-register the set of surfaces $\{f_1, \ldots, f_n\}$ while preserving the landmark correspondences. This problem can be written as the constrained minimization problem in Equation (6.2). To do so, we first select a reference surface, denoted by f_1, and then for every other surface f_i, find an initial diffeomorphism γ_0^i that aligns the landmarks of f_i onto those of f_1 using the approach described in Section 6.2.1. Next, one can use the approach described in Chapter 4, but instead of searching for the optimal diffeomorphism in Γ, we restrict the search to Γ_0.

Figure 6.8 shows four examples of computing such shape atlases in the landmark-constrained framework. For the cat and horse examples, we chose landmarks on the ears, face, paws (or hooves), and at the end and base of the tail. For the human body shapes, we chose landmarks at all of the extremities, the face, on each side of the neck and the rear. We note that in all of the presented examples, the computed average shape is a natural representative of the given surfaces. The pose of the atlases is an average of the poses of each of the shapes in the given sample. This is a very intuitive result and it is especially apparent in the horse example where the body of the average horse is in a neutral pose but its tail is in a pose that is an average of the three given horses.

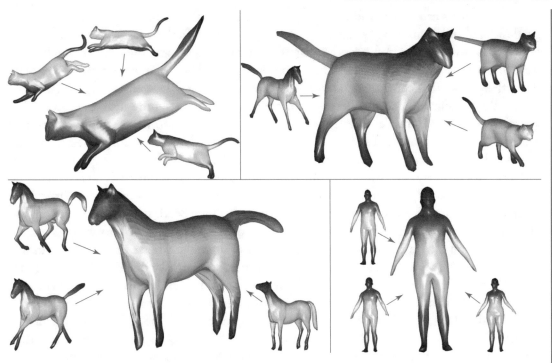

Figure 6.8: Examples of computing shape atlases for three cats in different poses, two cats and a horse in the same pose, three horses in different poses, and three humans with different body shapes.

6.5   BIBLIOGRAPHIC NOTES

Purely landmark-based analysis of shapes has been developed and discussed in several textbooks, including Dryden and Mardia [1998] and Kendall et al. [1999]. Landmarks have been also used for improving registration in functional data and image analysis [Glaunès et al., 2004]. The use of landmarks in shape analysis, especially for curves and surfaces, is a relatively more recent topic [Strait et al., 2016].

The framework described in this chapter was originally developed for the analysis of generic 3D objects of spherical topology and was presented in Kurtek et al. [2010]. The approach was later used to register and compute shape atlases of carpal bones in Banerjee et al. [2015]. In fact, the use of landmarks is highly desirable in many fields. In medical applications, for example, the landmarks correspond to points, curves, or anatomical regions manually labeled by a medical expert [Banerjee et al., 2015]. This chapter considered only point landmarks. It is however interesting to investigate whether the framework extends to more general landmarks such as curves or surface patches.

Landmarks can also benefit computer graphics applications where one needs to compute geodesics and deformation paths between very complex shapes. In these cases, geometric features only are not sufficient to find correct registrations between surfaces. Thus, it is natural to use a sparse set of landmarks to guide the registration and geodesic computation processes. Note that other works that compute geodesics between shapes, e.g., Heeren et al. [2012], Kilian et al. [2007], assume that a full one-to-one correspondence between the surfaces is given. The approach described in this chapter handles a wider range of deformations and requires only a sparse set of correspondences (4–10 landmark points). The lengths of the geodesics that are computed provide a formal distance that measures the difference between the shapes of the given surfaces. This quantity is very useful in different applications such as retrieval and classification.

The landmark detection and matching step can be automated in some cases, particularly when dealing with isometric 3D objects, i.e., objects that only bend. For example, one can use Heat Kernel Signatures (HKS) [Sun et al., 2009] to detect points of high curvature, especially those located on extremities such as the legs and tails of the cat and horse examples used in this chapter. The same geometric signatures may also be used to match landmark points across surfaces. We refer the reader to Guo et al. [2016] for a detailed survey and performance evaluation of various local geometric descriptors that can be used for establishing landmark correspondences.

Finally, the generic 3D models used in this chapter are from the SHREC07 benchmark [Giorgi et al., 2007] and the TOSCA database [Bronstein et al., 2008], while the ground truth correspondences were kindly made publicly available by the authors of Kim et al. [2011].

APPENDIX A

Differential Geometry

We start with some basic concepts in differential geometry that are useful in specifying shape spaces and in analyzing shapes as elements of these spaces.

A.1 DIFFERENTIABLE MANIFOLDS AND TANGENT SPACES

In differential geometry one performs differential and integral calculus on domains that are nonlinear, i.e., they are not vector spaces. These more general domains are termed manifolds, and we start with a simple definition.

Definition A.1 Manifold. A topological space M is called a **manifold** of dimension m if:

1. it is Hausdorff;

2. it has a countable basis; and

3. for each point $p \in M$, there is a neighborhood U of p that is homeomorphic to an open subset of $\mathbb{R}^m$.

In our applications of geometry, purely topological manifolds are not sufficient. We would like to be able to evaluate first and higher derivatives of functions on our manifold. A **differentiable manifold** is a manifold with a smoother structure that allows the definition of derivatives. We illustrate this with a few examples.

Example A.2

1. The Euclidean space $\mathbb{R}^m$ is an m-dimensional differentiable manifold.

2. Any open subset of a differentiable manifold is itself a differentiable manifold. Let $M(n)$ be the set of all $n \times n$ matrices; $M(n)$ can be identified with the set $\mathbb{R}^{n \times n}$ and is, therefore, a differentiable manifold. Define the subset $GL(n)$ as the set of non-singular matrices, i.e.,

$$GL(n) = \{A \in M(n) \mid \det(A) \neq 0\}, \tag{A.1}$$

where $\det(\cdot)$ denotes the determinant of a matrix. Since $GL(n)$ is an open subset of $M(n)$, it is also a differentiable manifold.

3. Any finite-dimensional sphere $\mathbb{S}^m \subset \mathbb{R}^{m+1}$ is a differentiable manifold.

4. Define $O(n)$ to be the set of all $n \times n$ invertible matrices A that satisfy $AA^T = I$. It can be shown that $O(n)$ is a differentiable manifold. Actually, $O(n)$ is not connected, but has two components: those orthogonal matrices with determinant $+1$, and those with determinant -1. The set of orthogonal matrices with determinant 1 is called the **special orthogonal group**, and is denoted by $SO(n)$. The dimension of $SO(n)$ is $n^2 - n(n + 1)/2 = n(n - 1)/2$.

In order to perform differential calculus, i.e., to compute gradients, directional derivatives, critical points, etc., of functions on manifolds, one needs to understand the tangent structure of those manifolds. There are several ways to define tangent spaces. One approach is to consider differentiable (C^1) curves on the manifold passing through the point of interest, and to study the velocity vectors of these curves at that point. Different velocity vectors, corresponding to all possible curves, will be tangential to the manifold at that point and form a vector space called the tangent space at that point. We will use $T_p(M)$ to denote the vector space tangent to M at a $p \in M$.

One may also think of the tangent space at a point as the set of infinitesimal movements one may make away from that point, or in other words, as the set of infinitesimal changes one may make to the point, or, even more suggestively for our application, as the set of infinitesimal "deformations" of a point.

Example A.3

1. In case of the Euclidean space $\mathbb{R}^n$, the tangent space $T_p(\mathbb{R}^n) = \mathbb{R}^n$ for all $p \in \mathbb{R}^n$.

2. For any $A \in GL(n)$, the space of non-singular matrices, the tangent space $T_A(GL(n))$ is all of $M(n)$.

3. The tangent space of $\mathbb{S}^n$ at any point p is the set of all velocity vectors associated with the C^1 curves passing through p. The resulting space is an n-dimensional hyperplane in $\mathbb{R}^{n+1}$ orthogonal to the vector p under the Euclidean metric:

$$T_p(\mathbb{S}^n) = \{v \in \mathbb{R}^{n+1} | \langle v, p \rangle = 0\} .$$

4. The tangent space of $SO(n)$ at the identity matrix, $T_I(SO(n))$, is the set of all $n \times n$ skew-symmetric matrices. For an arbitrary matrix $A \in SO(n)$, the tangent space $T_A(SO(n)) = \{AX : X$ is skew-symmetric$\}$.

Maps between Differentiable Manifolds

Now that we have seen the objects of differential geometry, we need to understand maps between these objects. In general, the maps between two differentiable manifolds are simply the differentiable maps. However, there is a class of such maps of special importance; its members are called *diffeomorphisms*.

Definition A.4 Diffeomorphism. A diffeomorphism $f : M \to N$ between two differentiable manifolds M and N is a differentiable bijection whose inverse is also differentiable.

Diffeomorphisms are isomorphisms of differentiable manifolds: if two differentiable manifolds are diffeomorphic, i.e., if there is a diffeomorphism between them, then they are essentially the same manifold up to a "relabeling" of their points. We will mostly be concerned with the set of diffeomorphisms of a manifold M to itself, $\text{Diff}(M)$. This set forms a group under inversion and composition of maps.

A.2 RIEMANNIAN MANIFOLDS, GEODESICS, AND THE EXPONENTIAL MAP

Differentiable manifolds are topological objects: they can be deformed by diffeomorphisms without changing their essential identity; in other words, they have no rigidity, or notion of distance. In order to define such a notion, we introduce an additional structure. This structure, called a *Riemannian metric*, can be thought of as measuring the distance between infinitesimally close points, or, alternatively, as measuring the "size" of an infinitesimal change in, or deformation of, a point. It does this by assigning an inner product to each tangent space of the manifold, thereby defining a norm on tangent vectors. A differentiable manifold with a Riemannian metric on it is called a **Riemannian manifold**.

To define a Riemannian metric, we begin by defining a bilinear form on a vector space. A **bilinear form** on a vector space V over $\mathbb{R}$ is a map $\langle\langle \cdot, \cdot \rangle\rangle : V \times V \to \mathbb{R}$, that satisfies the following requirements:

1. $\langle\langle c_1 v_1 + c_2 v_2, w \rangle\rangle = c_1 \langle\langle v_1, w \rangle\rangle + c_2 \langle\langle v_2, w \rangle\rangle$ and

2. $\langle\langle v, c_1 w_1 + c_2 w_2 \rangle\rangle = c_1 \langle\langle v, w_1 \rangle\rangle + c_2 \langle\langle v, w_2 \rangle\rangle$,

where $c_1, c_2 \in \mathbb{R}$ and $v, w, v_1, v_2, w_1, w_2 \in V$. A bilinear form is symmetric if $\langle\langle v, w \rangle\rangle = \langle\langle w, v \rangle\rangle$. A symmetric form becomes an inner product if it is positive definite, i.e., $\langle\langle v, v \rangle\rangle \geq 0$, and $\langle\langle v, v \rangle\rangle = 0 \iff v = 0$.

The norm $\|v\|$ of a tangent vector is then given by $\|v\|^2 = \langle\langle v, v \rangle\rangle$.

Definition A.5 Riemannian metric. A Riemannian metric on a differentiable manifold M is a map g that smoothly associates to each point $p \in M$ an inner product on the tangent space $T_p(M)$.

Example A.6

1. As stated in Example A.2, the tangent space at any point in $\mathbb{R}^n$ is $\mathbb{R}^n$ itself. It becomes a Riemannian manifold with the Riemannian metric $\langle\langle v_1, v_2 \rangle\rangle = \langle v_1, v_2 \rangle$, the standard Euclidean product.

2. For $SO(n)$, a standard Riemannian metric is defined as follows: for any $Y, Z \in T_A(O(n))$ set $\langle\langle Y, Z \rangle\rangle = \mathrm{trace}(YZ^T)$, where trace denotes the sum of diagonal elements. With this metric $SO(n)$ becomes a Riemannian manifold. This metric is preserved under left and right multiplication by elements of $SO(n)$:

$$\langle\langle AY, AZ \rangle\rangle = \mathrm{trace}(AY(AZ)^T) =$$
$$\mathrm{trace}(AYZ^T A^T) = \mathrm{trace}(AYZ^T A^{-1}) = \mathrm{trace}(YZ^T) = \langle\langle Y, Z \rangle\rangle .$$

3. For the unit sphere $\mathbb{S}^n$ and a point $p \in \mathbb{S}^n$, the Euclidean inner product on the tangent vectors makes $\mathbb{S}^n$ into a Riemannian manifold. That is, for any $v_1, v_2 \in T_p(\mathbb{S}^n)$, we use the Riemannian metric $\langle\langle v_1, v_2 \rangle\rangle = \langle v_1, v_2 \rangle$.

Maps Between Riemannian Manifolds

Having defined a new type of object, we can again ask about maps between these objects. The extra structure of a Riemannian metric introduces rigidity to differentiable manifolds, and enables us to define a more refined notation of isomorphism, called an *isometry*.

Definition A.7 Isometry. A diffeomorphism $f : M \to N$, where M and N are Riemannian manifolds, is an **isometry** if, for all $p \in M$ and all $u, v \in T_p(M)$:

$$\langle\langle u, v \rangle\rangle_p = \langle\langle df_p(u), df_p(v) \rangle\rangle_{f(p)}, \tag{A.2}$$

where the left inner product is computed using the Riemannian metric on M while the right one is computed using the metric on N.

Note that this implies that $\|v\|_p = \|df(u)\|_{f(p)}$, i.e., that isometries preserve the length of tangent vectors, or equivalently, preserve infinitesimal distances.

Example A.8   Consider the mapping from $\mathbb{R}^{n+1}$ to itself, given by $x \mapsto Ox$, for a fixed $O \in SO(n+1)$. Restricting it to the unit sphere $\mathbb{S}^n$, endowed with the Euclidean metric, we obtain a mapping $f : \mathbb{S}^n \to \mathbb{S}^n$ that is an isometry.

A.2.1 GEODESICS

Once we have a Riemannian metric, it becomes possible to define the length of a path on a manifold. Let $\alpha : [0, 1] \to M$ be a parameterized path on a Riemannian manifold M, such that α is differentiable everywhere on $[0, 1]$. Then $\dot{\alpha} \equiv \frac{d\alpha}{dt}$, the velocity vector at t, is an element of the tangent space $T_{\alpha(t)}(M)$. Its length is $\|\dot{\alpha}\|$. The length of the path α is then given by:

$$\mathcal{L}(\alpha) = \int_0^1 dt \, \|\dot{\alpha}(t)\|. \tag{A.3}$$

This is the integral of the lengths of the velocity vectors along α and, hence, is the length of the whole path α. For any two points $p, q \in M$, one can define the distance between them as the infimum of the lengths of all smooth paths on M that start at p and end at q:

$$d(p, q) = \inf_{\substack{\alpha:[0,1]\to M \\ \alpha(0)=p \\ \alpha(1)=q}} \mathcal{L}(\alpha). \tag{A.4}$$

This definition turns M into a metric space, with distance d.

Definition A.9 If there exists a path α^* that achieves the above minimum, then it is called a **geodesic** between p and q on M.

Very often the search for geodesics is handled by changing the objective functional from length to an energy functional given by:

$$E(\alpha) = \int_0^1 dt \, \langle\langle \dot{\alpha}(t), \dot{\alpha}(t) \rangle\rangle. \tag{A.5}$$

The only difference from the path length in Equation (A.3) is that the square root in the integrand has been removed. It can be shown that a critical point of this functional restricted to paths between p and q is a geodesic between p and q. Furthermore, of all the reparameterizations of a geodesic, the one with constant speed has the minimum energy.[1] As a result, for a minimizing path α^*, we have

$$E(\alpha^*) = \mathcal{L}(\alpha^*)^2. \tag{A.6}$$

Example A.10

1. Geodesics on $\mathbb{R}^n$ with the Euclidean metric are straight lines: $\alpha(t) = tq + (1-t)p, t \in [0, 1]$, is a geodesic between p and q. The length of this geodesic is $\int_0^1 dt \, |q - p| = |q - p|$. So the distance between points in $\mathbb{R}^n$, as we already know, is simply the (Euclidean) length of these straight lines.

---

[1]Constant-speed parameterization implies that $\|\dot{\alpha}_v(t)\| = \sqrt{g(\dot{\alpha}_v(t), \dot{\alpha}_v(t))}$ does not depend on t.

2. Geodesics on a unit sphere $\mathbb{S}^n$ are given by great circles. The distance minimizing geodesic between any two points is the shortest of the two arcs of a great circle joining them. If p and q are points on the unit sphere (with $p \neq \pm q$), then the path

$$\alpha(t) = \frac{1}{\sin(\vartheta)}(\sin(\vartheta(1-t))p + \sin(\vartheta t)q) \tag{A.7}$$

gives a constant-speed parameterization of the unique shortest geodesic (i.e., great circle arc) from p to q, where ϑ is determined by $\cos(\vartheta) = \langle p, q \rangle$ and $0 < \vartheta < \pi$.

A.2.2   EXPONENTIAL MAP

Let M be a Riemannian manifold. Given a point $p \in M$ and a tangent vector $v \in T_p(M)$, there exists a unique constant-speed parameterized geodesic $\alpha_v : (-\epsilon, \epsilon) \to M$, for some $\epsilon > 0$, such that $\alpha_v(0) = p$ and $\dot{\alpha}_v(0) = v$. If the manifold M is **geodesically complete**, the parameterized geodesic is defined for all $t \in \mathbb{R}$.

Definition A.11   Exponential map.   If M is a Riemannian manifold, $p \in M$, and $U \subset T_p(M)$ is an open neighborhood of 0, then the **exponential map** $\exp_p : U \to M$, is defined by $\exp_p(v) = \alpha_v(1)$ where α_v is as defined above.

The exponential map exp maps a vector $v \in T_p(M)$ to a point of M. In other words, to reach the point $\exp_p(v)$, one starts at p, and then moves for time 1 along the unique constant speed geodesic whose velocity vector at p is v. Note that if $v = 0$, the corresponding geodesic is just the constant path at p, so $\exp_p(0) = p$.

The inverse of an exponential map takes a point on the manifold M and maps it to an element (or multiple elements) of the tangent space $T_p(M)$. A vector v is said to be the inverse exponential of $q \in M$ at p if $\exp_p(v) = q$. It is denoted by $v = \exp_p^{-1}(q)$ and is often not a unique point: the inverse may be set-valued.

Example A.12

1. For $\mathbb{R}^n$, under the Euclidean metric, since geodesics are given by straight lines, the exponential map is a simple addition: $\exp_p(v) = p + v$, for $p, v \in \mathbb{R}^n$. The inverse exponential map is simply $\exp_p^{-1}(q) = q - p$. Similarly, for $M(n)$, the space of $n \times n$ matrices, the exponential map is given by a simple addition of matrices, i.e., $\exp_A(X) = A + X$, and the inverse exponential is $\exp_A^{-1}(B) = B - A$.

2. The geodesics on a sphere $\mathbb{S}^n$ under the Euclidean metric can also be parameterized in terms of a direction v in $T_p(\mathbb{S}^n)$:

$$\alpha_t(v) = \cos(t|v|)p + \sin(t|v|)\frac{v}{|v|}. \tag{A.8}$$

As a result, the exponential map, $\exp_p : T_p(\mathbb{S}^n) \mapsto \mathbb{S}^n$, has a simple expression:

$$\exp_p(v) = \cos(|v|)p + \sin(|v|)\frac{v}{|v|} . \tag{A.9}$$

The exponential map is a bijection if we restrict $|v|$ so that $|v| \in [0, \pi)$. For a point $q \in \mathbb{S}^n$ $(q \neq p)$, the inverse exponential map $\exp_p^{-1}(q)$ is given by u, where:

$$u = \frac{\theta}{\sin(\theta)}(q - \cos(\theta)p), \quad \text{where} \quad \theta = \cos^{-1}(\langle p, q \rangle) . \tag{A.10}$$

3. The exponential map for $SO(n)$ at any point $O \in SO(n)$ is given by $\exp_O : T_O(SO(n)) \to SO(n)$, $\exp_O(OX) = O \exp(X)$, where X is skew-symmetric and the last term is the matrix exponential. Note that this map is not one-to-one unless we restrict to a small enough neighborhood of O. The inverse exponential map on $O(n)$ is defined as follows: For $O_1, O_2 \in O(n)$, define $\exp_{O_1}^{-1}(O_2) = O_1 \log(O_1^T O_2)$, where this log is the matrix logarithm.

A.3   LIE GROUP ACTIONS AND QUOTIENT SPACES

So far we have discussed definitions and examples of manifolds and groups. In some cases, the sets have both structures: manifold and group; these sets are called Lie groups. In view of their dual structures, they are of great importance in algebra and pattern theory.

Definition A.13   Lie group.   A group G is a **Lie group**, if: (i) it is a smooth manifold, and (ii) the group operations $G \times G \to G$ defined by $(g, h) \to gh$ and $G \to G$ defined by $g \to g^{-1}$ are both smooth mappings. Most of the groups we have considered earlier are Lie groups.

Example A.14

1. The general linear group $GL(n)$, by virtue of being an open subset of $\mathbb{R}^{n \times n}$, is also a differentiable manifold. It is, therefore, a Lie group. Any subgroup of $GL(n)$, if it is also a submanifold of $GL(n)$, will be a Lie group. An important example in this category is the rotation group $SO(n)$.

2. The translation group $\mathbb{R}^n$ is both a manifold and a group (with addition operation). Therefore, it is a Lie group.

3. The scaling group, $R^\times$ with multiplication operation, is a Lie group.

4. The unit circle $\mathbb{S}^1$ is a group, although it is not straightforward to see why from its definition. Using the mapping $\mathbb{S}^1 \to SO(2)$ given by $(x_1, x_2) \mapsto \left(\begin{smallmatrix} x_1 & -x_2 \\ x_2 & x_1 \end{smallmatrix} \right)$, we can identify $\mathbb{S}^1$ with $SO(2)$. The latter is a group with matrix multiplication as the group operation. Through this identification, $\mathbb{S}^1$ also inherits a group structure. Since it is also a differentiable manifold, $\mathbb{S}^1$ becomes a Lie group. However, the two-dimensional sphere $\mathbb{S}^2$ is not a Lie group as it does not have a group structure.

Definition A.15 Group action.   Given a manifold M and a Lie group G, a **left group action** of G on M is a map $G \times M \to M$. We will write the pair and its image as $(g, p) \in M$. For all $p \in M$, and $g_1, g_2 \in G$, the map must satisfy:

1. $(g_2, (g_1, p)) = (g_2 g_1, p)$;

2. $(\mathrm{id}, p) = p$.

Similarly, a **right group action** is a map $M \times G \to M$, satisfying:

1. $((p, g_1), g_2) = (p, g_1 g_2)$;

2. $(p, \mathrm{id}) = p$.

We note that a left group action on M defines two other actions:

- On a space of maps $f : N \to M$, a left action given by $(g, f)(n) = (g, f(n))$, where $n \in N$;

- On a space of maps $f : M \to N$, a right action given by $(f, g)(m) = f((g, m))$.

These are frequently known as pushforwards and pullbacks, respectively.

Definition A.16   A group action of G on a Riemannian manifold M is called **isometric** if it preserves the Riemannian metric on M. In other words, for all $g \in G$, the map $M \to M$ given by $p \mapsto (g, p)$ is an isometry. For the same situation, we sometimes say that G acts on M by isometries.

It then also follows that for all $g \in G$ and $x, y \in M$, $d(x, y) = d((g, x), (g, y))$, where $d(x, y)$ is the distance function on M resulting from the Riemannian metric. Compare this with Definition A.7 that specifies an isometry between Riemannian manifolds. This is a specific case of that definition: here the mapping is from the manifold to itself, and it is defined by the group action.

Definition A.17 Orbit.   Assume that a group G acts on a manifold M. The group action defines an equivalence relation on M: two points p and p' are equivalent, $p \sim p'$ if and only if there exists a $g \in G$ such that $p' = (g, p)$. We denote the equivalence class of a point p by $[p]$. It is known as the **orbit** of p under the group action. It may equally be defined as the set $[p] \equiv (G, p) = \{(g, p) : g \in G\}$, i.e., it is the set of all possible points one can reach in M using the action of G on that point. The orbit of a point can vary in size from a single point to the entire manifold M. If the orbit of any $p \in M$ is the whole of M, then the group action is said to be **transitive**.

Example A.18   Let us now consider some examples to illustrate these definitions.

- **Translation Group**: The translation group $\mathbb{R}^n$ acts on the affine space $\mathbb{R}^n$ by the action $(v, y) = v + y$ for any $v, y \in \mathbb{R}^n$. This group action is transitive, since the orbit of any point y is the whole of $\mathbb{R}^n$, i.e., $[y] = \mathbb{R}^n$. The group action is also isometric, using the Euclidean structure on $\mathbb{R}^n$, since $|y_1 - y_2| = |(v + y_1) - (v + y_2)|$ for all $v, y_1, y_2 \in \mathbb{R}^n$.

  The translation group acts by pushforward on $\mathcal{F} = \mathrm{Map}(D, \mathbb{R}^n)$, the spaces of curves and surfaces considered in Chapter 2. For any $f \in \mathcal{F}$ and $v \in \mathbb{R}^n$, the translation of f by v is given by $\tilde{f}(p) = f(p) + v$, for all $p \in D$.

- **Scaling Group**: The scale group $\mathbb{R}^\times \equiv \mathbb{R}_{>0}$ acts on $\mathbb{R}^n$ by $(a, x) = ax$ for any $a \in \mathbb{R}^\times$ and $x \in \mathbb{R}^n$. This group action is not transitive on $\mathbb{R}^n$. Under the action, the orbit of the zero vector consists of the zero vector alone. The orbit of a nonzero vector is a straight line spanned by positive scalings of this vector. If we impose the Euclidean metric on $\mathbb{R}^n$ to make it a Riemannian manifold, then the action of $\mathbb{R}^\times$ on $\mathbb{R}^n$ is not isometric because $|x_1 - x_2| \neq |ax_1 - ax_2|$ for any $a \neq 1$.

  The scaling group acts by pushforward on $\mathcal{F}$. For any $f \in \mathcal{F}$ and $a \in \mathbb{R}^\times$, the scaling of f by a is given by $\tilde{f}(p) = af(p)$, for all $p \in D$.

- **Rotation Group**: The rotation group $SO(n)$ acts on $\mathbb{R}^n$ as $(O, x) = Ox$, the matrix-vector multiplication, for all $O \in SO(n)$ and $x \in \mathbb{R}^n$. The orbit of any vector x is simply a sphere centered at zero with radius $|x|$. Therefore, this group action is not transitive, but is isometric, under the Euclidean structure on $\mathbb{R}^n$, because $|x_1 - x_2| = |Ox_1 - Ox_2|$, for all $O \in SO(n), x_1, x_2 \in \mathbb{R}^n$.

  The rotation group acts by pushforward on $\mathcal{F}$. For any $f \in \mathcal{F}$ and $O \in SO(n)$, the rotation of f by O is given by $\tilde{f}(p) = Of(p)$, for all $p \in D$.

- **Diffeomorphism Group**: Let $\Gamma = \mathrm{Diff}(D)$ denote the set of orientation-preserving diffeomorphisms of D. This is a group under composition and inversion of maps. An orientation-preserving diffeomorphism is also called a *reparametrization* function, and Γ may be called the **reparametrization group**.

  By definition, Γ left acts on D: $(\gamma, p) = \gamma(p)$. It also right acts on $\mathcal{F}$ by pullback. For any $f \in \mathcal{F}$ and $\gamma \in \Gamma$, we have $(f, \gamma) = f \circ \gamma$. This action is called a *reparameterization* of f.

Definition A.19 Quotient space.   Given a set M, and an equivalence relation $\sim$ on M, we can divide M into equivalence classes. We will denote the equivalence class of a point $p \in M$ by $[p]$. The **quotient space** of M by $\sim$, denoted $M/\sim$ is defined to be the set of equivalence classes:

$$M/\sim = \{[p] \ : \ p \in M\}. \tag{A.11}$$

Now let M be a finite-dimensional manifold and G be a Lie group that acts on M. As we have seen, this action defines an equivalence relation, and so we can define the quotient space, now denoted M/G: it is the set of all orbits of the group action.

Example A.20   Let $X \in \mathbb{R}^{n \times k}$ be a matrix whose k columns denote k ordered points in $\mathbb{R}^n$. The action of $SO(n)$ on $\mathbb{R}^{n \times k}$ is defined in Example A.18, except that the same rotation is applied to all the columns, and this defines the orbit of X:

$$[X] = \{OX | O \in SO(n)\}.$$

This set consists of all $n \times k$ matrices whose columns can be obtained by simultaneously rotating the columns of X using the same rotation. Treating elements of $[X]$ as an equivalence class implies that all rotated versions of X are equivalent. The resulting quotient space is given by $\mathcal{L}_{n,k}/SO(n) = \{[X] | X \in \mathcal{L}_{n,k}\}$.

Definition A.21 Quotient metric.   If M happens to be a metric space, with distance d, then a distance may be induced on $M/\sim$ as follows. First, note that a pseudometric ρ on M defines an equivalence relation: two points are equivalent $p \sim p'$, if and only if $\rho(p, p') = 0$. The pseudometric also defines a metric on the resulting quotient space: $d([p], [p']) = \rho(p, p')$ (where we use the same symbol for the distance on $M/\sim$ as on M). So, given a metric space with an equivalence relation $\sim$, we can induce a distance on $M/\sim$ if we can find a pseudometric ρ on M such that $\rho(p, p') = 0$ if and only if $p \sim p'$. One possibility is:

$$\tilde{\rho}(p, p') = \begin{cases} 0 & p \sim p', \\ d(p, p') & \text{else}. \end{cases} \tag{A.12}$$

This defines a symmetric, non-negative function on $M \times M$, and clearly satisfies $\rho(p, p') = 0$ if and only if $p \sim p'$. However, it may not satisfy the triangle inequality and so may not be a pseudometric. To ensure that it is, we form:

$$\rho(p, p') = \inf_{\substack{n \in \mathbb{N} \\ \{p_i\} \in M^{n+1} \\ p_0 = p \\ p_n = p'}} \sum_{i=0}^{n-1} \tilde{\rho}(p_i, p_{i+1}), \tag{A.13}$$

i.e., we minimize over all finite chains of points connecting the two end points. This pseudo-metric then defines a *bona fide* distance on $M/\sim$.

Since every Riemannian manifold is naturally a metric space, we can in principle apply the above construction to turn the quotient M/G into a metric space. As elegant as this construction is, however, it is clearly not computationally feasible to minimize over all chains. Note at this point that one apparent solution, in which we define a distance on the quotient $M/\sim$ via:

$$d([p], [p']) = \inf_{\substack{p \in [p] \\ p' \in [p']}} d(p, p') \tag{A.14}$$

does *not* work in general. It is easy to construct examples in which the result does not satisfy the triangle inequality, and it is easy to see why: $[p]$ and $[p']$ may approach each other very closely, as may $[p']$ and $[p'']$, but at different points $p' \in [p']$; thus $[p]$ and $[p'']$ need never be very close. As an example, imagine the lines $y = -1$ and $y = 1$ in $\mathbb{R}^2$, and the curve $y = \tanh(x)$, viewed as equivalence classes of the points $(0, -1)$, $(0, 1)$, and $(0, 0)$. Clearly $d([(0, -1)], [(0, 0)]) = d([(0, 0)], [(0, 1)]) = 0$, while $d([(0, -1)], [(0, 1)]) = 1$, and so the triangle inequality is violated.

The violation occurs when the equivalence classes are not parallel, that is when $\inf_{p' \in [p']} d(p, p')$ and $\inf_{p \in [p]} d(p, p')$ are not independent of p and p' respectively. When they are parallel, then the infimum over both endpoints in Equation (A.14) can clearly be replaced by a single infimum over either of the endpoints, giving:

$$d([p], [p']) = \inf_{p' \in [p']} d(p, p') = \inf_{p \in [p]} d(p, p'). \tag{A.15}$$

It is then easy to see that the triangle inequality *is* satisfied:

$$d([p], [p']) + d([p'], [p'']) = \min_{p' \in [p']} d(p, p') + \min_{p'' \in [p'']} d(p', p'') \tag{A.16a}$$

$$= \min_{p \in [p]} d(p, p') + \min_{p'' \in [p'']} d(p', p'') \tag{A.16b}$$

$$= \min_{\substack{p \in [p] \\ p'' \in [p'']}} (d(p, p') + d(p', p'')) \tag{A.16c}$$

$$\geq \min_{\substack{p \in [p] \\ p'' \in [p'']}} d(p, p'') \tag{A.16d}$$

$$= \min_{p'' \in [p'']} d(p, p'') \tag{A.16e}$$

$$= d([p], [p'']) . \tag{A.16f}$$

Fortunately, these are the cases in which we will be interested. When a group acts by isometries, then the resulting equivalence classes are parallel.[2] Take two points $p_1, p_2 \in [p]$. By

---

[2]The following calculations use a left action; it is clear that the same conclusions follow from a right action.

definition of the orbit, there exists $g \in G$ such that $p_2 = (g, p_1)$. Then we have that

$$\inf_{p' \in [p']} d(p_2, p') = \inf_{p' \in (G, p')} d(p_2, p') \tag{A.17a}$$

$$= \inf_{g' \in G} d(p_2, (g', p')) \tag{A.17b}$$

$$= \inf_{g' \in G} d((g, p_1), (g', p')) \tag{A.17c}$$

$$= \inf_{g' \in G} d((g^{-1}, (g, p_1)), (g^{-1}, (g', p'))) \tag{A.17d}$$

$$= \inf_{g' \in G} d(p_1, (g^{-1}g', p')) \tag{A.17e}$$

$$= \inf_{g' \in G} d(p_1, (g', p')) \tag{A.17f}$$

$$= \inf_{p' \in [p']} d(p_1, p') . \tag{A.17g}$$

Thus the infimum is independent of the point in $[p]$, and of course the symmetric case follows as well. We can therefore turn the quotient space into a metric space via a single minimization over an equivalence class, as in Equation (A.15), but adapted to the case of a group action:

$$d([p], [p']) = \inf_{g \in G} d((g, p), p') = \inf_{g \in G} d(p, (g, p')) . \tag{A.18}$$

Definition A.22   Quotient Riemannian metric.   The above construction has an infinitesimal counterpart, using the Riemannian metric, as follows. Let M be a Riemannian manifold and let G act on M by isometries. The **quotient Riemannian metric** induced on the quotient space M/G is given as follows. For any $v_1, v_2 \in T_{[p]}(M/G)$, define

$$\langle\langle v_1, v_2 \rangle\rangle_{[p]} = \langle \tilde{v}_1, \tilde{v}_2 \rangle_p , \tag{A.19}$$

where $\tilde{v}_1, \tilde{v}_2$ are considered as elements of $N_p(M) \subset T_p(M)$ on the right side. Due to the isometry of the group action, it does not matter which $p \in [p]$ is selected for this definition. We can then define arc-length, geodesics, and a distance function on the manifold M/G using this inherited Riemannian metric.

The definition of a quotient distance given in Equation (A.18) applies to any metric space; in particular, M/G need not be a smooth manifold. This is relevant because in general there is no guarantee that the quotient of a smooth manifold by a smooth group action will itself be a smooth manifold.[3] Often this arises because some points in M are preserved by a subgroup of the group G. The quotient space at such a point may have a different dimensionality to the quotient space at generic points that are not preserved by any subgroup, and hence the manifold structure is lost. Such points tend to form a set of measure zero in M, however; in our case, they may, for example, represent shapes with particular symmetry properties, for example a circle or a square. As such, they can often be ignored; Equation (A.19) can still be used for generic points.

[3]If G is compact, and its action is free (i.e., no $g \in G$ preserves any $p \in M$), then the quotient is a manifold.

APPENDIX B

Differential Geometry of Surfaces

In this appendix, we take a careful look at the differential geometry of 2D surfaces. Since we are dealing with spherically parameterized surfaces, which can be viewed as immersions or embeddings of the unit sphere $\mathbb{S}^2$ in $\mathbb{R}^3$, we start with $\mathbb{S}^2$, but almost all that follows applies to other two-dimensional domains D, and, *mutatis mutandis*, to other dimensions as well.

The set $\mathbb{S}^2$ can be coordinatized in many ways. A convenient system of coordinates is the polar system (u, v) where $u \in [0, \pi]$ denotes the elevation angle and $v \in [0, 2\pi)$ denotes the azimuthal angle, but what follows applies to an arbitrary coordinate system.[1] For any $s = (u, v) \in \mathbb{S}^2$, the tangent space $T_s(\mathbb{S}^2)$ is spanned by the basis vectors $\partial_u = \frac{\partial}{\partial u}$ and $\partial_v = \frac{\partial}{\partial v}$. Let f be a smooth map from $\mathbb{S}^2$ to $\mathbb{R}^3$, given by $f(u, v) = (f_1(u, v), f_2(u, v), f_3(u, v))$. Due to the smoothness assumption, the partial derivatives of f with respect to u and v are well defined. They are given by:

$$f_u = \partial_u f = \frac{\partial f}{\partial u} = \left(\frac{\partial f_1}{\partial u}, \frac{\partial f_2}{\partial u}, \frac{\partial f_3}{\partial u} \right) \in \mathbb{R}^3$$

$$f_v = \partial_v f = \frac{\partial f}{\partial v} = \left(\frac{\partial f_1}{\partial v}, \frac{\partial f_2}{\partial v}, \frac{\partial f_3}{\partial v} \right) \in \mathbb{R}^3 \ .$$

The differential of f at a point $s \in \mathbb{S}^2$ is a mapping df_s from $T_s(\mathbb{S}^2)$ to $\mathbb{R}^3$ given by:

$$df_s(\partial_u) = \partial_u f(s)$$

$$df_s(\partial_v) = \partial_v f(s) \ .$$

Intuitively, two infinitesimally close points in D are mapped to two infinitesimally close points in $\mathbb{R}^3$. We can express the map as a 3×2 matrix with columns given by the two vectors listed above.

Definition B.1 Immersions.   A smooth map f from $\mathbb{S}^2$ to $\mathbb{R}^3$ is called an **immersion** if the differential $df_s : \mathbb{R}^2 \to \mathbb{R}^3$ is one-to-one for all $s \in \mathbb{S}^2$.

---

[1]Note that we do not distinguish carefully between the coordinates of a point and the point itself; to do so would needlessly increase the complexity of the notation, with no benefit. We also pay no attention to the fact that manifolds may, and $\mathbb{S}^2$ in particular does, require several coordinate patches to avoid coordinate singularities; for $\mathbb{S}^2$ this only occurs at one point, and this may be dealt with on an *ad hoc* basis.

The (unnormalized) normal vector to a surface f at a point $s = (u, v)$ is given by:

$$n(s) = \partial_u f(s) \times \partial_v f(s) \, .$$

When f is an immersion, the normal vector does not vanish at any point, and one can define a unit normal vector field:

$$\hat{n}(s) = \frac{n(s)}{|n(s)|} \, .$$

Here $| \cdot |$ represents the Euclidean vector norm.

The immersion f may still have self intersections. To avoid them, one often restricts to a smaller class of maps.

Definition B.2   Embeddings.   An immersion f from $\mathbb{S}^2$ to $\mathbb{R}^3$ is called an **embedding** if f is a homeomorphism from $\mathbb{S}^2$ to the set $f(\mathbb{S}^2)$, i.e., embeddings are bijective immersions.

In this manuscript, we will restrict to those surfaces that are represented as embeddings of $\mathbb{S}^2$ in $\mathbb{R}^3$. For any such f, its image $f(\mathbb{S}^2)$ is an unparameterized surface S. The mapping f is also called a *parametrization* of S. If f is an embedding, then the surface $f(\mathbb{S}^2)$ is naturally oriented by the frame $\{f_u, f_v\}$, or equivalently by the normal vector field n.

We define the space of all such parameterized surfaces as $\mathcal{F} = \{f : \mathbb{S}^2 \to \mathbb{R}^3 : f$ is an embedding$\}$. The set $\mathcal{F}$ is itself a manifold, as an open subset of the linear space $C^\infty(\mathbb{S}^2, \mathbb{R}^3)$ of smooth functions from $\mathbb{S}^2$ to $\mathbb{R}^3$. The tangent space to $\mathcal{F}$ at f, denoted by $T_f(\mathcal{F})$, is therefore just $C^\infty(\mathbb{S}^2, \mathbb{R}^3)$.

We will need to be able to measure distances and areas on the surface, and to measure how curved the surface is, and for that we need to define several other quantities. We start with distances.

Definition B.3   Induced or pullback Riemannian metric and measure.   Consider a parametrized surface $f : D \to \mathbb{R}^3$, where, for example, $D = \mathbb{S}^2$. There is a Riemannian metric on $\mathbb{R}^3$ given at each point by the usual Euclidean inner product $\langle \cdot, \cdot \rangle$. We can use the map f to induce a Riemannian metric on D, as follows.

We use coordinates $(u, v) = (u_1, u_2) = u_i$ for $i \in \{1, 2\}$ on D, with basis vectors $\partial_i = \partial_{u_i} = (\partial_{u_1}, \partial_{u_2})$. A tangent vector to D at a point s can be mapped to a tangent vector to $\mathbb{R}^3$ at the point $f(s)$ by the derivative map $df_s = df_{s,i}$ whose components in the above basis are $f_i = (f_1, f_2) = (f_{u_1}, f_{u_2}) = (f_u, f_v)$. The inner product of two tangent vectors to D at s can then be defined to be the inner product of the corresponding tangent vectors to $\mathbb{R}^3$ at $f(s)$; effectively, we use Equation (A.2) to *define* its left hand side. An inner product can therefore be defined at each point of D, i.e., we have defined a Riemannian metric. This metric is called the **induced** or **pullback** metric.

If we express this inner product in the coordinate basis ∂_i, we find the metric components in this basis. They are given by

$$g_{ij} = \begin{pmatrix} g_{11} & g_{12} \\ g_{12} & g_{22} \end{pmatrix} = \langle f_i, f_j \rangle = \begin{pmatrix} \langle f_u, f_u \rangle & \langle f_u, f_v \rangle \\ \langle f_v, f_u \rangle & \langle f_v, f_v \rangle \end{pmatrix} = (\langle df_s, df_s \rangle)_{ij} .$$

The Riemannian metric g is also called the **first fundamental form** of f.

The square-root of the determinant of g, $\sqrt{\det(g)}$, often notated $\sqrt{g}$ or $|g|^{\frac{1}{2}}$, is the density, with respect to the measure $du\,dv$, of the **induced area measure** on D, also notated r. It measures area on the embedded surface. Note that the norm of the unnormalized normal vector, n, is given by $|n| = r = |g|^{\frac{1}{2}}$.

Definition B.4 Gauss map.   Earlier, we saw that an embedding, or more generally an immersion, has a unit normal vector field $\hat{n}$. When $D = \mathbb{S}^2$, this is a map from $\mathbb{S}^2$ to itself; it is called the **Gauss map**.

The differential of the Gauss map is a (self-adjoint) linear mapping $d\hat{n}_s : T_s(\mathbb{S}^2) \to T_{\hat{n}(s)}(\mathbb{S}^2)$. Since ∂_u, ∂_v forms a basis for the tangent space $T_s(\mathbb{S}^2)$, this linear mapping is completely specified by its evaluation on the basis elements:

$$d\hat{n}_s(\partial_u) = \partial_u \hat{n}_s$$
$$d\hat{n}_s(\partial_v) = \partial_v \hat{n}_s .$$

In other words, any arbitrary element $c_1\partial_u + c_2\partial_v$ of $T_s(\mathbb{S}^2)$ is mapped under $d\hat{n}_s$ to $c_1\partial_u\hat{n}_s + c_2\partial_u\hat{n}_s$.

This differential of the Gauss map at s is useful in characterizing the shape of a small patch at the point $f(s)$ as follows.

Definition B.5 Second fundamental form.   Using the differential of the Gauss map, one can define the **second fundamental form** of a surface f as a quadratic form: $L : T_s(\mathbb{S}^2) \to \mathbb{R}$ given by $L(v) = \langle d\hat{n}_s(v), df_s(v) \rangle$.

Alternatively, it can also be specified using the second derivatives of the embedding f. The second fundamental form of f at a point p can be written as a 2×2 matrix:

$$\Pi = \begin{pmatrix} \Pi_{11} & \Pi_{12} \\ \Pi_{12} & \Pi_{22} \end{pmatrix} , \tag{B.1}$$

where $\Pi_{ij} = \langle \partial_i \partial_j f, \hat{n} \rangle$.

A physical interpretation of these variables is that the graph of the surface can be approximated locally around $(u, v) = (0, 0)$ up to second order using:

$$f(u, v) \approx f(0, 0) + \frac{1}{2} \sum_{ij} u_i \Pi_{ij} u_j . \tag{B.2}$$

Definition B.6   Curvature.   One aspect of the shape of f at a point $f(s)$ is its curvature. There are several ways of capturing this local curvature. One of them is the *extrinsic curvature*, also known as the *shape operator*. At a point $f(s) \in S$, this operator is a 2×2 matrix given by:

$$L = g^{-1}\Pi .$$

(B.3)

The eigenvalues of L provide measures of the curvature of f. The Gaussian curvature of S at $f(s)$ is the product of the eigenvalues, or the determinant of L:

$$K = \det(L) = \frac{\det(\Pi)}{\det(g)} .$$

(B.4)

Similarly, the average of the eigenvalues of L provides the mean curvature of f at s:

$$K_m = \frac{1}{2}\mathrm{tr}L .$$

(B.5)

The curvature descriptors are invariant to the parameterization of S. This is an important property for shape analysis, as discussed in Chapter 2.

APPENDIX C

Spherical Parametrization of Triangulated Meshes

Often, the boundary f of a 3D object is represented as a piecewise linear surface in the form of a triangulated mesh M, i.e., a set of vertices $P = \{p_1, \cdots, p_n\}$ and triangles $\mathcal{T} = \{T_1, \cdots, T_m\}$ such that the triangles intersect only at common vertices or edges [Floater and Hormann, 2005]. Such a representation is suitable for rendering and visualization. Shape analysis tasks, such as the ones discussed in this book, require parameterized surfaces that are represented as an embedding of a domain D in $\mathbb{R}^3$. The goal of parameterization is to find a suitable continuous domain D, referred to as *the parameterization domain*, and then estimate the underlying continuous surface $f : D \to \mathbb{R}^3$. If M is a disk-like surface, then D can be chosen as a simply-connected region of the plane, e.g., the unit disk. When dealing with closed genus-0 surfaces then the unit sphere $\mathbb{S}^2$ is the natural parameterization domain. In what follows, we will discuss a few methods that have been used in the literature for parameterizing closed genus-0 surfaces. Thus, we have $D = \mathbb{S}^2$. These methods are referred to as *spherical parameterization* methods.

Spherical parameterization is performed in a two-step process: first, find a continuous mapping $\Phi : M \to \mathbb{S}^2$ that is uniquely determined by the images $\Phi(p_i) \in \mathbb{S}^2$ where $p_i \in P$ are the vertices of the triangulated mesh M. Next, for each point $s = (u, v) \in \mathbb{S}^2$, estimate its corresponding surface point $p = f(s) = \Phi^{-1}(s)$, which is uniquely determined by the vertices $p_i, p_j, p_k \in P$ of a triangle $T \in \mathcal{T}$ such that the polygon formed by $\Phi(p_i), \Phi(p_j)$, and $\Phi(p_k)$ encloses p.

Spherical parameterization proves to be very challenging in practice. First, parameterization algorithms should be robust, preventing parametric foldovers and thus guaranteeing one-to-one spherical maps. The second challenge is to create parameterizations that adequately sample all surface regions with minimum distortion. This is particularly difficult since genus-0 surfaces can contain complex parts that are highly deformed. A good parameterization is a one-to-one map that minimizes these distortions in some sense [Floater and Hormann, 2005]. Many approaches for achieving this have been proposed in the literature. In this Appendix, we will discuss three methods that are commonly used in the literature.

The first one, which is simple and fast, is the *Gauss map* (see Definition B.4). It maps every point of M onto its unit normal vector at that point. Naturally, this mapping is one-to-one only in the case of star-shaped surfaces. By a star-shaped surface we mean a surface f that, up to a translation, can be written in the form $f(u, v) = \rho(u, v)n(u, v)$, where $\rho(u, v) \in \mathbb{R}_{\geq 0}$, and $n(u, v) \in \mathbb{S}^2$ is the unit normal vector in $\mathbb{R}^3$ given in Euclidean coordinates by $n(u, v) = (\cos(u)\sin(v), \sin(u)\sin(v), \cos(v))$.

The second one, called *conformal spherical mapping*, has nice mathematical properties but in practice, it is only suitable for blobby surfaces (e.g., anatomical organs) since it introduces large distortions for surfaces that contain complex elongated parts (e.g., human shapes). The last method uses a coarse-to-fine strategy to optimize a stretch-based metric. It is robust and adequately samples all surface regions. All results presented in this book have been obtained using this parameterization method. Below we discuss the last two methods since the first one is straightforward.

C.1   CONFORMAL SPHERICAL MAPPING

We will first review some definitions and then lay down the conformal spherical parameterization algorithm.

Definition C.1   Conformal mapping.   A mapping $\Phi : M \rightarrow \mathbb{S}^2$ is conformal, or angle-preserving, if the angle of intersection of every pair of intersecting arcs on $\mathbb{S}^2$ is the same as that of the corresponding pre-images on M at the corresponding point.

Definition C.2   String energy.   The string energy of a mapping $\Phi : M \rightarrow \mathbb{S}^2$ is defined as:

$$E(\Phi) = \sum_{e_{ij}=(p_i,p_j)\in K} w_{ij}\|\Phi(p_i) - \Phi(p_j)\|^2, \tag{C.1}$$

where p_i and p_j are vertices of M, and K is the set of edges $e_{ij} = (p_i, p_j)$.

When $w_{ij} = 1$ for every edge e_{ij}, then the String energy is known as the *Tuette* energy. The Tuette mapping is the mapping that minimizes the Tuette energy obtained by setting the weights of Equation (C.1) to one.

Definition C.3   Harmonic energy.   Harmonic energy is a special case of the string energy where the weights w_{ij} are constructed using the cotangent of the angles α_{ij} and β_{ij} opposite to the edge e_{ij} (see Figure C.1):

$$w_{ij} = \cot \alpha_{ij} + \cot \beta_{ij}. \tag{C.2}$$

A mapping Φ with zero harmonic energy is called a *harmonic mapping*. Geometrically, Φ is harmonic if at each point $p \in M$, the Laplace-Beltrami vector $\Delta_M \Phi(p)$ is perpendicular to the tangent plane of $\mathbb{S}^2$ at $\Phi(p)$ [Floater and Hormann, 2005]. In other words, the tangential component of the Laplace-Beltrami vector field $\Delta_M \Phi$ vanishes.

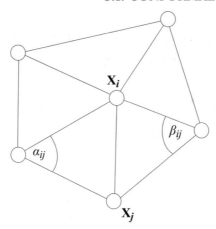

Figure C.1: The angles used for computing the weights of the harmonic energy of Equation (C.2).

An important key observation made by Gu et al. [2004] is that in the case of closed sphere-like (i.e., genus-0) surfaces, harmonic mapping and conformal mapping are the same. Gu et al. [2004] used this property and proposed an iterative method, which builds an approximate conformal map of closed genus-0 surfaces without splitting or cutting the surfaces. The algorithm, summarized in Algorithm C.1, starts with an initial mapping Φ_0, and iteratively updates it using a gradient descent-like approach. At each iteration, the estimated map Φ is updated by subtracting a proportion δ_t of the tangential component, $D\Phi$, of its Laplacian, hereinafter referred to as the absolute derivative and defined as follows:

$$D\Phi(p) = \Delta\Phi(p) - \langle \Delta\Phi(p), \hat{n}(\Phi(p)) \rangle \, \hat{n}(\Phi(p)), \qquad (C.3)$$

where $\hat{n}(\Phi(p))$ is the unit normal vector to $\mathbb{S}^2$ at $\Phi(p)$. δ_t is referred to as the step size. Gu et al. [2004] also enforces an additional zero-mass condition to improve the convergence and to ensure the uniqueness of the solution.

The speed of convergence of Algorithm C.1 depends on the initial map Φ_0 and on the step size δ_t. Gu et al. [2004] showed that by carefully choosing the step size, the energy can be decreased monotonically at each iteration. For the initial map Φ_0, one can use the Gauss map Φ_N or a Tuette map. The former will require more iterations for the conformal mapping algorithm to converge. Since conformal mapping iterations are computationally expensive, initializing the algorithm with a Tuette map would significantly reduce the computation time. Algorithm C.2 details the Tuette mapping algorithm. Note that the Tuette algorithm converges rapidly, and more importantly, it has a unique minimum.

Algorithm C.1 Spherical conformal mapping.

Input: Triangulated mesh M, step size δt, and energy difference threshold δE.

Output: A mapping $\Phi : M \to \mathbb{S}^2$ that minimizes the harmonic energy and satisfies the zero-mass center constraint.

1: Compute Tuette map $\Phi_t : M \to \mathbb{S}^2$.
2: Let $\Phi = \Phi_t$. Compute the harmonic energy E_0.
3: For each vertex p of M, compute the absolute derivative $D\Phi(p)$.
4: Update $\Phi(p)$ with $\delta\Phi(p) = -D\Phi(p)\delta_t$.
5: Ensure that Φ satisfies the zero-mass condition:

  • Compute the mass center $c = \int_{\mathbb{S}^2} \Phi(s)ds$, where $ds = d\phi d\theta \sin(\theta)$ is the standard Lebesgue norm on $\mathbb{S}^2$.

  • For all $p \in M$, $\Phi(p) = \Phi(p) - c$.

  • For all $p \in M$, $\Phi(p) = \Phi(p)/\|\Phi(p)\|$.

6: Compute the harmonic energy E.
7: If $\|E - E_0\| < \delta E$, return Φ. Otherwise assign E to E_0 and repeat Step 3–Step 7.

Algorithm C.2 Tuette mapping.

Input: Triangulated mesh M, step size δt, and energy difference threshold δE.

Output: A mapping $\Phi : M \to \mathbb{S}^2$ that minimizes the Tuette energy.

1: Compute Gauss map $\Phi_N : M \to \mathbb{S}^2$.
2: Let $\Phi = \Phi_N$. Compute the Tuette energy E_0.
3: For each vertex p of M, compute the absolute derivative $D\Phi(p)$.
4: Update $\Phi(p)$ with $\delta\Phi(p) = -D\Phi(p)\delta_t$.
5: Compute the Tuette energy E.
6: If $\|E - E_0\| < \delta E$, return Φ. Otherwise assign E to E_0 and repeat Steps 3–6.

C.2 COARSE-TO-FINE MINIMAL STRETCH EMBEDDING

In practice, genus-0 surfaces, which are essentially deformed spheres, can be highly complex. Conformal spherical mapping algorithms undersample highly deformed regions. Praun and Hoppe [2003] introduced an algorithm that achieves robustness using a coarse-to-fine optimization strategy, and penalizes undersampling using a stretch-based parametrization metric. The metric measures how distances in the domain get scaled onto the surface. Large stretch in any direction around a surface point implies that the reconstruction of the surface signal from a domain-uniform sampling will lose high-frequency surface details [Praun and Hoppe, 2003].

Let $\Phi : M \rightarrow \mathbb{S}^2$ be a mapping from the surface of a triangulated mesh M onto the unit sphere. Let J_Φ denote the Jacobian of Φ with λ_1 and λ_2 its eigenvalues. The stretch over a triangle T of M is defined as

$$(L^2(T))^2 = \frac{1}{A_{M_T}} \iint_{(s,t) \in T} \left(\frac{1}{\lambda_1^2} + \frac{1}{\lambda_2^2} \right) dA_{M_T}(s,t) + \epsilon \left(\frac{A_M}{4\pi} \right)^{\frac{p}{2}+1} \lambda_1^p. \qquad (C.4)$$

Here (s,t) is a local orthonormal coordinate frame on a triangle T of M, A_{M_T} denotes the area of T, and $dA_{M_T}(s,t)$ the differential mesh triangle area. The second term of Equation (C.4) is a small regularization term introduced to avoid oversampling when $\lambda_1 \ll \lambda_2$. Experimentally, Praun and Hoppe [2003] found that $\epsilon = 0.0001$ and $p = 6$ provide good results for many complex genus-0 surfaces.

Praun and Hoppe [2003] proposed a robust algorithm for creating a spherical map that minimizes the stretch energy of Equation (C.4) using a coarse-to-fine strategy. The idea is to create a multiresolution mesh, embed first the base mesh, i.e., the one with lowest resolution, and then progressively insert new vertices while optimizing their position on the sphere. Below we detail each step of the algorithm.

- **Coarse-to-fine strategy.** The first step is to simplify the input triangulated mesh M to a tetrahedron while creating a progressive mesh. The algorithm starts by mapping the base tetrahedron to the sphere. The progressive mesh is then traversed, inserting vertices on the sphere while maintaining an embedding, by avoiding foldovers, and minimizing the stretch metric.

- **Vertex insertion.** Each vertex split in the progressive mesh specifies a ring of vertices that will be the neighbors of the new vertex. This vertex ring forms a spherical polygon. The kernel of this spherical polygon is defined as the intersection of the open hemispheres defined by the polygon edges. To maintain an embedding (i.e., avoid flipped or degenerate triangles), a new vertex is always inserted inside this kernel. Note that if the mapping is an embedding prior to the vertex insertion, the kernel cannot be empty.

- **Vertex position optimization.** After inserting a new vertex, the positions of the vertices in the neighborhood of the inserted vertex are optimized one at a time. The optimization is performed by minimizing the stretch metric of Equation (C.4) summed on its adjacent triangles. This is done using great-circle searches in random directions on the sphere, using bracketed parabolic minimization. To prevent flipping, a vertex is only perturbed within the kernel of its 1-ring. Note that degenerate triangles are avoided since they have infinite stretch energy. Each time the number of vertices has increased by a constant factor, the algorithm sweeps through all mesh vertices and optimizes each one at a time.

- **Stopping criterion.** The algorithm stops when the largest change in the vertex positions on the sphere is below a predefined threshold.

We refer the reader to Praun and Hoppe [2003] for more details. All of the spherically parame-terized surfaces used in this book have been obtained using this algorithm. Note that for simple blobby surfaces, such as the ones that are commonly used in medical imaging, one can use spher-ical conformal or Gauss maps. For more general surfaces, such as the ones used in this book, the algorithm of Praun and Hoppe [2003] results in less distortion and thus better preserves the surface details.

In terms of computation time, the parameterization of a mesh with 15 K vertices takes less than 5 m on a 3.06 GHz Intel Core 2 Duo with 8 GB memory and running Windows. All of the parameterization code is written in C++ running entirely on a CPU.

APPENDIX D

Landmark Detection

We consider the problem of detecting and matching landmarks on certain types of objects. In what follows, we assume that the surfaces being analyzed have been normalized for translation and scale. Thus, they are elements of the preshape space $\mathcal{C}_f$.

D.1 LANDMARK DETECTION USING HEAT KERNEL SIGNATURES

We are particularly interested in landmark points that correspond to extremal features of high curvature such as the tips of protruding parts in a human shape or a carpal bone. Such landmarks are often stable across different poses of a shape. They can be obtained in various ways, depending on the application at hand and on the type of 3D models being analyzed. In medical applications, for example, they are often manually marked and annotated by professionals or medical practitioners. For general 3D objects such as human shapes and other natural objects that are commonly used in graphics applications, (semi-)automatic techniques can be used to assist in the detection and matching process. In particular, one can use the Heat Kernel Signature (HKS) [Sun et al., 2009] to detect landmarks that correspond to tips of protrusions of the shapes.

The HKS at a point s on a surface $f \in \mathcal{C}_f$ is a multi-scale descriptor defined with respect to a time parameter τ as follows:

$$h(s) = (h_\tau(s, s), \tau \in [\tau_0, \tau_1]), \text{ where } h_\tau(s_1, s_2) = \sum_{i=0}^{K} e^{-\lambda_i \tau} \Phi_i(s_1) \Phi_i(s_2)$$

is the heat kernel associated with the positive-semidefinite Laplace-Beltrami operator Δ_f of the surface f, and λ and Φ are the eigenvalues and eigenfunctions of Δ_f, respectively. For small values of τ, the function $h_\tau(s, \cdot)$ is mainly determined by a small neighborhood around s. Thus, it only reflects local properties of the shape around s. This neighborhood grows bigger as τ increases. Sun et al. [2009] showed that for small τ, $h_\tau(s, \cdot)$ is directly related to the Gaussian curvature of a surface. The local maxima of the HKS function for a large time parameter correspond to stable feature points of interest.

In what follows, for a given surface $f_i \in \mathcal{C}_f$, the locations of the detected landmarks on f_i are denoted by $\{f_i(s_1^i), \cdots, f_i(s_m^i)\}$. Their corresponding locations on $\mathbb{S}^2$ under the current parameterization are $\{s_1^i, \cdots, s_m^i\}$.

D.2   LANDMARK CORRESPONDENCES

When given two surfaces f_1, $f_2 \in C_f$ that undergo nearly isometric deformations, one can use HKS to detect landmarks and then use Möbius voting [Lipman and Funkhouser, 2009] to put the detected landmarks in correspondence. This procedure is performed as follows. For each landmark on the source surface f_1, we find $k = 3$ candidate correspondences from the landmarks detected on the target surface f_2 by matching their Heat Kernel Signatures. These are then used as input to a Möbius voting procedure that produces a fuzzy correspondence matrix $C = (C_{k,l})$ where $C_{k,l}$ indicates the confidence of the k-th landmark on f_1 being in correspondence with the l-th landmark on f_2. The following algorithm provides more details.

- Sample one random triplet from the landmarks on f_1 and another from the landmarks on f_2. Let (s_1^i, s_2^i, s_3^i) be these triplets, with $i = 1$, 2. The triplets on the target surface are chosen from the $k = 3$ candidate correspondences of the landmarks on f_1.

- The sampled pair of triplet points defines a Möbius transform, denoted by ψ_m, that aligns these points, i.e., ψ_m transforms s_k^2 into $\psi_m(s_k^2) = s_k^1, k = 1$, 2, 3, and transforms all of the other surface points into a common domain.

- We then compute an alignment error, which measures how well mutually close landmarks align in that domain. The inverse of the alignment error can be interpreted as the confidence of the k-th landmark on f_1 being in correspondence with the l-th landmark on f_2.

- This process is repeated a certain number of iterations and the correspondence confidences are accumulated in a fuzzy correspondence matrix C.

- Finally, the fuzzy correspondence matrix C is processed to produce a discrete set of correspondences with high confidence. This step is a standard assignment problem, which can be efficiently solved using the Hungarian algorithm [Kuhn, 1955].

Let $\tilde{s}_k^2 = \psi_m(s_k^2)$ and let s_j^1 be the closest landmark to $\tilde{s}_k^2$ in terms of arc-length distance on $\mathbb{S}^2$. Then, the alignment error E can be measured as the length of the shortest arc on $\mathbb{S}^2$ that connects $\tilde{s}_k^2$ to s_j^1. For each Möbius transform, we update the confidence matrix by adding the quantity $1/(\epsilon + E/n)$ to the entries $C_{k,l}$, where k, l are the computed pairs of correspondences, n here is the number of computed pairs of correspondences, and ϵ is some small number.

For more details about this procedure, we refer the reader to the paper by Lipman and Funkhouser [2009]. Figure 6.1 shows examples of landmarks automatically detected and matched across complex surfaces that undergo nearly isometric motion. In these examples, the HKS are computed after normalizing the shapes to have unit surface area and use the uniform value of $\tau = 0.1$ across all shapes. In a final post-processing step, we filter the detected features by keeping one feature point in a neighborhood of size $r = 0.1\delta$ where δ is the length of the longest geodesic on the surface f.

It is important to point out that this procedure is suitable for matching landmarks on surfaces that undergo nearly isometric deformations. When the shapes undergo elastic deformations or contain missing parts, the isometry assumption is no longer valid and both the HKS signatures as well as the Möbius voting procedure do not provide reliable correspondences. In these cases, while the landmarks can be automatically detected, the correspondences have to be manually specified.

Bibliography

Kinetsu Abe and Joseph Erbacher. Isometric immersions with the same Gauss map. *Mathematische Annalen*, 215(3):197–201, 1975. DOI: 10.1007/bf01343889. 30, 35

Dror Aiger, Niloy J. Mitra, and Daniel Cohen-Or. 4-points congruent sets for robust pairwise surface registration. *ACM Transactions on Graphics*, 27(3):85:1–85:10, 2008. DOI: 10.1145/1360612.1360684. 8

Ibraheem Alhashim, Kai Xu, Yixin Zhuang, Junjie Cao, Patricio Simari, and Hao Zhang. Deformation-driven topology-varying 3D shape correspondence. *ACM Transactions on Graphics*, 34(6):236:1–236:13, 2015. DOI: 10.1145/2816795.2818088. 9

Brett Allen, Brian Curless, and Zoran Popović. Articulated body deformation from range scan data. *ACM Transactions on Graphics*, 21(3):612–619, 2002. DOI: 10.1145/566654.566626. 113

Brett Allen, Brian Curless, and Zoran Popović. The space of human body shapes: Reconstruction and parameterization from range scans. *ACM Transactions on Graphics*, 22(3):587–594, 2003. DOI: 10.1145/882262.882311. 113

Brett Allen, Brian Curless, Zoran Popović, and Aaron Hertzmann. Learning a correlated model of identity and pose-dependent body shape variation for real-time synthesis. In *ACM SIGGRAPH/Eurographics Symposium on Computer Animation*, pages 147–156, 2006. 113

Brian Amberg, Sami Romdhani, and Thomas Vetter. Optimal step nonrigid ICP algorithms for surface registration. In *IEEE Conference on Computer Vision and Pattern Recognition*, pages 1–8, 2007. DOI: 10.1109/cvpr.2007.383165. 9

Dragomir Anguelov, Praveen Srinivasan, Daphne Koller, Sebastian Thrun, Jim Rodgers, and James Davis. SCAPE: Shape completion and animation of people. *ACM Transactions on Graphics*, 24(3):408–416, 2005. DOI: 10.1145/1073204.1073207. 113

Vladimir Arnold. Ten problems. *Advances in Soviet Mathematics*, 1:1–8, 1990. 35

Vladimir Arnold. *Arnold's Problems*. Springer Berlin Heidelberg, 2004. DOI: 10.1007/b138219. 35

Imon Banerjee, Hamid Laga, Giuseppe Patanè, Sebastian Kurtek, Anuj Srivastava, and Michela Spagnuolo. Generation of 3D canonical anatomical models: An experience on carpal bones.

In *International Conference on Image Analysis and Processing*, pages 167–174, 2015. DOI: 10.1007/978-3-319-23222-5_21. 127

Martin Bauer, Martins Bruveris, and Peter W. Michor. Uniqueness of the Fisher-Rao metric on the space of smooth densities. *Bulletin of the London Mathematical Society*, 48(3):499–506, 2016. DOI: 10.1112/blms/bdw020. 24

Benjamin Berkels, Tom Fletcher, Behrend Heeren, Martin Rumpf, and Benedikt Wirth. Discrete geodesic regression in shape space. In *International Conference on Energy Minimization Methods in Computer Vision and Pattern Recognition*, 2013. DOI: 10.1007/978-3-642-40395-8_9. 114

Paul J. Besl and Neil D. McKay. A method for registration of 3D shapes. *IEEE Transactions on Pattern Analysis and Machine Intelligence*, 14(2):239–256, 1992. DOI: 10.1109/34.121791. 8, 92, 99, 113

Volker Blanz and Thomas Vetter. A morphable model for the synthesis of 3D faces. In *SIG-GRAPH*, pages 187–194, 1999. DOI: 10.1145/311535.311556. 7, 8

William M. Boothby. *An Introduction to Differentiable Manifolds and Riemannian Geometry*. Academic Press, 1975. DOI: 10.1016/s0079-8169(08)x6065-9. 62

Sylvain Bouix, Jens C. Pruessner, Donald L. Collins, and Kaleem Siddiqi. Hippocampal shape analysis using medial surfaces. *NeuroImage*, 25(4):1077–1089, 2005. DOI: 10.1016/j.neuroimage.2004.12.051. 7

Christian Brechbühler, Guido Gerig, and Olaf Kübler. Parametrization of closed surfaces for 3D shape description. *Computer Vision and Image Understanding*, 61(2):154–170, 1995. DOI: 10.1006/cviu.1995.1013. 8

Alexander M. Bronstein, Michael M. Bronstein, and Ron Kimmel. *Numerical Geometry of Non-rigid Shapes*. Springer Science and Business Media, 2008. DOI: 10.1007/978-0-387-73301-2. 114, 124, 128

Alexander M. Bronstein, Michael M. Bronstein, and Ron Kimmel. Topology-invariant similarity of nonrigid shapes. *International Journal of Computer Vision*, 81(3):281–301, 2009. DOI: 10.1007/s11263-008-0172-2. 7

Alexander M. Bronstein, Michael M. Bronstein, Ron Kimmel, Mona Mahmoudi, and Guillermo Sapiro. A Gromov-Hausdorff framework with diffusion geometry for topologically-robust non-rigid shape matching. *International Journal of Computer Vision*, 89(2–3):266–286, September 2010. DOI: 10.1007/s11263-009-0301-6. 7

Matthew J. Burden, Joseph L. Jacobson, Alissa Westerlund, Leslie H. Lundahl, Audrey Morrison, Neil C. Dodge, Rafael Klorman, Charles A. Nelson, Malcolm J. Avison, and Sandra W. Jacobson. An event-related potential study of response inhibition in ADHD with and without prenatal alcohol exposure. *Alcoholism: Clinical and Experimental Research*, 34(4):617–627, 2010. DOI: 10.1111/j.1530-0277.2009.01130.x. 114

Will Chang and Matthias Zwicker. Automatic registration for articulated shapes. *Computer Graphics Forum*, 27(5):1459–1468, 2008. DOI: 10.1111/j.1467-8659.2008.01286.x. 9

Chu-Song Chen, Yi-Ping Hung, and Jen-Bo Cheng. RANSAC-based DARCES: A new approach to fast automatic registration of partially overlapping range images. *IEEE Transactions on Pattern Analysis and Machine Intelligence*, 21(11):1229–1234, 1999. DOI: 10.1109/34.809117. 8

Yang Chen and Gérard Medioni. Object modelling by registration of multiple range images. *Image and Vision Computing*, 10(3):145–155, 1992. DOI: 10.1016/0262-8856(92)90066-c. 8

Brian Clarke. The metric geometry of the manifold of Riemannian metrics over a closed manifold. *Calculus of Variations and Partial Differential Equations*, 39(3–4):533–545, 2010. DOI: 10.1007/s00526-010-0323-5. 28

Timothy F. Cootes, Christopher J. Taylor, David H. Cooper, and Jm Graham. Active shape models-their training and application. *Computer Vision and Image Understanding*, 61(1):38–59, 1995. DOI: 10.1006/cviu.1995.1004. 7, 8

Bryce S. DeWitt. Quantum theory of gravity. I. The canonical theory. *Physical Review*, 160(5):1113–1148, 1967. DOI: 10.1103/physrev.171.1834.2. 27

Ian L. Dryden and Kanti V. Mardia. *Statistical Shape Analysis*. John Wiley & Sons, 1998. 7, 82, 95, 127

David G. Ebin. On the space of Riemannian metrics. *Bulletin of the American Mathematical Society*, 74(5):1001–1003, 1968. DOI: 10.1090/s0002-9904-1968-12115-9. 28

Jost-Hinrich Eschenburg, B. S. Kruglikov, Vladimir S. Matveev, and Renato Tribuzy. Compatibility of Gauss maps with metrics. *Differential Geometry and its Applications*, 28(2):228–235, 2010. DOI: 10.1016/j.difgeo.2009.10.004. 35

Michael S. Floater and Kai Hormann. Surface parameterization: A tutorial and survey. In *Advances in Multiresolution for Geometric Modelling*, pages 157–186, 2005. DOI: 10.1007/3-540-26808-1_9. 145, 146

Oren Freifeld and Michael J. Black. Lie bodies: A manifold representation of 3D human shape. In *European Conference on Computer Vision*, pages 1–14, 2012. DOI: 10.1007/978-3-642-33718-5_1. 114

Olga Gil-Medrano and Peter W. Michor. The Riemannian manifold of all Riemannian metrics. *Quarterly Journal of Mathematics*, 42:183–202, 1991. DOI: 10.1093/qmath/42.1.183. 28

Daniela Giorgi, Silvia Biasotti, and Laura Paraboschi. Shape retrieval contest 2007: Watertight models track. *SHREC Competition*, 8, 2007. 10, 43, 91, 94, 114, 128

Joan Glaunès, Marc Vaillant, and Michael I. Miller. Landmark matching via large deformation diffeomorphisms on the sphere. *Journal of Mathematical Imaging and Vision*, 20(1–2):179–200, 2004. DOI: 10.1023/B:JMIV.0000011323.32914.f3. 118, 119, 127

Kevin Gorczowski, Martin Styner, Ja Yeon Jeong, J. S. Marron, Joseph Piven, Heather C. Hazlett, Stephen M. Pizer, and Guido Gerig. Multi-object analysis of volume, pose, and shape using statistical discrimination. *IEEE Transactions on Pattern Analysis and Machine Intelligence*, 32(4):652–661, 2010. DOI: 10.1109/tpami.2009.92. 7

John C. Gower and Garmt B. Dijksterhuis. *Procrustes Problems*, volume 3. Oxford University Press Oxford, 2004. DOI: 10.1093/acprof:oso/9780198510581.001.0001. 8

Xianfeng Gu, Yalin Wang, Tony F. Chan, Paul M. Thompson, and Shing-Tung Yau. Genus zero surface conformal mapping and its application to brain surface mapping. *IEEE Transactions on Medical Imaging*, 23(8):949–958, 2004. DOI: 10.1109/tmi.2004.831226. 147

Yulan Guo, Mohammed Bennamoun, Ferdous Sohel, Min Lu, Jianwei Wan, and Ngai Ming Kwok. A comprehensive performance evaluation of 3D local feature descriptors. *International Journal of Computer Vision*, 116(1):66–89, 2016. DOI: 10.1007/s11263-015-0824-y. 128

Nils Hasler, Carsten Stoll, Bodo Rosenhahn, Thorsten Thormählen, and Hans-Peter Seidel. Estimating body shape of dressed humans. *Computers and Graphics*, 33(3):211–216, 2009a. DOI: 10.1016/j.cag.2009.03.026. 10

Nils Hasler, Carsten Stoll, Martin Sunkel, Bodo Rosenhahn, and H.-P. Seidel. A statistical model of human pose and body shape. *Computer Graphics Forum*, 28(2):337–346, 2009b. DOI: 10.1111/j.1467-8659.2009.01373.x. 100, 114

Behrend Heeren, Martin Rumpf, Max Wardetzky, and Benedikt Wirth. Time-discrete geodesics in the space of shells. *Computer Graphics Forum*, 31(5):1755–1764, 2012. DOI: 10.1111/j.1467-8659.2012.03180.x. 114, 128

Behrend Heeren, Martin Rumpf, Peter Schröder, Max Wardetzky, and Benedikt Wirth. Exploring the geometry of the space of shells. *Computer Graphics Forum*, 33(5):247–256, 2014. DOI: 10.1111/cgf.12450. 114

David A. Hoffman and Robert Osserman. The Gauss map of surfaces in R3 and R4. *Proc. of the London Mathematical Society*, 3(1):27–56, 1985. DOI: 10.1112/plms/s3-50.1.27. 35

Sandra W. Jacobson, Joseph L. Jacobson, Robert J. Sokol, Lisa M. Chiodo, and Raluca Corobana. Maternal age, alcohol abuse history, and quality of parenting as moderators of the effects of prenatal alcohol exposure on 7.5-year intellectual function. *Alcoholism: Clinical and Experimental Research*, 28(11):1732–1745, 2004. DOI: 10.1097/01.alc.0000145691.81233.fa. 114

Ian H. Jermyn, Sebastian Kurtek, Eric Klassen, and Anuj Srivastava. Elastic shape matching of parameterized surfaces using square root normal fields. In *European Conference on Computer Vision*, pages 804–817, 2012. DOI: 10.1007/978-3-642-33715-4_58. 37, 46, 79

Shantanu H. Joshi, Eric Klassen, Anuj Srivastava, and Ian H. Jermyn. A novel representation for efficient computation of geodesics between *n*-dimensional curves. In *IEEE Conference on Computer Vision and Pattern Recognition*, 2007. 46

Michael Kazhdan, Thomas Funkhouser, and Szymon Rusinkiewicz. Rotation invariant spherical harmonic representation of 3D shape descriptors. In *Symposium on Geometry Processing*, volume 6, pages 156–164, 2003. 6

András Kelemen, Gábor Székely, and Guido Gerig. Elastic model-based segmentation of 3D neuroradiological data sets. *IEEE Transactions on Medical Imaging*, 18(10):828–839, 1999. DOI: 10.1109/42.811260. 99

David G. Kendall. The diffusion of shape. *Advances in Applied Probability*, 9(3):428–430, 1977. DOI: 10.2307/1426091. 6, 7, 50

David G. Kendall, Dennis Barden, T. K. Carne, and Huiling Le. *Shape and Shape Theory*. Wiley, 1999. DOI: 10.1002/9780470317006. 7, 95, 127

Martin Kilian, Niloy J. Mitra, and Helmut Pottmann. Geometric modeling in shape space. *ACM Transactions on Graphics*, 26(3), 2007. DOI: 10.1145/1239451.1239515. 114, 128

Vladimir G. Kim, Yaron Lipman, and Thomas Funkhouser. Blended intrinsic maps. *ACM Transactions on Graphics*, 30(4):79:1–79:12, 2011. DOI: 10.1145/2010324.1964974. 124, 125, 126, 128

Eric Klassen. Private communication, January 2011. 35

Eric Klassen and Anuj Srivastava. Geodesics between 3D closed curves using path-straightening. In *European Conference on Computer Vision*, pages 95–106, 2006. DOI: 10.1007/11744023_8. 79

Harold W. Kuhn. The Hungarian method for the assignment problem. *Naval Research Logistics Quarterly*, 2(1–2):83–97, 1955. DOI: 10.1002/nav.3800020109. 152

Sebastian Kurtek and Anuj Srivastava. Elastic symmetry analysis of anatomical structures. In *Mathematical Methods in Biomedical Image Analysis*, pages 33–38, 2012. DOI: 10.1109/mmbia.2012.6164739. 114

Sebastian Kurtek, Eric Klassen, Zhaohua Ding, and Anuj Srivastava. A novel Riemannain framework for shape analysis of 3D objects. In *IEEE Conference on Computer Vision and Pattern Recognition*, pages 1625–1632, 2010. DOI: 10.1109/cvpr.2010.5539778. 25, 46, 79, 95, 127

Sebastian Kurtek, Eric Klassen, Zhaohua Ding, Malcom J. Avison, and Anuj Srivastava. Parameterization-invariant shape statistics and probabilistic classification of anatomical surfaces. In *Information Processing in Medical Imaging*, volume 6801, pages 147–158, Springer, 2011a. DOI: 10.1007/978-3-642-22092-0_13. 46, 95, 114

Sebastian Kurtek, Eric Klassen, Zhaohua Ding, Sandra W. Jacobson, Joseph B. Jacobson, Malcolm J. Avison, and Anuj Srivastava. Parameterization-invariant shape comparisons of anatomical surfaces. *IEEE Transactions on Medical Imaging*, 30(3):849–858, 2011b. DOI: 10.1109/tmi.2010.2099130. 46, 55, 56, 79, 95, 114

Sebastian Kurtek, Eric Klassen, John C. Gore, Zhaohua Ding, and Anuj Srivastava. Elastic geodesic paths in shape space of parameterized surfaces. *IEEE Transactions on Pattern Analysis and Machine Intelligence*, 34(9):1717–1730, 2012a. DOI: 10.1109/tpami.2011.233. 46, 65, 79, 95, 114

Sebastian Kurtek, Anuj Srivastava, Eric Klassen, and Zhaohua Ding. Statistical modeling of curves using shapes and related features. *Journal of American Statistical Association*, 107(499):1152–1165, 2012b. DOI: 10.1080/01621459.2012.699770. 46, 95

Sebastian Kurtek, Anuj Srivastava, Eric Klassen, and Hamid Laga. Landmark-guided elastic shape analysis of spherically-parameterized surfaces. *Computer Graphics Forum*, 32:429–438, 2013. DOI: 10.1111/cgf.12063. 95, 114

Sebastian Kurtek, Hamid Laga, and Qian Xie. Elastic shape analysis of boundaries of planar objects with multiple components and arbitrary topologies. In *Asian Conference on Computer Vision*, pages 424–439, 2014. DOI: 10.1007/978-3-319-16808-1_29. 114

Sebastian Kurtek, Qian Xie, Chafik Samir, and Michel Canis. Statistical model for simulation of deformable elastic endometrial tissue shapes. *Neurocomputing*, 173(P1):36–41, 2016. DOI: 10.1016/j.neucom.2015.03.098. 46, 79

Hamid Laga and Masayuki Nakajima. Supervised learning of similarity measures for content-based 3D model retrieval. *Large-Scale Knowledge Resources*, pages 210–225, 2008. DOI: 10.1007/978-3-540-78159-2_20. 6

Hamid Laga, Hiroki Takahashi, and Masayuki Nakajima. Spherical wavelet descriptors for content-based 3D model retrieval. In *IEEE International Conference on Shape Modeling and Applications*, pages 15–25, 2006. DOI: 10.1109/smi.2006.39. 6

Hamid Laga, Masayuki Nakajima, and Kunihiro Chihara. Discriminative spherical wavelet features for content-based 3D model retrieval. *International Journal of Shape Modeling*, 13(1):51–72, 2007. DOI: 10.1142/s0218654307000944. 6

Hamid Laga, Sebastian Kurtek, Anuj Srivastava, Mahmood Golzarian, and Stanley J. Miklavcic. A Riemannian elastic metric for shape-based plant leaf classification. In *Digital Image Computing Techniques and Applications*, pages 1–7, 2012. DOI: 10.1109/dicta.2012.6411702. 9, 46

Hamid Laga, Sebastian Kurtek, Anuj Srivastava, and Stanley J. Miklavcic. Landmark-free statistical analysis of the shape of plant leaves. *Journal of Theoretical Biology*, 363:41–52, 2014. DOI: 10.1016/j.jtbi.2014.07.036. 10, 46

Hamid Laga, Qian Xie, Ian H. Jermyn, and Anuj Srivastava. Numerical inversion of SRNF maps for elastic shape analysis of genus-zero surfaces. *IEEE Transactions on Pattern Analysis and Machine Intelligence*, In Press, 2017. DOI: 10.1109/tpami.2016.2647596. 46, 79, 95, 114

Sayani Lahiri, Daniel Robinson, and Eric Klassen. Precise matching of PL curves in R^N in the square root velocity framework. *arXiv:1501.00577v1*, 2015. DOI: 10.4310/gic.2015.v2.n3.a1. 13

Guillaume Lavoué. Combination of bag-of-words descriptors for robust partial shape retrieval. *The Visual Computer*, 28(9):931–942, 2012. DOI: 10.1007/s00371-012-0724-x. 95

Huiling Le. Locating Frèchet means with application to shape spaces. *Advances in Applied Probability*, 33(2):324–338, 2001. DOI: 10.1017/s0001867800010818. 82

Huiling Le and David G. Kendall. The Riemannain structure of Euclidean shape spaces: A novel environment for statistics. *The Annals of Statistics*, 21(3):1225–1271, 1993. DOI: 10.1214/aos/1176349259. 7

Yaron Lipman and Thomas Funkhouser. Möbius voting for surface correspondence. *ACM Transactions on Graphics*, 28(3):72:1–72:12, 2009. DOI: 10.1145/1531326.1531378. 8, 124, 152

Yaron Lipman, Raif M. Rustamov, and Thomas A. Funkhouser. Biharmonic distance. *ACM Transactions on Graphics*, 29(3):27:1–27:11, 2010. DOI: 10.1145/1805964.1805971. 7

Matthew Loper, Naureen Mahmood, Javier Romero, Gerard Pons-Moll, and Michael J. Black. SMPL: A skinned multi-person linear model. *ACM Transactions on Graphics*, 34(6):248:1–248:16, 2015. DOI: 10.1145/2816795.2818013. 114

Marco Lorenzi, Nicholas Ayache, and Xavier Pennec. Schildś ladder for the parallel transport of deformations in time series of images. In *Information Processing in Medical Imaging*, pages 463–474, Springer, 2011. DOI: 10.1007/978-3-642-22092-0_38. 114

Nicolas Mellado, Dror Aiger, and Niloy J. Mitra. Super 4PCS fast global pointcloud registration via smart indexing. *Computer Graphics Forum*, 33(5):205–215, 2014. DOI: 10.1111/cgf.12446. 8

Peter Michor and Robert Bryant. Representing immersions from a surface into 3-space, 2013. https://mathoverflow.net/questions/128441/representing-immersions-from-a-surface-into-3-space 35

Washington Mio, Anuj Srivastava, and Shantanu H. Joshi. On shape of plane elastic curves. *International Journal of Computer Vision*, 73(3):307–324, 2007. DOI: 10.1007/s11263-006-9968-0. 46

Niloy J. Mitra, Mark Pauly, Michael Wand, and Duygu Ceylan. Symmetry in 3D geometry: Extraction and applications. In *Eurographics STARs*, 2012. DOI: 10.1111/cgf.12010. 109, 110, 114

Marcin Novotni and Reinhard Klein. 3D Zernike descriptors for content based shape retrieval. In *ACM Symposium on Solid Modeling and Applications*, pages 216–225, 2003. DOI: 10.1145/781636.781639. 6

Robert Osada, Thomas Funkhouser, Bernard Chazelle, and David Dobkin. Shape distributions. *ACM Transactions on Graphics*, 21(4):807–832, 2002. DOI: 10.1145/571647.571648. 6

Chavdar Papazov and Darius Burschka. Stochastic global optimization for robust point set registration. *Computer Vision and Image Understanding*, 115(12):1598–1609, 2011. DOI: 10.1016/j.cviu.2011.05.008. 8

Xavier Pennec and Marco Lorenzi. Which parallel transport for the statistical analysis of longitudinal deformations? In *Colloque GRETSI*, 2011. 28, 114

Gerard Pons-Moll, Javier Romero, Naureen Mahmood, and Michael J. Black. Dyna: A model of dynamic human shape in motion. *ACM Transactions on Graphics*, 34(4):120:1–120:14, 2015. DOI: 10.1145/2766993. 114

Emil Praun and Hugues Hoppe. Spherical parameterization and remeshing. *ACM Transactions on Graphics*, 22(3):340–349, 2003. DOI: 10.1145/882262.882274. 148, 149, 150

Emanuele Rodolà, Andrea Albarelli, Filippo Bergamasco, and Andrea Torsello. A scale independent selection process for 3D object recognition in cluttered scenes. *International Journal of Computer Vision*, 102(1–3): 129–145, 2013. DOI: 10.1007/s11263-012-0568-x. 8

Szymon Rusinkiewicz and Marc Levoy. Efficient variants of the ICP algorithm. In *International Conference on 3D Digital Imaging and Modeling*, pages 145–152, 2001. DOI: 10.1109/im.2001.924423. 8

Chafik Samir, Anuj Srivastava, Mohamed Daoudi, and Sebastian Kurtek. On analyzing symmetry of objects using elastic deformations. In *VISAPP*, pages 194–200, 2009. DOI: 10.5220/0001797201940200. 114

Chafik Samir, Sebastian Kurtek, Anuj Srivastava, and Michel Canis. Elastic shape analysis of cylindrical surfaces for 3D/2D registration in endometrial tissue characterization. *IEEE Transactions on Medical Imaging*, 33(5):1035–1043, 2014. DOI: 10.1109/tmi.2014.2300935. 46, 66, 79

Kaleem Siddiqi, Juan Zhang, Diego Macrini, Ali Shokoufandeh, Sylvain Bouix, and Sven Dickinson. Retrieving articulated 3D models using medial surfaces. *Machine Vision and Applications*, 19(4):261–275, 2008. DOI: 10.1007/s00138-007-0097-8. 7

Christopher Small. *The Statistical Theory of Shape*. Springer, 1996. DOI: 10.1007/978-1-4612-4032-7. 7, 95

Anuj Srivastava and Eric Klassen. *Functional and Shape Data Analysis*. Springer Series in Statistics, 2016. DOI: 10.1007/978-1-4939-4020-2. 46, 79, 95

Anuj Srivastava, Shantanu H. Joshi, Washington Mio, and Xiuwen Liu. Statistical shape analysis: Clustering, learning, and testing. *IEEE Transactions on Pattern Analysis and Machine Intelligence*, 27(4):590–602, 2005. DOI: 10.1109/tpami.2005.86. 95

Anuj Srivastava, Eric Klassen, Shantanu H. Joshi, and Ian H. Jermyn. Shape analysis of elastic curves in Euclidean spaces. *IEEE Transactions on Pattern Analysis and Machine Intelligence*, 33(7):1415–1428, 2011. DOI: 10.1109/tpami.2010.184. 9, 46, 95

Justin Strait, Sebastian Kurtek, Emily Bartha, and Steven N. MacEachern. Landmark-constrained elastic shape analysis of planar curves. *Journal of the American Statistical Association*, DOI: 10.1080/01621459.2016.1236726. 127

Martin Styner, Ipek Oguz, Shun Xu, Christian Brechbühler, Dimitrios Pantazis, James J. Levitt, Martha E. Shenton, and Guido Gerig. Framework for the statistical shape analysis of brain structures using SPHARM-PDM. *The Insight Journal*, 1071:242–250, 2006. 8, 99, 113

Jian Sun, Maks Ovsjanikov, and Leonidas Guibas. A concise and provably informative multi-scale signature based on heat diffusion. *Computer Graphics Forum*, 28(5):1383–1392, 2009. DOI: 10.1111/j.1467-8659.2009.01515.x. 128, 151

Hedi Tabia and Hamid Laga. Covariance-based descriptors for efficient 3D shape matching, retrieval and classification. *IEEE Transactions on Multimedia*, 17(9):1591–1603, 2015. DOI: 10.1109/tmm.2015.2457676. 6, 95

Hedi Tabia and Hamid Laga. Learning shape retrieval from different modalities. *Neurocomputing*, 253:24–33, 2017. DOI: 10.1016/j.neucom.2017.01.101. 98, 113

Hedi Tabia, Mohamed Daoudi, Jean-Philippe Vandeborre, and Olivier Colot. A new 3D-matching method of nonrigid and partially similar models using curve analysis. *IEEE Transactions on Pattern Analysis and Machine Intelligence*, 33(4):852–858, 2011. DOI: 10.1109/tpami.2010.202. 95

Hedi Tabia, Hamid Laga, David Picard, and Philippe-Henri Gosselin. Covariance descriptors for 3D shape matching and retrieval. In *IEEE Conference on Computer Vision and Pattern Recognition*, pages 4185–4192, 2014. DOI: 10.1109/cvpr.2014.533. 6, 95

Gary K. L. Tam, Zhi-Quan Cheng, Yu-Kun Lai, Frank C. Langbein, Yonghuai Liu, David Marshall, Ralph R. Martin, Xian-Fang Sun, and Paul L. Rosin. Registration of 3D point clouds and meshes: A survey from rigid to nonrigid. *IEEE Transactions on Visualization and Computer Graphics*, 19(7):1199–1217, 2013. DOI: 10.1109/tvcg.2012.310. 52

Alice Barbara Tumpach, Hassen Drira, Mohamed Daoudi, and Anuj Srivastava. Gauge invariant framework for shape analysis of surfaces. *IEEE Transactions on Pattern Analysis and Machine Intelligence*, 38(1):46–59, 2015. DOI: 10.1109/tpami.2015.2430319. 34

Oliver van Kaick, Hao Zhang, Ghassan Hamarneh, and Daniel Cohen-Or. A survey on shape correspondence. *Computer Graphics Forum*, 30(6):1681–1707, 2011. DOI: 10.1111/j.1467-8659.2011.01884.x. 52

Qian Xie, Sebastian Kurtek, Huiling Le, and Anuj Srivastava. Parallel transport of deformations in shape space of elastic surfaces. In *International Conference on Computer Vision*, 2013. DOI: 10.1109/iccv.2013.112. 34, 46, 79, 114

Qian Xie, Ian Jermyn, Sebastian Kurtek, and Anuj Srivastava. Numerical inversion of SRNFs for efficient elastic shape analysis of star-shaped objects. In *European Conference on Computer Vision*, pages 485–499, 2014. DOI: 10.1007/978-3-319-10602-1_32. 46, 95

Boon Thye Thomas Yeo, Wanmei Ou, and Polina Golland. On the construction of invertible filter banks on the 2-sphere. *IEEE Transactions on Image Processing*, 17(3):283–300, 2008. DOI: 10.1109/tip.2007.915550. 40

Li Yi, Hao Su, Xingwen Guo, and Leonidas Guibas. SyncSpecCNN: Synchronized spectral CNN for 3D shape segmentation. *arXiv:1612.00606*, 2016. 98, 113

Laurent Younes. Computable elastic distance between shapes. *SIAM Journal of Applied Mathematics*, 58(2):565–586, 1998. DOI: 10.1137/s0036139995287685. 46

Laurent Younes, Peter W. Michor, Jayant Shah, and David Mumford. A metric on shape space with explicit geodesics. *Matematica E Applicazioni*, 19(1):25–57, 2008a. DOI: 10.4171/rlm/506. 46

Laurent Younes, Anqi Qiu, Raimond L. Winslow, and Michael I. Miller. Transport of relational structures in groups of diffeomorphisms. *Journal of Mathematical Imaging and Vision*, 32(1):41–56, 2008b. DOI: 10.1007/s10851-008-0074-5. 114

Hao Zhang, Alla Sheffer, Daniel Cohen-Or, Quan Zhou, Oliver Van Kaick, and Andrea Tagliasacchi. Deformation-driven shape correspondence. *Computer Graphics Forum*, 27(5):1431–1439, 2008. DOI: 10.1111/j.1467-8659.2008.01283.x. 9

Authors' Biographies

IAN H. JERMYN

Ian H. Jermyn received a B.A. Honours degree (First Class) in Physics from Oxford University, and a Ph.D. in Theoretical Physics from the University of Manchester, UK. After working as a postdoc at the International Centre for Theoretical Physics in Trieste, Italy, he studied for and received a Ph.D. in Computer Vision from the Computer Science department of the Courant Institute of Mathematical Sciences at New York University. He then joined the Ariana research group at INRIA Sophia Antipolis, France, first as a postdoctoral researcher, and then as a Senior Research Scientist. Since September 2010, he has been Associate Professor (Reader) in Statistics in the Department of Mathematical Sciences at Durham University. His research concerns statistical geometry: the statistical modeling of shape and geometric structure, particularly using random fields with complex interactions and Riemannian geometry. This work is motivated by problems of shape and texture modelling in image processing, computer vision, and computer graphics. Using a Bayesian approach, it has been extensively applied to different types of images, including biological and remote sensing imagery. He is also interested in information geometry as applied to inference.

SEBASTIAN KURTEK

Sebastian Kurtek is currently an Assistant Professor in the Department of Statistics at The Ohio State University, which he joined in 2012. He received a B.S. degree in Mathematics from Tulane University in 2007, and M.S. and Ph.D. degrees in Biostatistics from Florida State University in 2009 and 2012, respectively. His main research interests include statistical shape analysis, functional data analysis, statistical image analysis, statistics on manifolds, medical imaging, and computational statistics. In particular, he is interested in the interplay between statistics and Riemannian geometry, and their role in developing solutions to various applied problems. He is a member of the American Statistical Association, Institute of Mathematical Statistics, and the IEEE.

HAMID LAGA

Hamid Laga received his Ph.D. degree in Computer Science from Tokyo Institute of Technology in 2006. He is currently an Associate Professor at Murdoch University (Australia) and an Adjunct Associate Professor with the Phenomics and Bioinformatics Research Centre (PBRC) of the University of South Australia (UniSA). His research interests span various fields of computer vision, computer graphics, and image processing, with a special focus on the 3D acquisition, modeling, and analysis of the shape of static and deformable 3D objects.

ANUJ SRIVASTAVA

Anuj Srivastava is a Professor of Statistics and a Distinguished Research Professor at the Florida State University. He obtained his Ph.D. degree in Electrical Engineering from Washington University in St. Louis in 1996 and was a visiting research associate at the Division of Applied Mathematics at Brown University during 1996–1997. He joined the Department of Statistics at the Florida State University in 1997 as an Assistant Professor, and was promoted to full Professor in 2007. He has held visiting positions at INRIA, France, University of Lille, France, and Durham University, UK. His areas of research interest include statistics on nonlinear manifolds, statistical image understanding, functional data analysis, and statistical shape theory. He has published more than 200 papers in refereed journals and proceedings of refereed international conferences. He has been an associate editor for leading journals in computer vision and image processing, including IEEE PAMI, IEEE TIP, JMIV, and CVIU. He is a fellow of IEEE, IAPR, and ASA.